A NEW APPROACH TO TIME-HONORED DESIGN

Nostalgia
HOME PLANS COLLECTION™

70 DESIGNS

design basics inc.®
HOME PLAN DESIGN SERVICE

Over the years, we at Design Basics have been bringing people home with many of America's most popular home plans. Our company began as a custom home plan design firm for the professional builders of our local community, Omaha, NE. As the popularity of our designs increased, we expanded our focus from designing for the local market only, to designing plans that would be adaptable anywhere. Since then, builder as well as consumer interest in our plans has grown tremendously in all 50 states and countries around the world.

Today we are one of the nation's largest home plan design companies, nationally recognized through numerous awards in design, business management, corporate growth and the development of effective marketing products. We offer a variety of home plans as well as products and services which include color renderings, estimator's material lists, plan changes and more.

Whether it's a product, service or one of our home plans, we take pride in serving you with our very best.

Nostalgia

Nostalgia
HOME PLANS COLLECTION™

A NEW APPROACH TO TIME-HONORED DESIGN

Publisher Dennis Brozak
Associate Publisher Linda Reimer

Editor Carol Stratman Shea
Managing Editor Kevin Blair
Plans Editor Tina Leyden
Circulation Manager Priscilla Ivey
Art Director Sheri Potter
Graphic Artists Heather Bettinger
Gloria A. Chavez
Yen Gutowski
Production Assistants Oanh Heiser
Brooke Pfutzenreuter
Rendering Colorization Alva Louden
Rendering Illustrator Perry M. Gauthier
Interior Perspectives Shawn Doherty
Furniture Layouts Sherri Rydl
Design Team Leader Jody Marker
Sharon Fustos
Ron Kreutzian
Adam Marquart
Bill Martin
Sherri Rydl

CEO Dennis Brozak
President Linda Reimer
Director of Marketing Kevin Blair
Director of Business Development Paul Foresman
Controller Janie Murnane

Text and Design © 1998 by Design Basics Inc.
All rights reserved.

No part of this publication may be reproduced in any form or by any means without prior written permission of the publisher.

Library of Congress Number: 97-077469
ISBN: 9647658-8-8

Table of Contents

One-Story Homes
8

1 1/2-Story Homes
48

Two-Story Homes
106

Product & Services Information 154-160
Home Plan Information 156
Design Basics Planbooks 159
Customized Plan Changes 157
Order Form 160

Home Plan Index

One-Story home plans

Plan #	Plan Name	Sq. ft.	Page #
5180	Holbrook	1339	10-11
5034	Payson	1472	12-13
5035	Canton	1552	14-15
5179	Spenlow	1650	16-17
5001	Anson	1653	18-19
5080	Thomaston	1660	20-21
5177	Cedric	1679	22-23
4948	Bradbury	1758	24-25
5181	Vautrin	1806	26-27
4953	Morenci	1853	28-29
5135	Hayden	1894	30-31
5090	Simeon	1920	32-33
4644	Elving	1971	34-35
4951	Aldrich	2039	36-37
4208	Creighton	2057	38-39
5036	Cameron	2167	40-41
4998	Holden	2227	42-43
5141	Enfield	2242	44-45
5003	Saybrooke	2750	46-47

1 1/2 - Story home plans

Plan #	Plan Name	Sq. ft.	Page #
5151	Sedona	1755	50-51
5160	Tecoma	1762	52-53
4133	Marcell	1772	54-55
5079	Cumberland	1851	56-57
4646	Kirkwood	1853	58-59

1 1/2 - Story home plans

Plan #	Plan Name	Sq. ft.	Page #
5159	Blaire	2118	60-61
5131	Chambers	2143	62-63
5161	Auburn	2167	64-65
5149	Camrose	2190	66-67
5136	Stanfield	2221	68-69
5148	Bowden	2339	70-71
4082	Kenneth	2351	72-73
5162	Calidore	2393	74-75
5150	Magrath	2421	76-77
5158	Carey	2512	78-79
5146	Ellsworth	2536	80-81
4081	Hanna	2576	82-83
4134	Schuyler	2613	84-85
5178	Rowena	2637	86-87
5210	Colette	2681	88-89
5157	Reston	2738	90-91
4641	Nicole	2781	92-93
5185	Wayland	2820	94-95
5105	Mahoning	2826	96-97
5000	Middleboro	2989	98-99
4144	Marlow	3040	100-101
4089	Eleanor	3103	102-103
5142	Landreth	3480	104-105

Two - Story home plans

Plan #	Plan Name	Sq. ft.	Page #
4999	Sanders	1628	108-109
4642	Ackerly	1712	110-111
4997	Rocklund	1778	112-113
5084	Cohasset	1893	114-115
5085	Branford	1928	116-117
4949	Darius	1938	118-119
4996	Amesbury	2069	120-121
4952	Caldera	2144	122-123
5002	Rochdale	2224	124-125
4105	Eldon	2282	126-127
4145	Ainsley	2332	128-129
4135	Gerard	2349	130-131
5086	Patagonia	2417	132-133
5049	Norwood	2475	134-135
5132	Castine	2506	136-137
4125	Emery	2523	138-139
5209	Laveen	2531	140-141
4156	Karlynda	2558	142-143
5037	Suffolk	2560	144-145
4106	Calabretta	2613	146-147
4147	Sutter	2642	148-149
5083	Attleboro	2752	150-151
4950	Neville	2808	152-153

Built by Dan Lowe Construction. For more information about the Marcell #4133, see page 52.

A NEW APPROACH TO TIME-HONORED DESIGN

What is it we find so deeply alluring about homes of the past? Is it the beauty of their intricately crafted details? Is it their sheer presence that speaks of the fullness of their character? Is it their striking stature, yet the warmth of their nature that invites us inside? Is it the nostalgic feelings they stir in our memories that inevitably remind us of the homes we grew up in?

It is all of these things and more. It is the way in which a row of these one-of-a-kind classics seem to "live" together in a tight-knit neighborhood. It is the way they show off the skills of their craftsmen – the sometimes simple detailing that so subtly can make a prominent statement. It is the influence they've had on our lives and the impact they've had on our culture. They are homes that are as beautiful as they are nurturing. Homes that make us relish our childhood years because they made us feel sheltered, cared for and secure. They are homes that in a sudden wave of sentiment, will inevitably prompt us to lament, "They sure don't make 'em like they used to."

Turn the pages and go back there. Design Basics' Nostalgia Home Plans Collection™ was created to help you rediscover the home of yesteryear – homes distinguished by the rich architectural traditions of countless classic, romantic and revival eras. These designs will more than likely remind you of homes you've admired while driving through the old neighborhoods of town, or of ones you've seen on the pages of a historical homes magazine. They were not meant to replicate authentic historical architecture. Rather, they borrow the time-honored warmth and detail of the homes of the past to create something altogether unique. As varied as our culture is, so are these designs, revealing everyone's individual desire for choice and freedom in their home.

Throughout the following pages you will discover the comfortable familiarity of cherished detailing you've all but forgotten – entablatures, batten board shutters, corner boards and balustrades. You will, possibly for the first time, appreciate the steep massing of a roof and its brackets, fascias and cornices. These are style-conscious designs, steeped in historical shapes. These are homes that will inevitably bring families back together again and again, and leave them with an aching knot in their throat when it comes time to sell. They are homes, that as much as they express their character, they build it into its builders and occupants. They are homes with "fingerprints" – a built-in cabinet, a certain double-hung window, or an attic – destined to become a part of your daily life. Destined, in fact, to become your very definition of home.

Our own definition of home went into designing each of the 70 home plans from 1,339 - 3,480 square feet in this collection. It's a definition that lies at the heart of our mission at Design Basics: "Bringing People Home." Whether you're building a home for yourself or someone else, and whether you're looking for a one-story, 1½-story or two-story home, Nostalgia Home Plans can help you discover the warmth and beauty of designs you can be proud to build and live to fulfillment in. Turn the pages and allow us to bring you back home.

Exterior and Interior Photos: Phil Bell
The home in these photographs may be altered from the original plan.

ABOVE: MASTER BEDROOM
In the master bedroom, the use of scrolling wrought iron dictates the romantic flair of the past along with the knotted drapery – an updated version of bygone tassels.

ABOVE: KITCHEN
Wood tones were typically finished in oak, but the Marcell's updated kitchen uses a darker wood which still emits a warm nostalgic feeling.

BELOW: GREAT ROOM
The great room's vintage wall color was lighted for an updated look. The floral upholstery on the sofas and chairs was modernized with lighter colors and a less decorative pattern.

The Nostalgic touch INSIDE and OUT

"Marble slab mantels graced fireplaces..."

Homes from the early part of this century were known for their eclectic decor – their use of a variety of finishes and textures. As a result, the homes often contained styles that didn't always compliment each other. Today's updated version of this styling embraces a mix of such elements, yet downplays the elaborate detailing to make everything work together. While any decorating style will complement Nostalgia Home Plans, the following ideas provide ways you can bring a sense of this "time-honored" design styling throughout the interior and exterior of your home.

Interiors

Ceilings were high, halls were narrow and rooms were dimly lit. Today's interiors offer tall ceilings, yet forgo the dimly-lit rooms by providing a variety of natural light sources. The use of subdued interior coloring, however, still emits the warmth of a dimly-lit room. Contrasting ceiling heights and the use of sloped ceilings help bring back the quaint feeling of narrow halls, doorways and stairwells.

Woodwork

Interior trim included paneled wainscotting, beamed ceilings, heavy wooden trim and massive mouldings. While much of this wood was shown in darker tones, today's mouldings and wainscotting are painted or updated with lighter tones of wood.

Fireplaces

Marble slab mantels graced fireplaces, which often had ornamental arched openings. A luxury item today, marble can still add an old-world feel to a home through the substitution of a painted faux finish.

Kitchens

The common use of golden oak in kitchens and other cabinetry was a sign of respectability in a home, emitting a sense of richness to a room. Today's kitchens are given a time-worn feel through washed paint and distressed woodwork.

Windows

Windows had heavy draperies, swags, valances and jabots, enriched with tassels and heavy fringes. Today's windows are drastically simplified, often decorated with a swag or sheer treatment covering pleated shades or blinds. The tassels and heavy fringes of the past are being reintroduced in more delicate and subdued versions.

Exterior Facade

On the exteriors of homes you would find steep gabled roofs, corner towers, balconies and scalloped shingles as well as brick detail applied in patterns. Since much of this exterior detail has been omitted over the years because of its expense, builders and designers are using more of a vignette (and toned-down) approach with window trim, decorative ironwork and copper roofs. Other detailing on the exterior can also add a special old-fashioned touch such as, half-round gutters and round downspouts.

Landscaping

The homes of yesterday were also well-integrated with their neighborhoods and streets. The use of brick or cobblestone to pave the walkway into the home or out to the sidewalk brings back that feeling of nostalgia today. Incorporating a street lamp and wrought-iron bench into the landscaping adds to the warmth of a front elevation. Other garden-style touches such as free-standing gazebos and sundials additionally contribute an old-world feel to your home's surroundings.

Colors

Interior colors were often dark and neutralized, such as Mulberry, Bottle Green, Tobacco Brown, and Dull Red. They were colors with muddy, time-worn hues that diffuse an essence of affluence. These same colors applied today are toned-down and lightened to coincide with simplified interiors.

Furniture

Furniture of the early part of the century included legs with a turned treatment. The revival of these elements brings cherished antiques back to life in a home. Pairing them with a few modern pieces brings a fresh updated look to furnishings.

Upholstery

Upholstered furniture contained elaborate cord, fringe, button and tassel trims to match the elaborate window treatments of the time. Today's upholstery is less elaborate and may only contain hints of the past, such as sofas with high backs and carved feet. Furniture upholstered in the fabrics and colors of the time, but with a modern shape and design is another great way to mesh old and new styling.

"Furniture of the early part of the century included legs with a turned treatment."

Nostalgic INTERIOR colors

| mulberry | bottle green | tobacco brown | dull red |

"Interior colors were often dark and neutralized, such as Mulberry, Bottle Green, Tobacco Brown, and Dull Red."

In the **Nostalgia** *Collection you will find...*

SEPARATE LAUNDRY ROOMS

If there's one comment we've heard over and over through the years, it's that the laundry room placement is very important in the home. In these designs, we've taken special care to provide separate laundry room facilities. And in the few exceptions where this wasn't possible, we tried to design the laundry room large enough to accommodate the traffic and also serve as a mud room.

SIMPLER FOUNDATIONS

While buyers will appreciate the old-world feel of these homes, I think they will also appreciate the lengths we went to, throughout the design process, to save them money on the construction of the home. For example, any protrusion or 'jog' in the foundation costs money. The simpler the foundation, the less costly it becomes. As much as we could, we tried to limit any protrusions in the foundation to the front of the home, to focus the most dramatic effects there. Conversely, we often squared off the foundations in the back for cost effectiveness.

One-story Homes

Plan Index

Plan #	Plan Name	Sq. Ft.	Page #
5180	Holbrook	1339	10-11
5034	Payson	1472	12-13
5035	Canton	1552	14-15
5179	Spenlow	1650	16-17
5001	Anson	1653	18-19
5080	Thomaston	1660	20-21
5177	Cedric	1679	22-23
4948	Bradbury	1758	24-25
5181	Vautrin	1806	26-27
4953	Morenci	1853	28-29
5135	Hayden	1894	30-31
5090	Simeon	1920	32-33
4644	Elving	1971	34-35
4951	Aldrich	2039	36-37
4208	Creighton	2057	38-39
5036	Cameron	2167	40-41
4998	Holden	2227	42-43
5141	Enfield	2242	44-45
5003	Saybrooke	2750	46-47

Holbrook

❶ This home provides the efficiency of today's lifestyle needs with the detailing and charisma of homes typically larger.

❷ An angled counter in the kitchen helps define the space and organize the working areas.

❸ The large great room draws guests inside with its fireplace and access to a nearby bookshelf.

❹ A full bath serves the main floor as well as the second bedroom.

❺ A large walk-in closet is located off the master bath creating a private dressing area to avoid disturbing a sleeping spouse.

❻ The garage offers an alcove to build a work bench or shelves.

ALL PLANS COPYRIGHTED

For More Information on our Copyrights see page 154.

Nostalgia

9K-5180 PRICE CODE 13

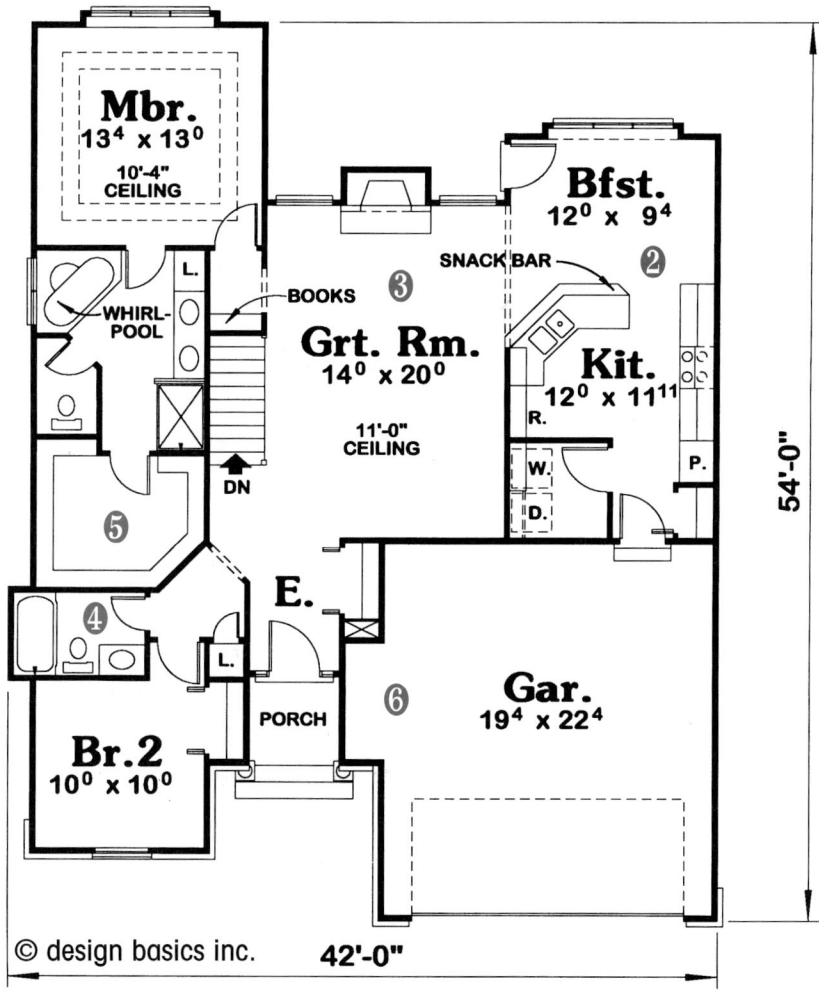

1339 Finished Sq. Ft.

NOTE: 9 ft. main level walls

EXTERIOR HIGHLIGHT

Since a deep covered stoop, such as the one on this home, has the potential to "hide" the front door, this home's entry was elevated to give it stature. Columns and a circle-top window draw further eye-catching appeal.

TO ORDER THIS PLAN CALL
1-800-947-7526

design basics inc.
HOME PLAN DESIGN SERVICE

Nostalgia

Payson

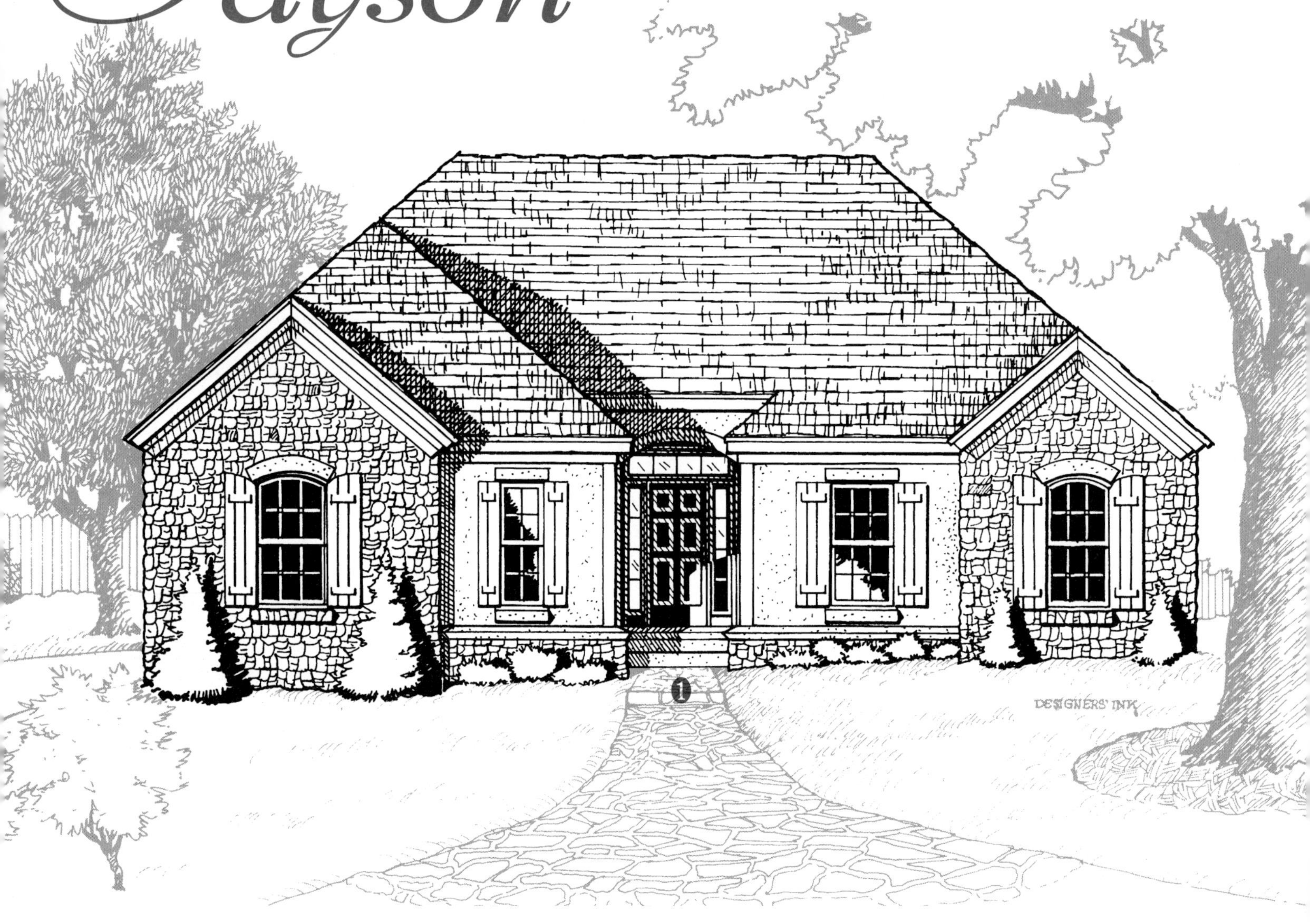

❶ This country cottage is updated with a hip roof and eyebrow arches.

❷ Traffic flows neatly through the den just inside the entry.

❸ With no wasted space, the kitchen and breakfast area function as a large living area organized with a island counter.

❹ His and her walk-in closets offer plenty of practical storage options in the master suite.

❺ An optional finished basement provides the possibility of creating an apartment for a live-in relative.

❻ Extra bedrooms in the basement are perfect for occasional visits from friends and relatives.

AVAILABLE FOR ALL PLANS

For More Information on Reverse Plans see page 158.

9K-5034 PRICE CODE 14

MAIN FLOOR

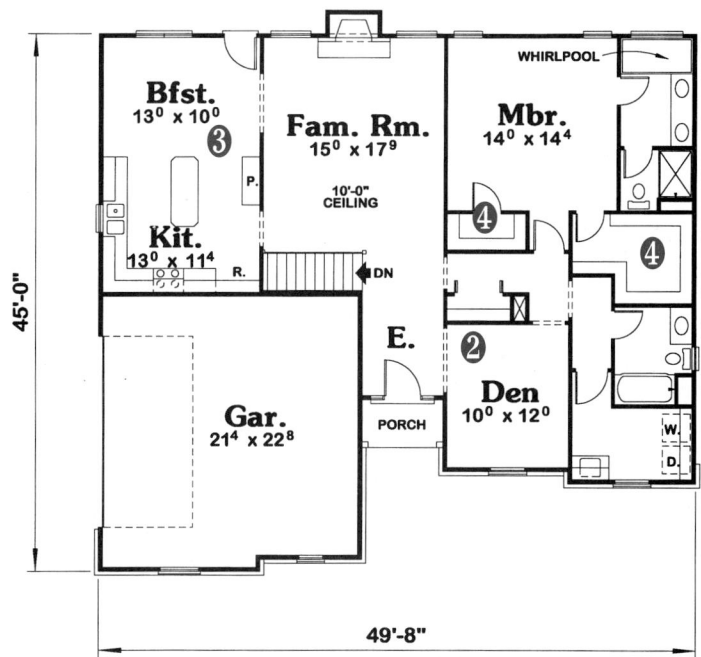

1472 Finished Sq. Ft.

NOTE: 9 ft. main level walls

LOWER FLOOR

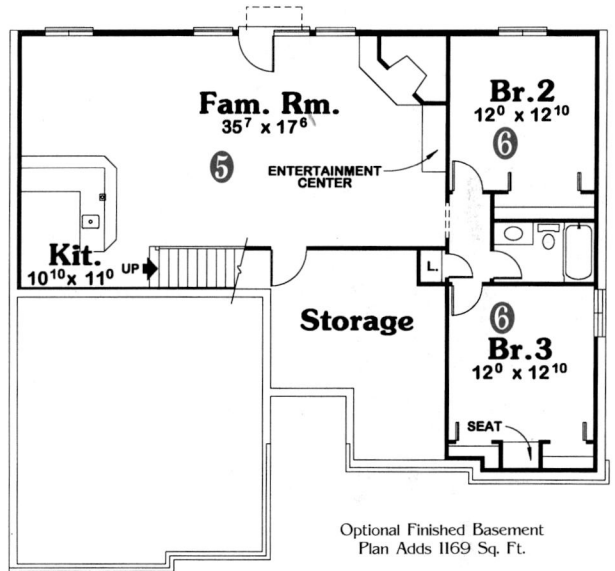

Optional Finished Basement Plan Adds 1169 Sq. Ft.

EXTERIOR HIGHLIGHT

Designing stone to stucco helps comfortably move the eye to the central focus of this design - the front door. Other detailing, such as batten board shutters and decorative lintels add a French country flair.

TO ORDER THIS PLAN CALL
1-800-947-7526

Nostalgia

Canton

❶ Columns atop pedestals captivate the recessed covered stoop on this home's facade.

❷ The master suite is a haven for time alone with its own covered porch, corner whirlpool tub and large shower.

❸ A separate laundry room keeps clothes from view and has space for an ironing board.

❹ 11-foot ceilings in the entry and great room bring a sense of airiness.

❺ A corner walk-in pantry, utility closet, and snack bar help organize the wide kitchen.

❻ Linen closets in both the master bath and main bath accommodate a place for toiletries.

AVAILABLE FOR ALL PLANS

Roof Construction Package

For More Information on our Roof Construction Package see page 158.

9K-5035 PRICE CODE 15

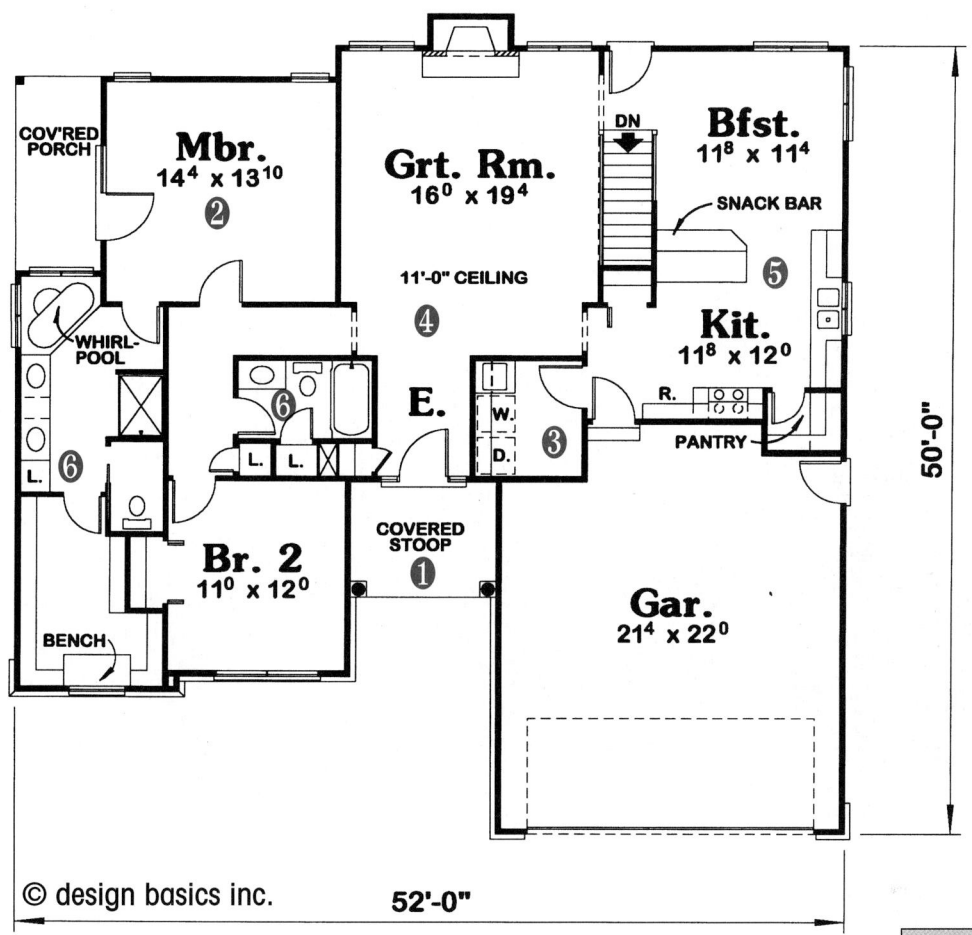

1552 Finished Sq. Ft.
NOTE: 9 ft. main level walls

INTERIOR VIEW

MASTER WALK-IN CLOSET - A sense of spaciousness is added to the walk-in closet of the master suite through a large window with curving arch. Its picturesque window seat is perfect for resting to put on one's shoes or deciding an outfit for the day.

TO ORDER THIS PLAN CALL
1-800-947-7526

design basics inc.
HOME PLAN DESIGN SERVICE

Nostalgia

Spenlow

❶ This home is distinguished by a decorative dormer and a dropped roof over four garage windows that are anchored with brackets.

❷ The dining room is located within close proximity to the kitchen and is defined with a boxed ceiling.

❸ At 11 feet in height, the great room establishes a haven for welcome and family activity.

❹ Accompanying the master bedroom, is a large walk-in closet, whirlpool and dual-lav vanity.

❺ The efficient kitchen is equipped with counter space that's useful when serving formal meals in the dining room.

❻ Coat closets located in the front and garage entries are convenient for guests and family.

AVAILABLE FOR ALL PLANS

For More Information on Parade Home Packages see page 158.

Nostalgia

9K-5179 PRICE CODE 16

EXTERIOR HIGHLIGHT

Lap siding and corner boards, especially visible here in the entry, eloquently express the simplicity of this one-story home.

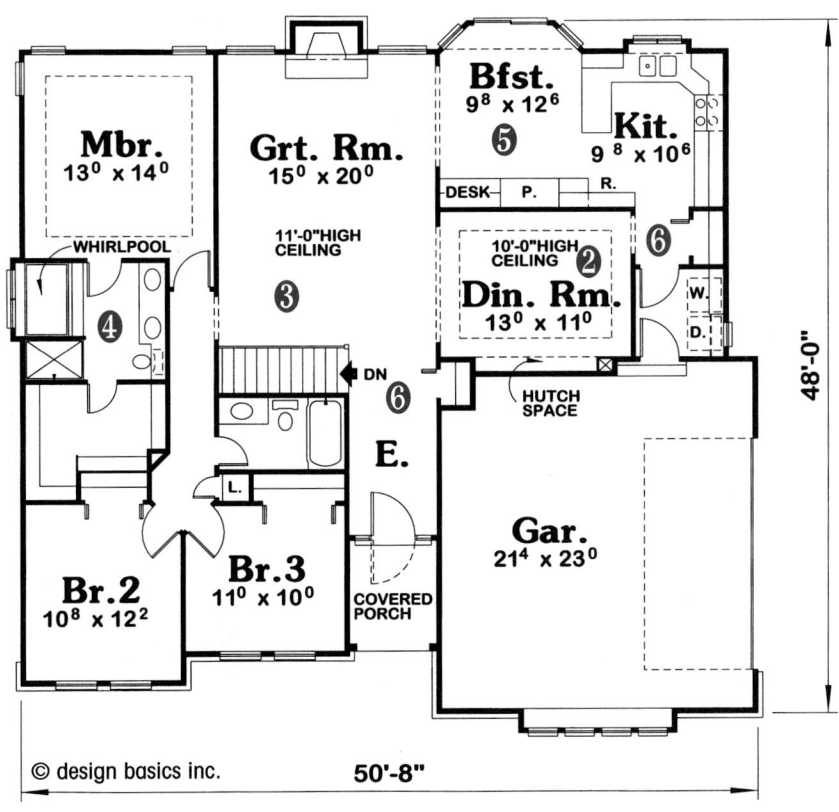

1650 Finished Sq. Ft.

NOTE: 9 ft. main level walls

© design basics inc.

TO ORDER THIS PLAN CALL
1-800-947-7526

design basics inc.
HOME PLAN DESIGN SERVICE

Nostalgia

Anson

❶ A front porch reminiscent of the 1920s sets the tone on this charming one-story home.

❷ Walking into this home reveals twin coat closets in the entry and an inviting great room with fireplace.

❸ Plenty of extra space in the master bath leaves room to fully utilize the corner make-up counter and his and her vanities.

❹ With the option of converting to a bedroom, the den offers a bayed window overlooking the charming front porch.

❺ A built-in workbench in the garage provides a place for tools.

❻ The spacious kitchen and dinette facilitate good circulation for daily use.

AVAILABLE FOR ALL PLANS

For More Information on Reverse Plans see page 158.

Nostalgia

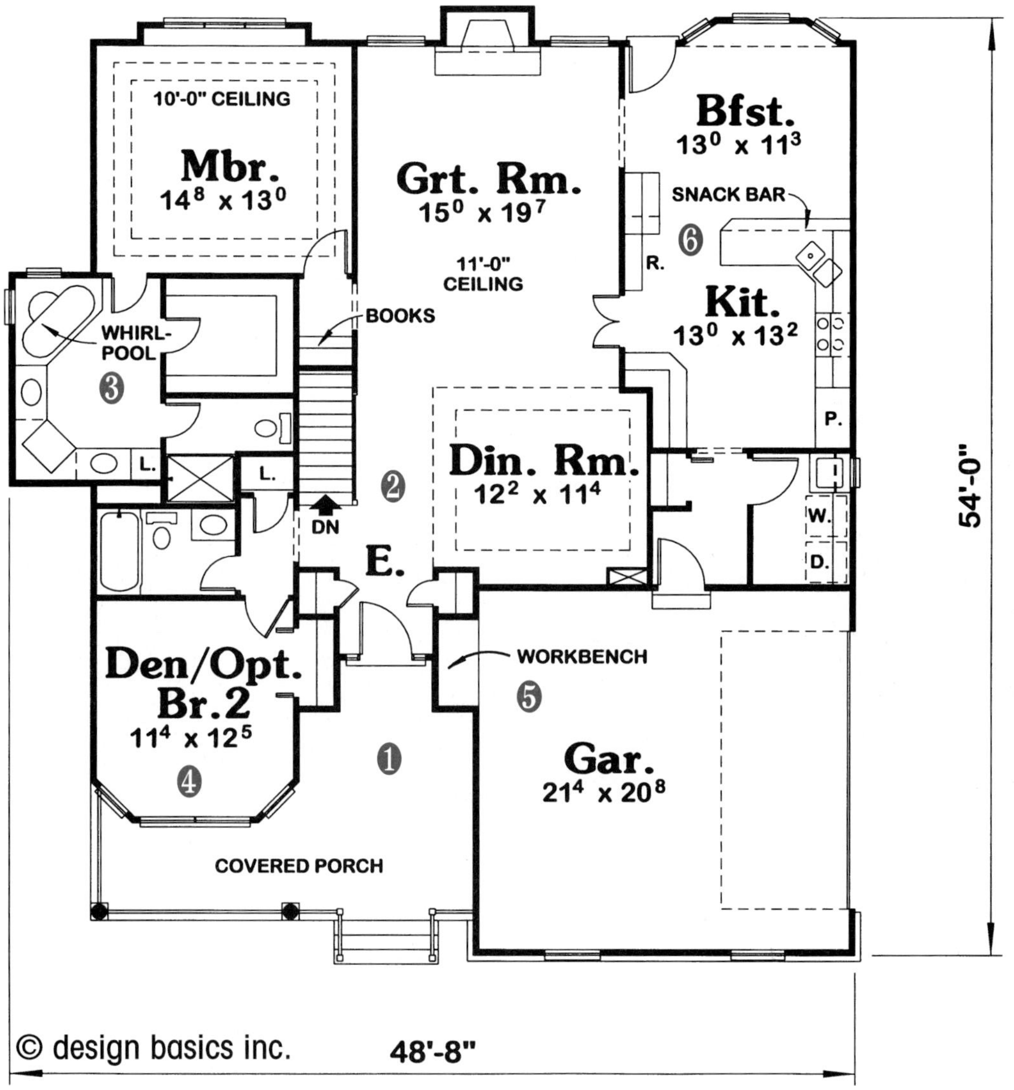

9K-5001 PRICE CODE 16

Mbr. 14⁸ x 13⁰ — 10'-0" CEILING

Grt. Rm. 15⁰ x 19⁷ — 11'-0" CEILING

Bfst. 13⁰ x 11³

SNACK BAR

Kit. 13⁰ x 13²

WHIRLPOOL

BOOKS

Din. Rm. 12² x 11⁴

Den/Opt. Br.2 11⁴ x 12⁵

WORKBENCH

Gar. 21⁴ x 20⁸

COVERED PORCH

54'-0"

48'-8"

© design basics inc.

1653 Finished Sq. Ft.
NOTE: 9 ft. main level walls

EXTERIOR HIGHLIGHT

A multi-paned front door is a beautiful addition to this home's entry. A deep front porch was designed to amply accommodate the protruding bay window.

TO ORDER THIS PLAN CALL
1-800-947-7526

Nostalgia

Thomaston

❶ Traditional styling can be found in this home's mouldings, corner boards and double-hung windows.

❷ The dining room could easily convert into a family computer/homework area.

❸ An ample corridor leads to the bedroom wing with the master suite and two bedrooms.

❹ A large walk-in closet, whirlpool, and dual-lav vanity assist getting ready in the master bath.

❺ The kitchen and dinette are well-integrated to function for everyday activity.

❻ A pocket door encloses the laundry room, which includes a linen closet and soaking sink.

AVAILABLE FOR ALL PLANS

For More Information on our Custom Changes see page 157.

Nostalgia

9K -5080 PRICE 16 CODE

MAIN FLOOR

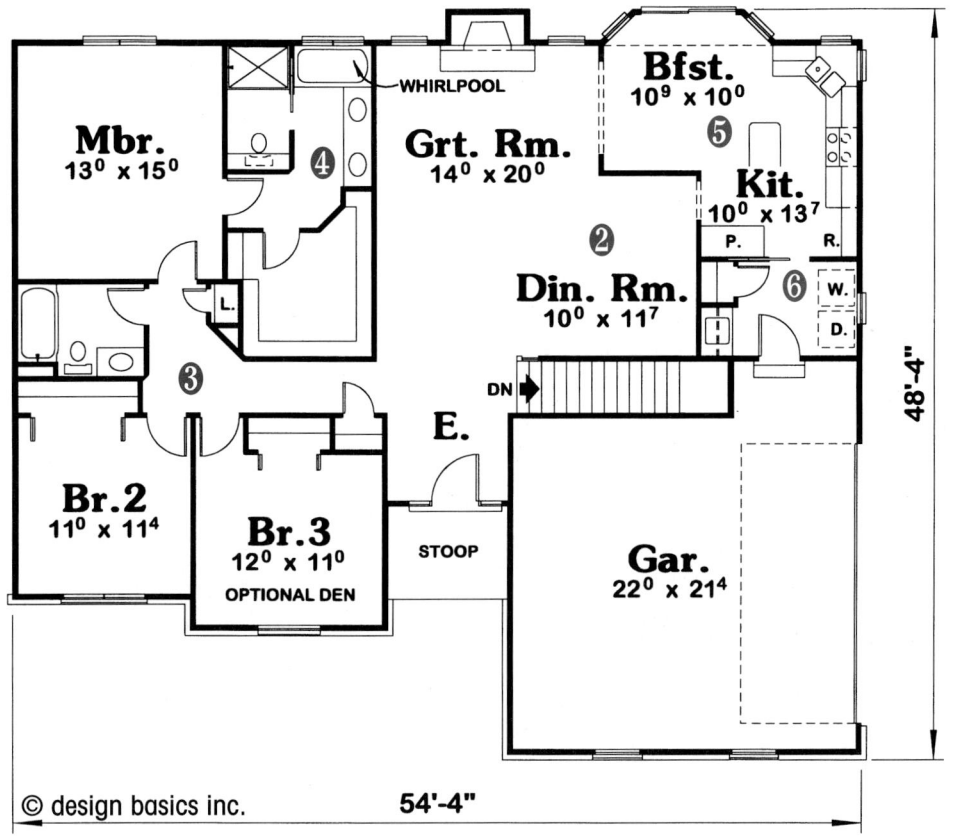

1660 Finished Sq. Ft.

NOTE: 9 ft. main level walls

DECORATOR DESIGN TIPS

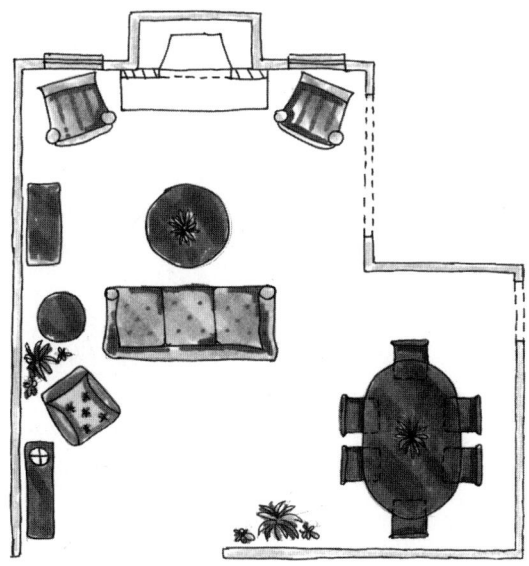

GREAT/DINING ROOMS - With a great room that is as long and extended as this one, the space needs to be divided. The furniture placement allows all seats to see the entertainment unit on the left side, and it allows the traffic to stay clear of the TV/conversation area. Floating the sofa allows a secondary space to be created behind it. The chair angled next to the bookcase makes a great reading spot.

TO ORDER THIS PLAN CALL
1-800-947-7526

Cedric

❶ Brick pedestals anchoring tapered columns and a detailed entablature provide the framework of this nostalgic front porch.

❷ Bedroom 3 could easily become a den with double doors opening to the entry.

❸ Both the dining room and breakfast area are near the kitchen and readily expand into one another.

❹ A boxed ceiling offers beauty in the master bedroom which also features a large walk-in closet and whirlpool tub.

❺ Extra counter area in the laundry room extends its available working space.

❻ A bench near the garage entry provides a place to take off one's muddy shoes.

ALL PLANS COPYRIGHTED

For More Information on our Copyrights see page 154.

9K -5177 PRICE CODE 16

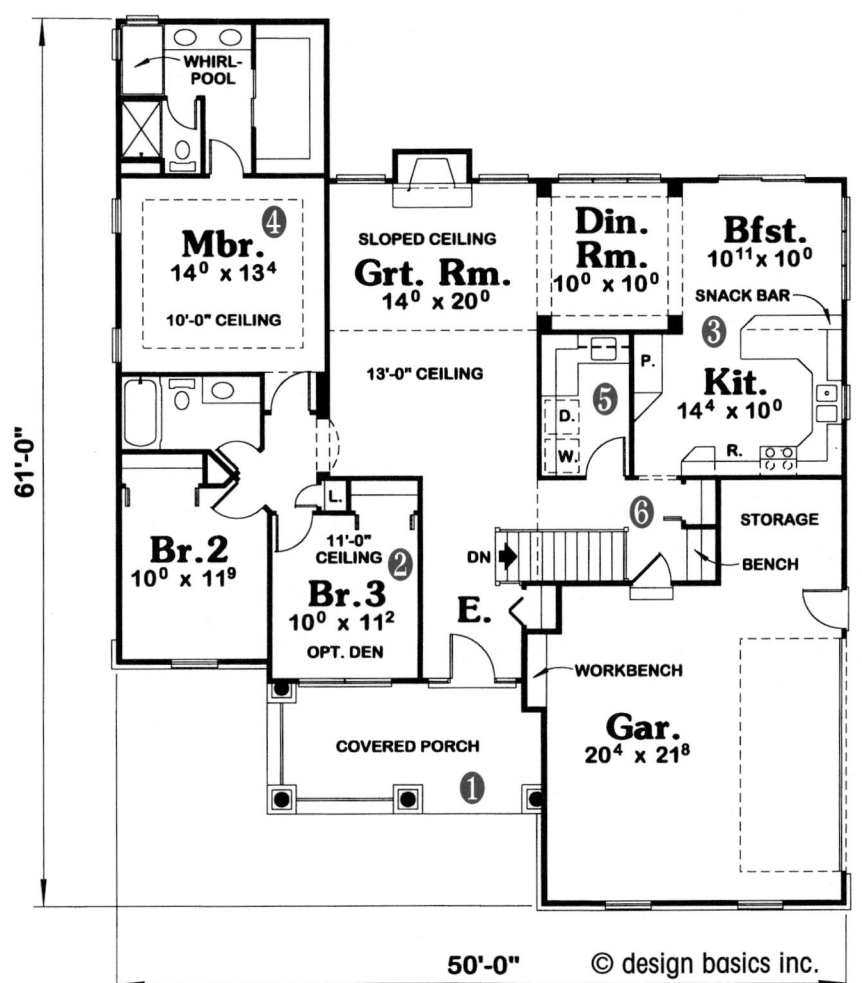

1679 Finished Sq. Ft.
NOTE: 9 ft. main level walls

© design basics inc.

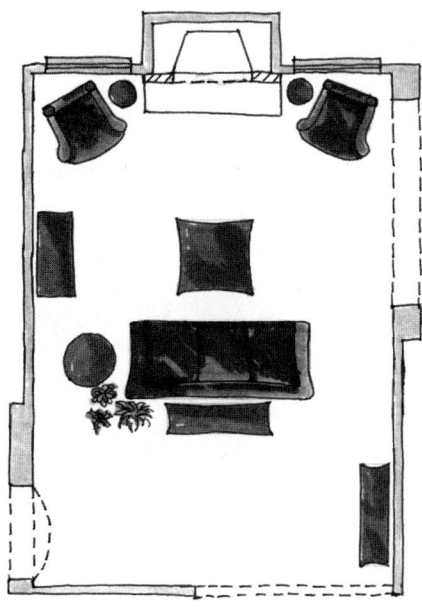

DECORATOR DESIGN TIPS

GREAT ROOM - Traffic flow is driven behind the main focal area and sets up a space conducive for TV watching or fireplace enjoyment. If a room like this were arranged with furniture along the walls, proximity to each other between the TV area and fireplace becomes a problem.

TO ORDER THIS PLAN CALL
1-800-947-7526

design basics inc.
HOME PLAN DESIGN SERVICE

Nostalgia

Bradbury

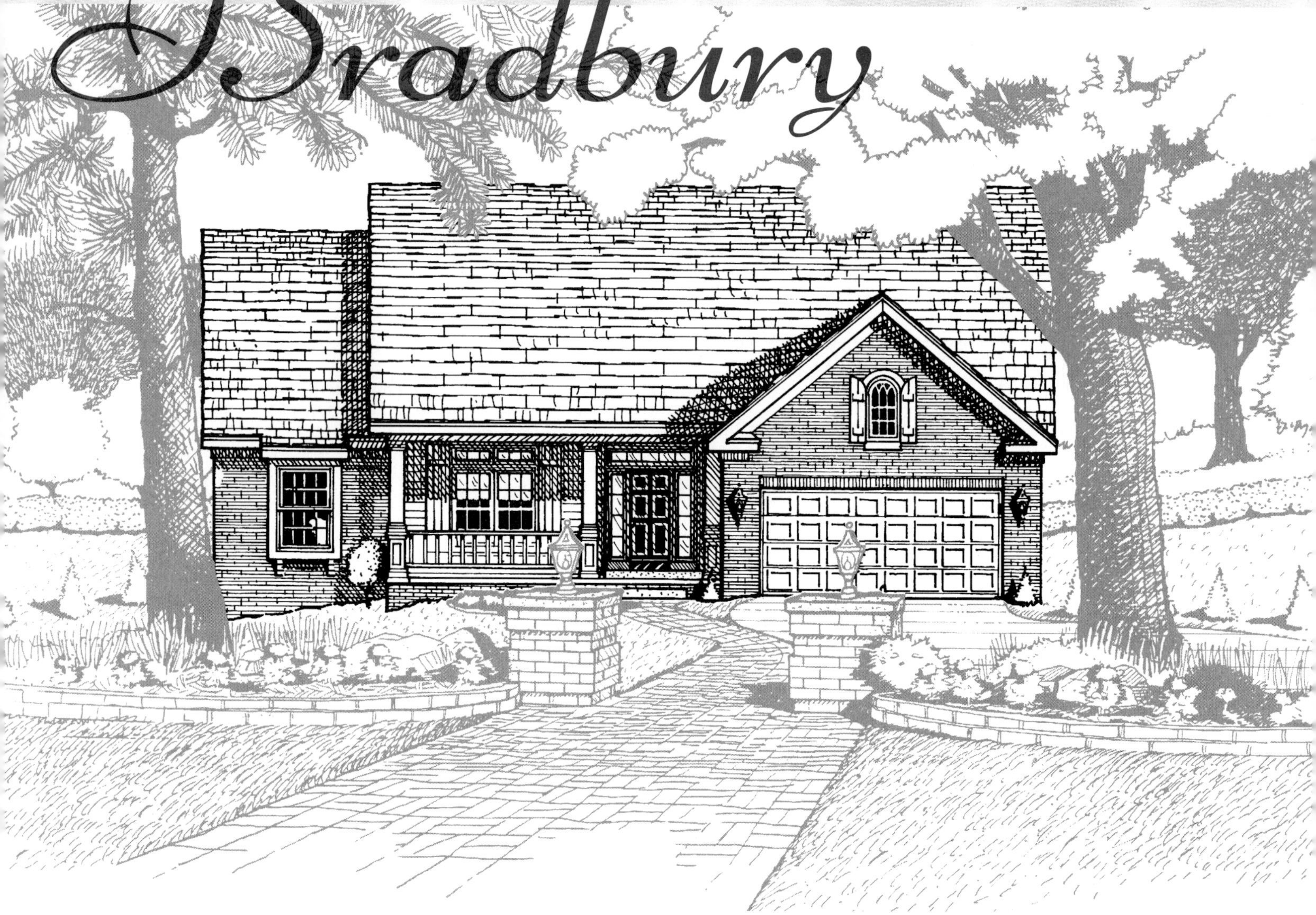

❶ The entry opens dramatically to an impressive volume great room.

❷ The kitchen has a snack bar, breakfast area and pantry, and is near a convenient laundry room off the garage.

❸ The large great room is further volumized by a stairway to the lower level and 11-foot ceiling.

❹ Along with angled entries, bedrooms 2 and 3 enjoy roomy closets and access to a full bath.

❺ The master suite welcomes a shower and whirlpool tub, dual lavs, compartmental stool and a large walk-in closet.

❻ A rear covered stoop makes a perfect garden center or sitting porch.

AVAILABLE FOR ALL PLANS

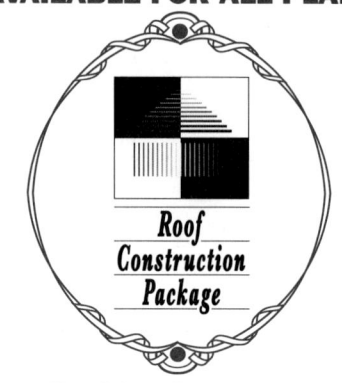

For More Information on our Roof Construction Package see page 158.

9K-4948 PRICE CODE 17

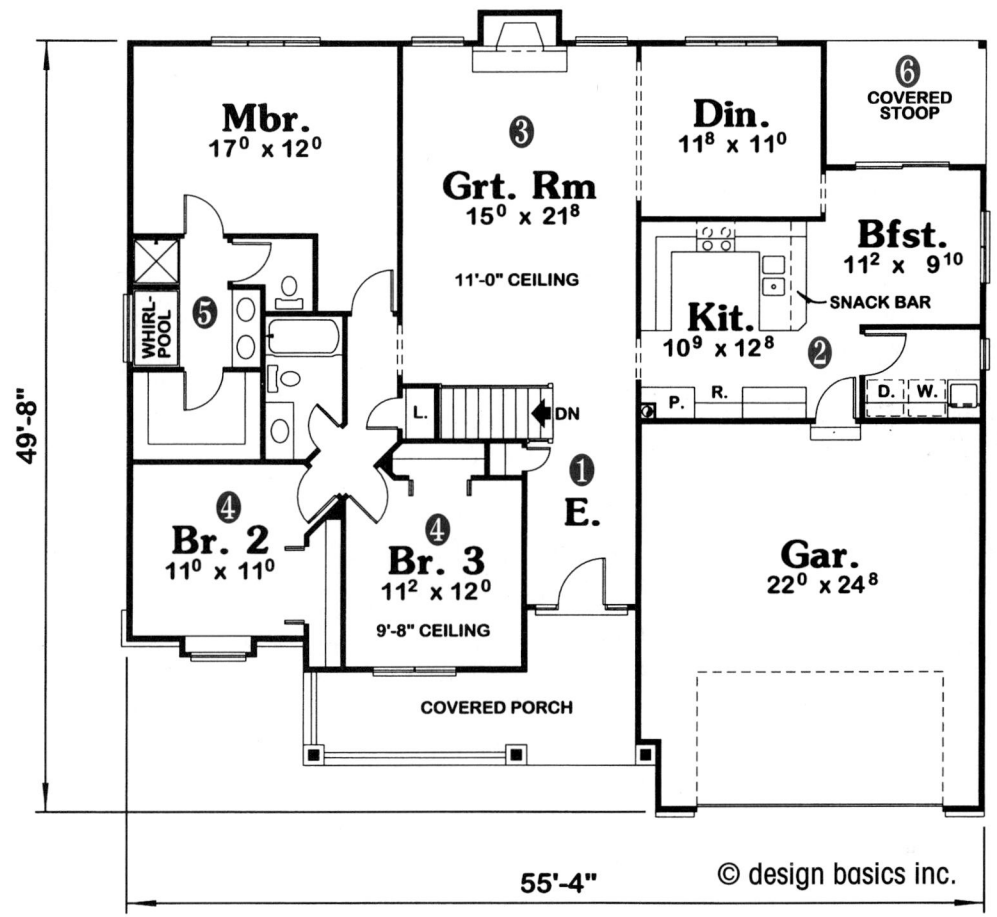

1758 Finished Sq. Ft.

NOTE: 9 ft. main level walls

EXTERIOR HIGHLIGHT

To give this home the ease of a calming one-story, a front porch was included with deep overhanging eaves. Sidelights and a transom call attention to the front door.

TO ORDER THIS PLAN CALL
1-800-947-7526

design basics inc.
HOME PLAN DESIGN SERVICE

Nostalgia

Vautrin

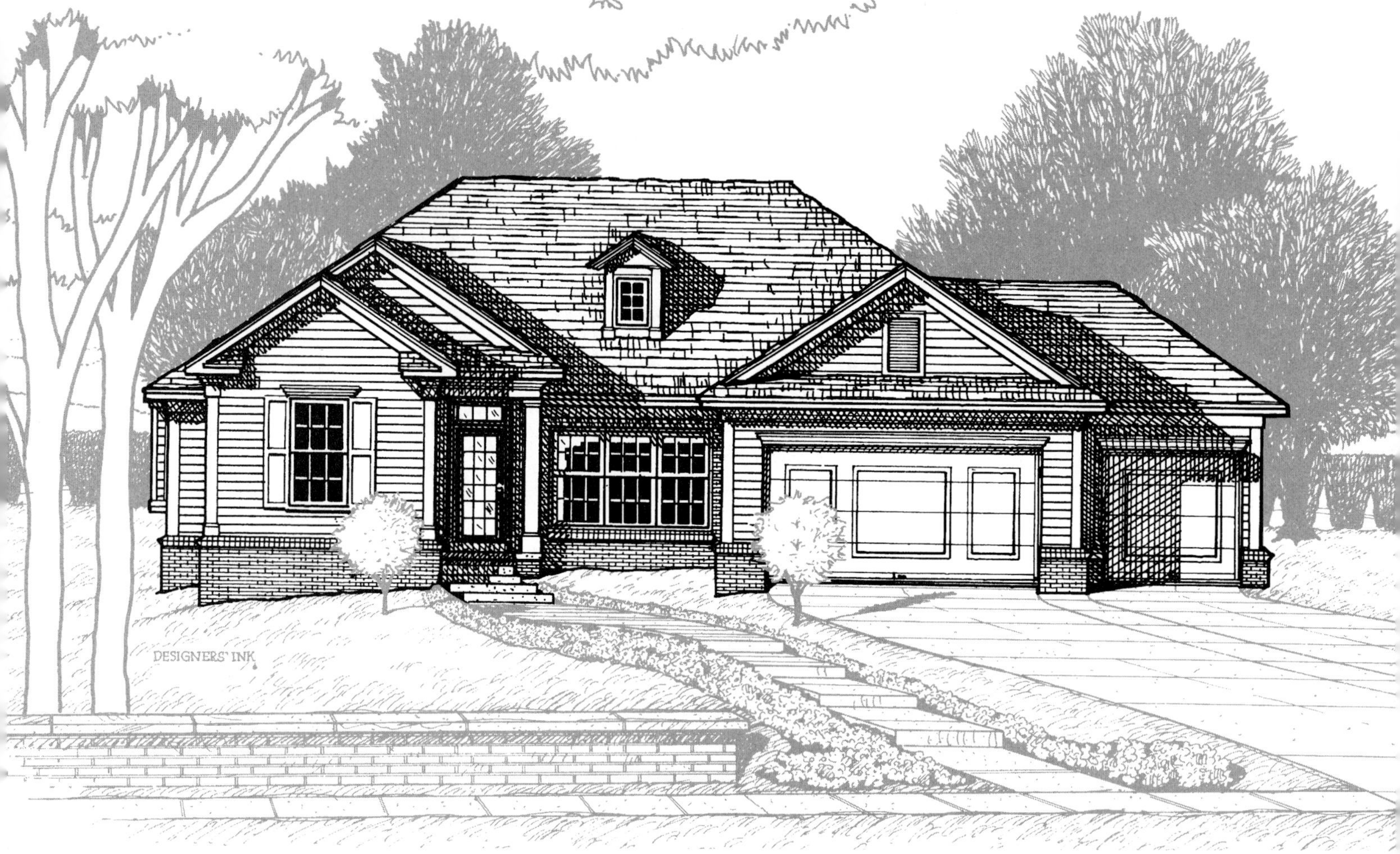

❶ Formal meals in the dining room will be easy with a nearby servery.

❷ An angled snack bar in the kitchen offers service to both the breakfast area and great room.

❸ Deep window sills create a picturesque atmosphere in the breakfast area.

❹ Just off the dinette, a covered porch is a great place to relax in the evening.

❺ A third bedroom is functional as a den and is within steps of a full bath with linen closet.

❻ A volume ceiling adds even more spaciousness to the pampering master suite.

AVAILABLE FOR ALL PLANS

For More Information on Parade Home Packages see page 158.

9K-5181 PRICE CODE 18

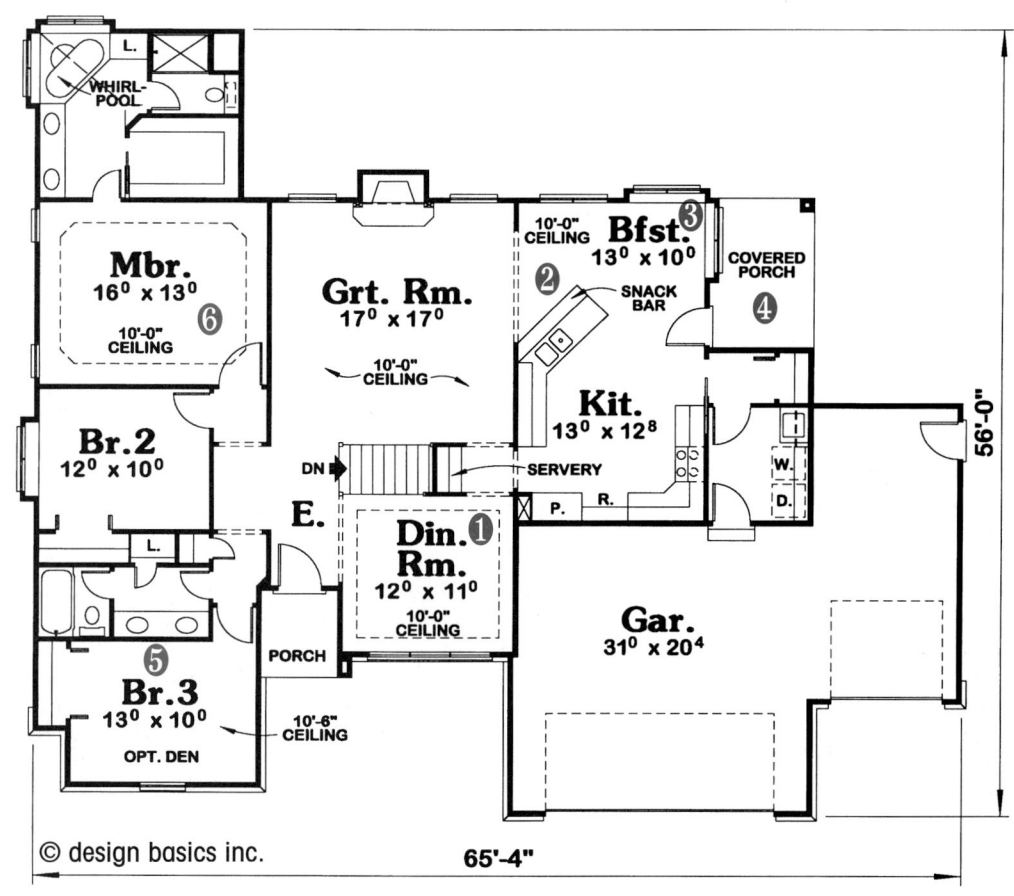

1806 Finished Sq. Ft.

NOTE: 9 ft. main level walls

EXTERIOR HIGHLIGHT

Pilasters set in a double gable join with a single dormer to draw attention to the entry. A triple-wide window is also complementary to this design's exterior.

TO ORDER THIS PLAN CALL
1-800-947-7526

Nostalgia

Morenci

❶ Corner boards and squared columns accent this enchanting one-story home.

❷ The large great room is ideally suited to accommodate guests from the entry as well as the dining room.

❸ An angled snack bar in the kitchen makes a great place for an informal meal.

❹ Perfect as a den or in-law suite, bedroom 4 is secluded and offers a 3/4 bath and walk-in closet.

❺ On the opposite end of the home, the master bedroom is organized with a compartmentalized shower and dressing area.

❻ Two secondary bedrooms easily accommodate guests or a hobby, such as sewing.

AVAILABLE FOR ALL PLANS

For More Information on our Custom Changes see page 157.

Nostalgia

9K-4953 PRICE CODE 18

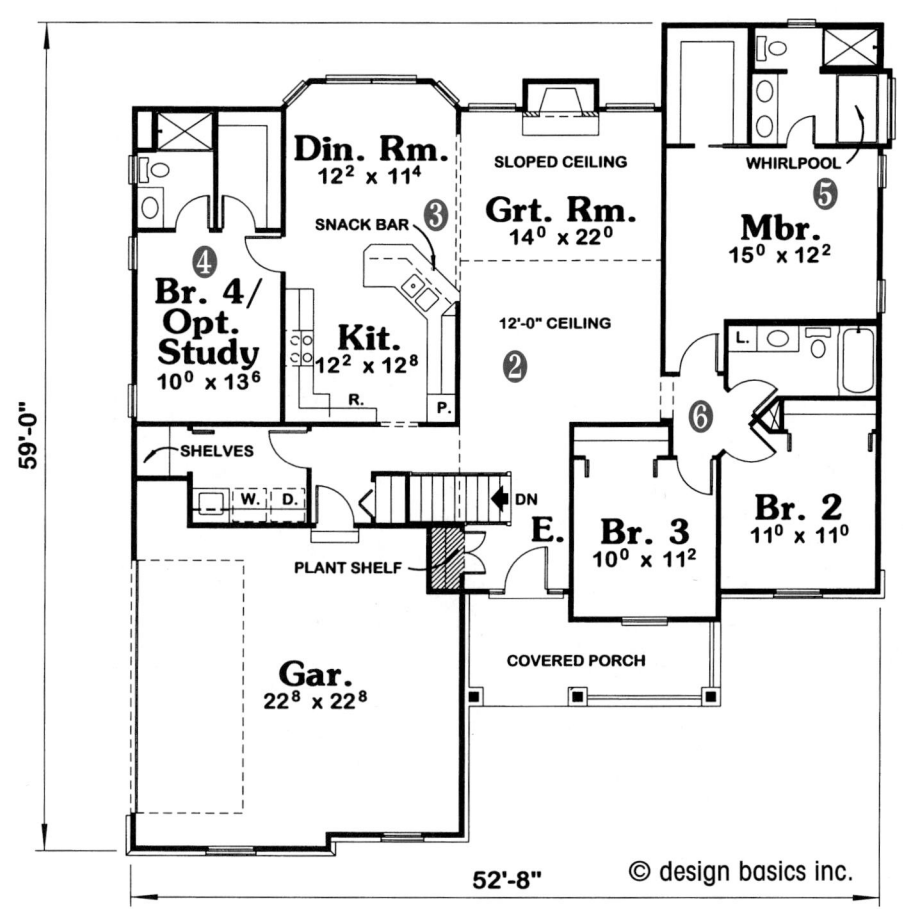

1853 Finished Sq. Ft.

NOTE: 9 ft. main level walls

INTERIOR VIEW

GREAT ROOM - A difference in ceiling heights, accentuated by a sloped ceiling in the great room, helps define the open spaces in this home. The integration of the kitchen, great room and dining room cuts down on room-to-room traffic and promotes family interaction.

TO ORDER THIS PLAN CALL
1-800-947-7526

Nostalgia

Hayden

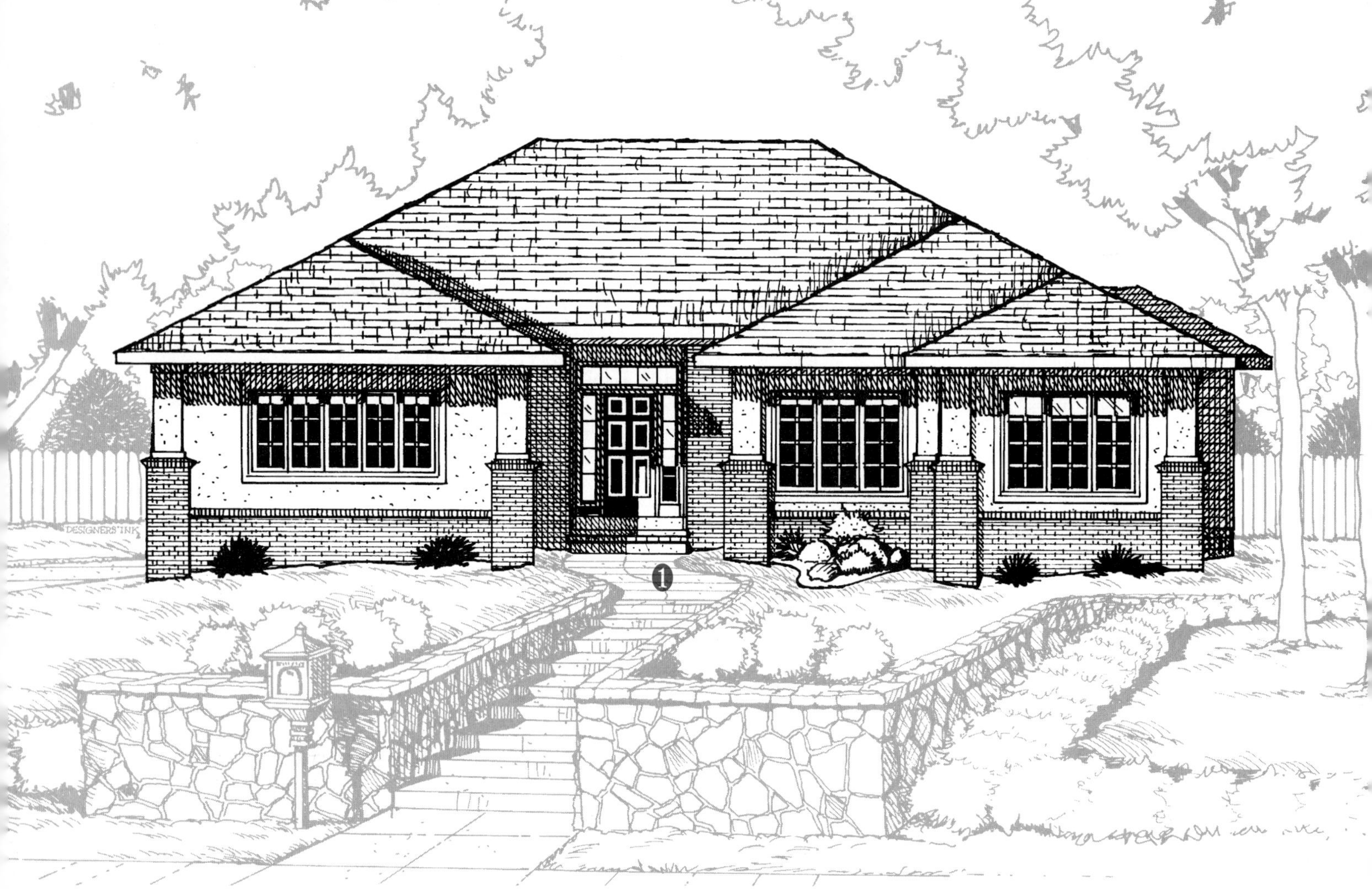

❶ Sturdy columns framing the wall corners give geometric balance to this home.

❷ A tiered entrance brings an old-world feel to the dining room which is optional as a living room.

❸ Traffic flow is enhanced through two entrances into the kitchen which includes an island counter and snack bar.

❹ A large laundry room accommodates a soaking sink and freezer space.

❺ A large master suite is enhanced with a vaulted ceiling and other amenities such as a walk-in closet, whirlpool tub, and separate shower.

❻ An alcove in the garage provides a place for a workbench.

ALL PLANS COPYRIGHTED

For More Information on our Copyrights see page 154.

9K-5135 PRICE CODE 18

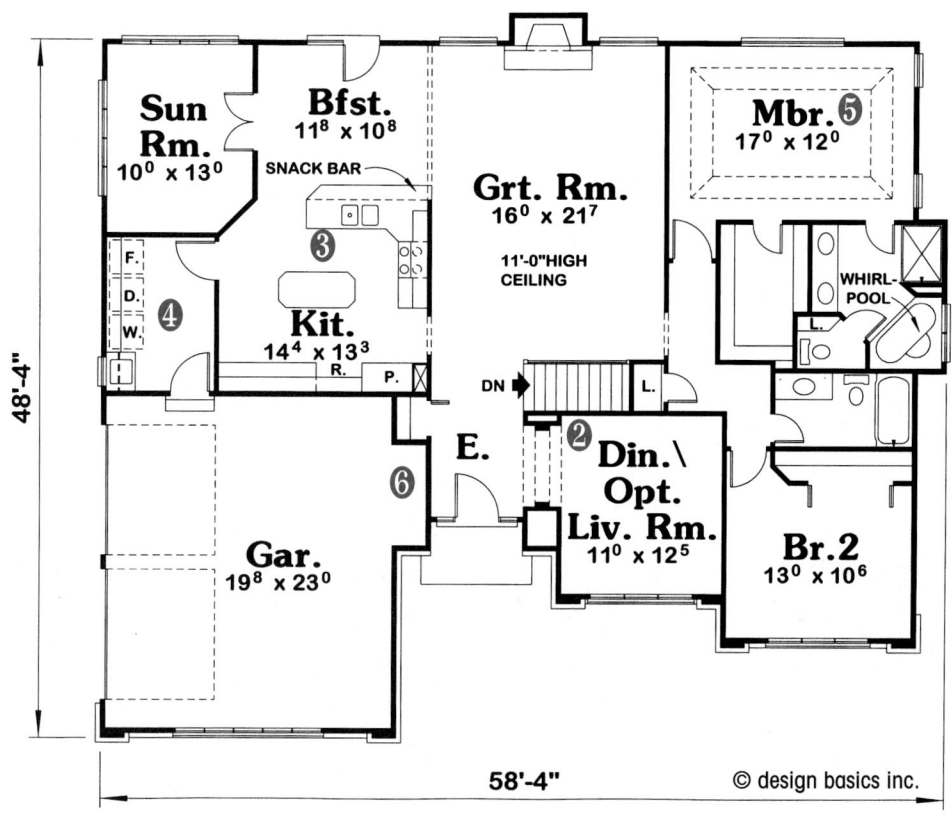

1894 Finished Sq. Ft.
NOTE: 9 ft. main level walls

INTERIOR VIEW

SUNROOM - Plentiful windows make this room a great haven for plants. Serving as a second living space, it is a great place to entertain guests without interrupting family activity.

TO ORDER THIS PLAN CALL
1-800-947-7526

Simeon

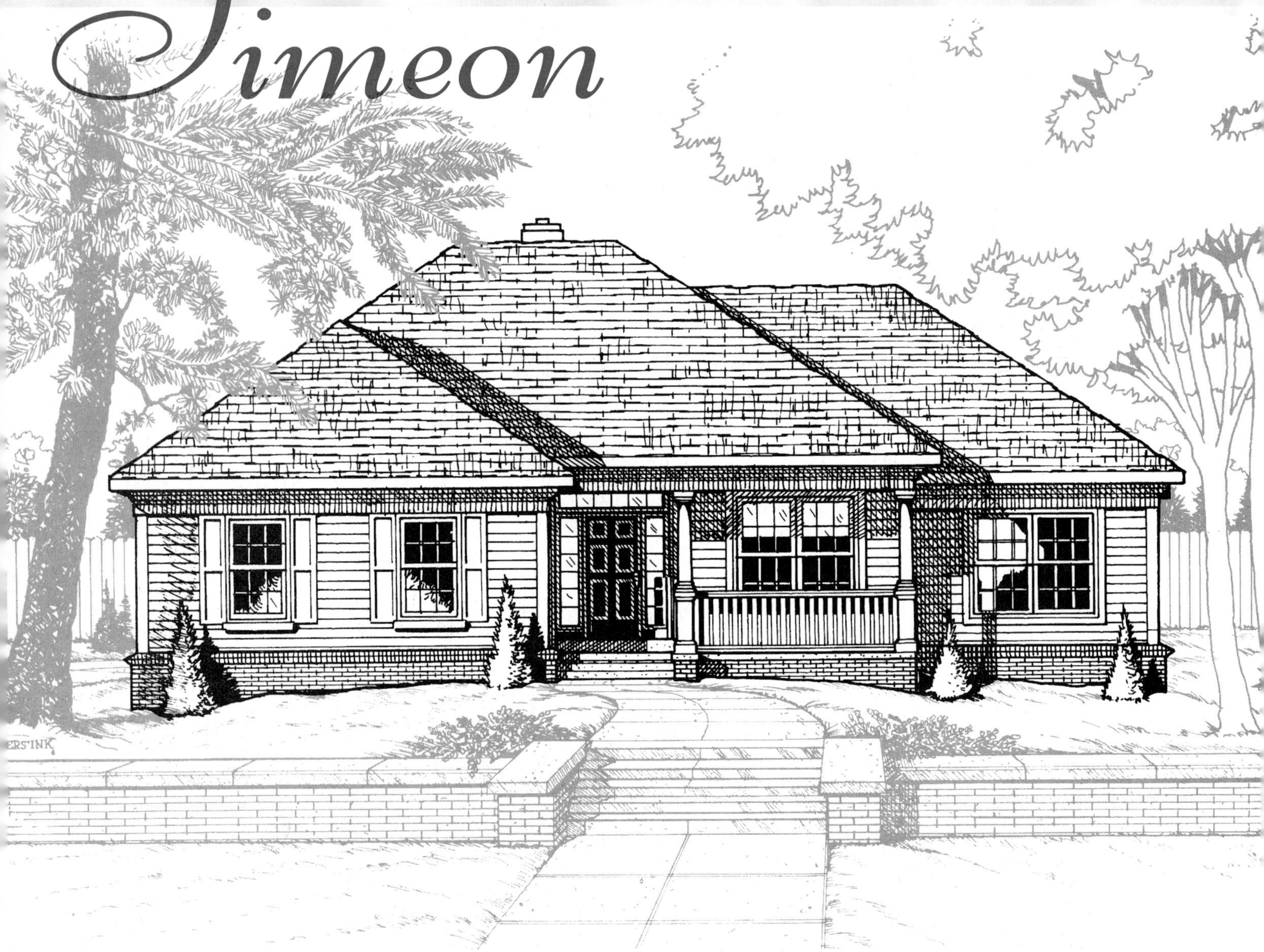

❶ A 10-foot ceiling on the front porch lends a spacious quality to this steadfast icon.

❷ The living room provides a number of options including use as a third bedroom.

❸ Mingling together in an open area, the kitchen and breakfast area create a haven for today's lifestyles.

❹ A walk-in pantry is located near the kitchen, and it could also be used for household storage.

❺ Accompanying the master bedroom, a private bath includes a walk-in closet, dual-sink vanity and whirlpool tub.

❻ A soaking sink is an added benefit to the laundry room.

AVAILABLE FOR ALL PLANS

For More Information on Reverse Plans see page 158.

9K-5090 PRICE CODE 19

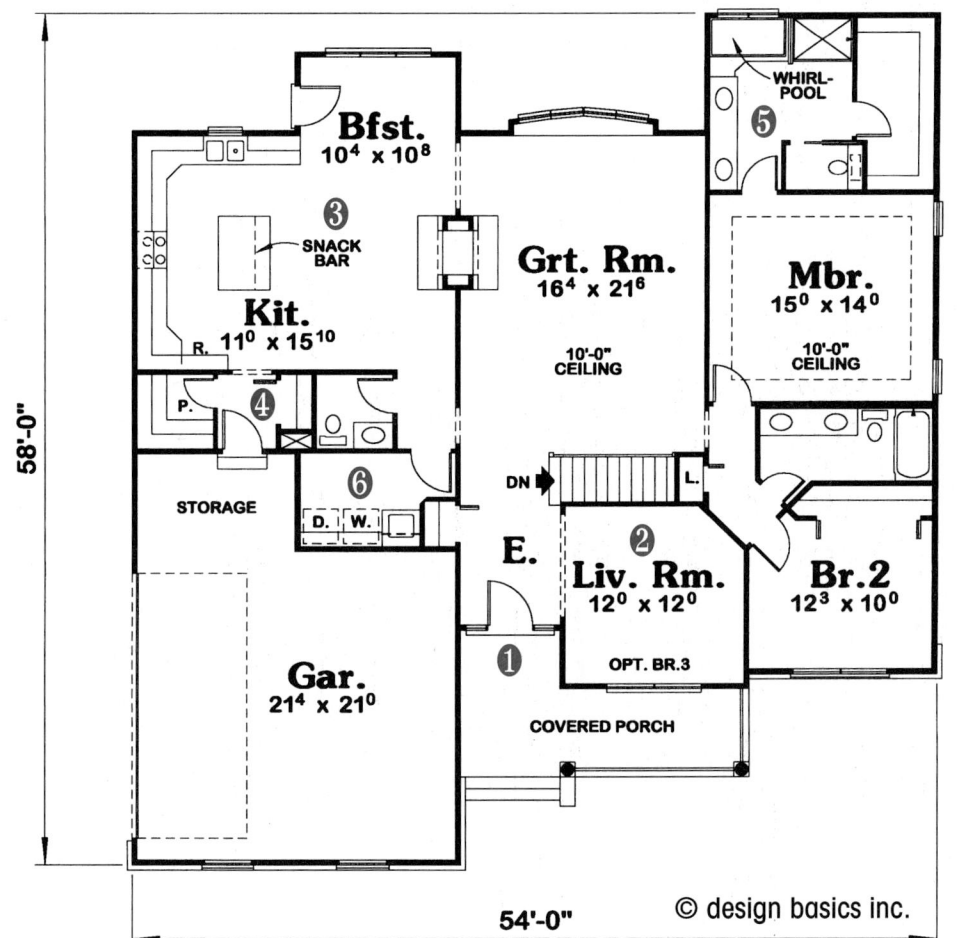

1920 Finished Sq. Ft.

NOTE: 9 ft. main level walls

DECORATOR DESIGN TIPS

KITCHEN/BREAKFAST AREA - Kitchens often serve as a "hub" within a home. Two wing-style chairs flanking each side of the fireplace are positioned to face the kitchen area, so that this "hub" can be viewed from all angles. One may find the chairs a nice, cozy place for reading or curling up by the fire. A bookcase full of books adds a warm touch to the room. This space can also readily accommodate a desk where one may study, use a computer, or make a grocery list.

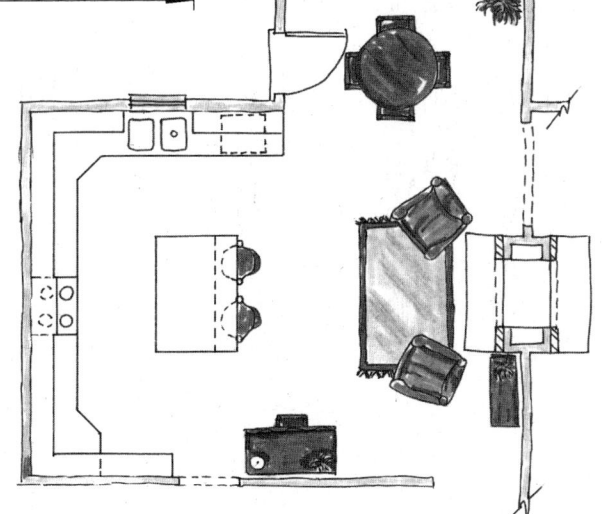

TO ORDER THIS PLAN CALL
1-800-947-7526

Nostalgia

Elving

❶ The stately brick exterior of this home beckons interest and attention.

❷ The formal dining room just off the hearth room features a convenient servery for special occasions.

❸ The great room, charmed by a sloped ceiling, shares a lovely see-thru fireplace with the hearth room and kitchen.

❹ A peninsula snack bar in the cozy kitchen serves the breakfast area, which has a sloped ceiling and atrium door to the outside.

❺ The master suite is secluded off the great room and offers private access to outside.

❻ Near the kitchen is an efficient laundry room with soaking sink.

AVAILABLE FOR ALL PLANS

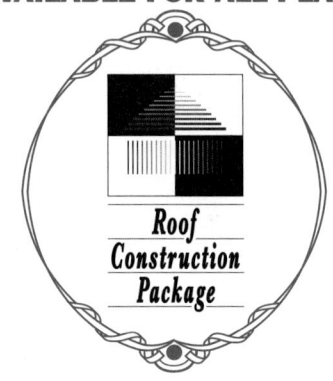

Roof Construction Package

For More Information on our Roof Construction Package see page 158.

9K-4644 PRICE CODE 19

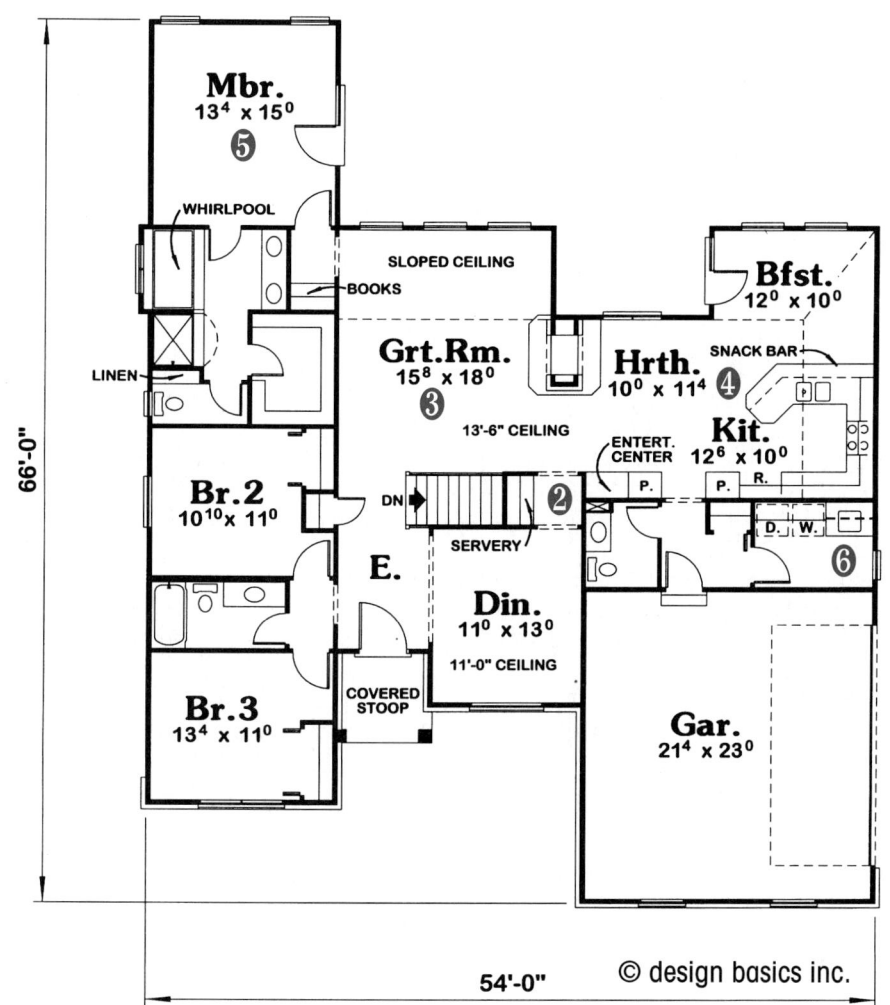

1971 Finished Sq. Ft.

NOTE: 9 ft. main level walls

EXTERIOR HIGHLIGHT

The use of a copper-clad roof and an oversized arched window were designed to draw attention to the elevation. The effect is also unpretentious which is the perfect atmosphere for a one-story of this size.

TO ORDER THIS PLAN CALL
1-800-947-7526

Nostalgia
35

Aldrich

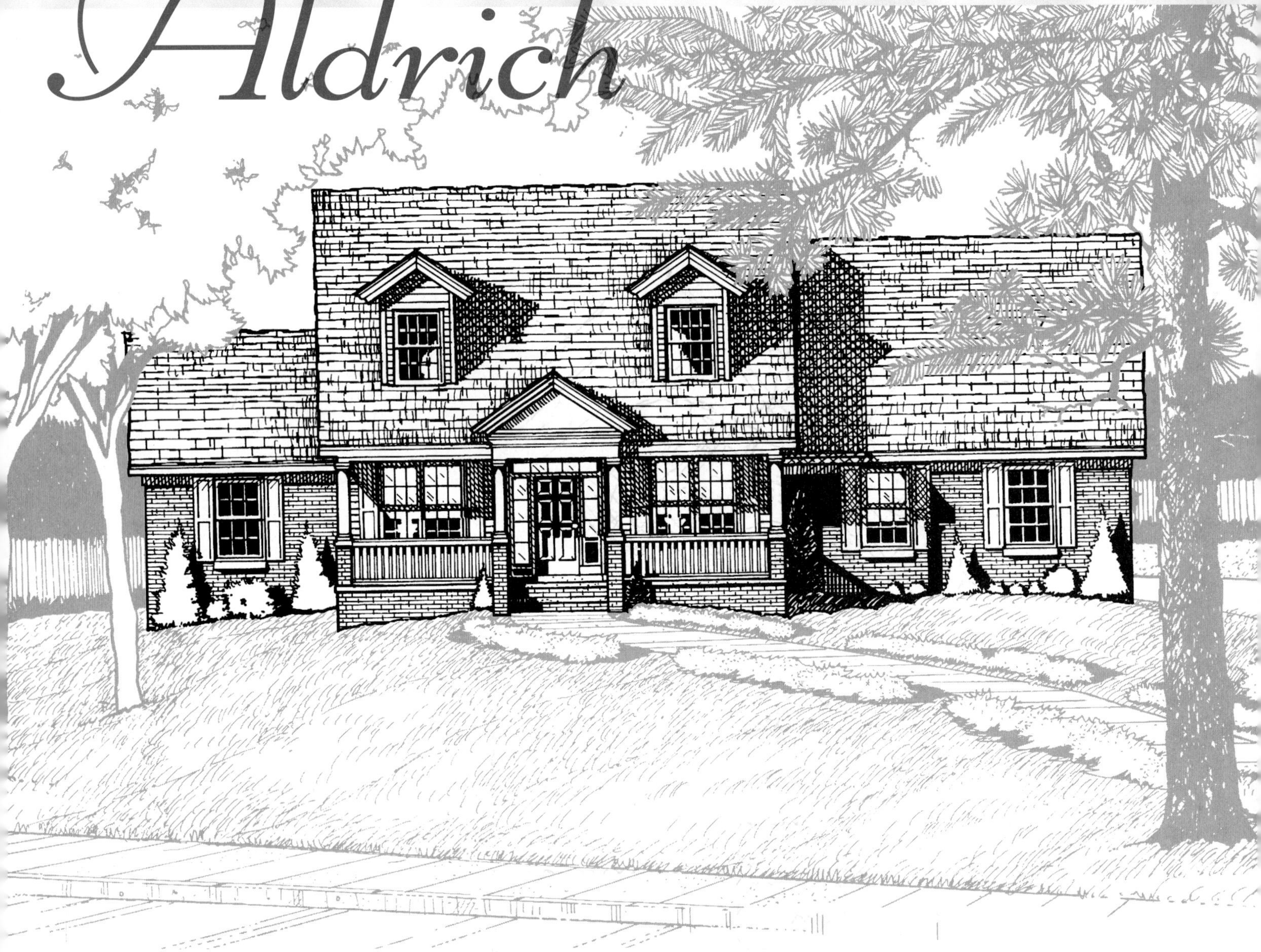

❶ Upon walking in, large formal rooms help define the stylish appeal of this design.

❷ Oak flooring is abundant throughout the main floor, creating a cozy yet dignified feel.

❸ The master bedroom affords privacy and luxury, located on an opposite wing of the home and furnished with luxurious amenities.

❹ A walk-in closet and dressing area in the master bath are served by a large linen closet opened by beautiful double doors.

❺ Bedroom 2 has as much privacy as the master suite, with its own full bath across the hall.

❻ An unfinished attic with adorable dormers could be used as a quaint office or guest suite.

AVAILABLE FOR ALL PLANS

For More Information on Parade Home Packages see page 158.

EXTERIOR HIGHLIGHT

Southern Colonial front porches are notable for their charm. This one was designed with crown moulding and smooth Doric columns on a square brick column base.

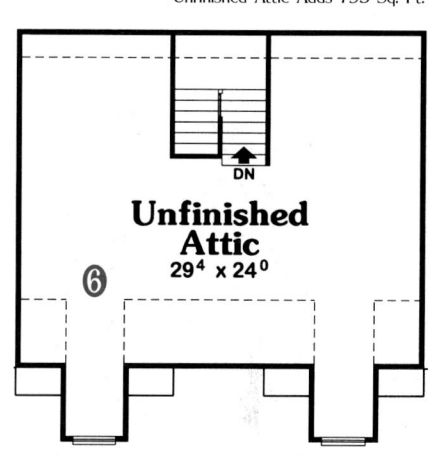

Unfinished Attic Adds 795 Sq. Ft.

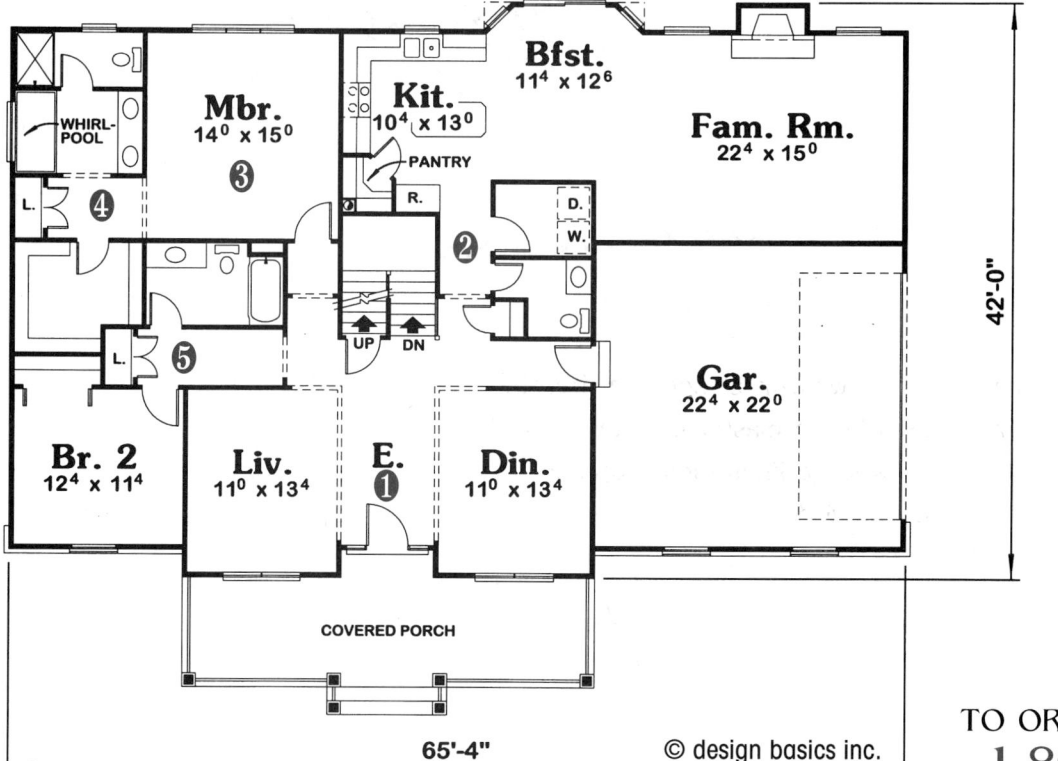

2039 Finished Sq. Ft.

NOTE: 9 ft. main level walls

MAIN FLOOR

TO ORDER THIS PLAN CALL
1-800-947-7526

Nostalgia
37

Creighton

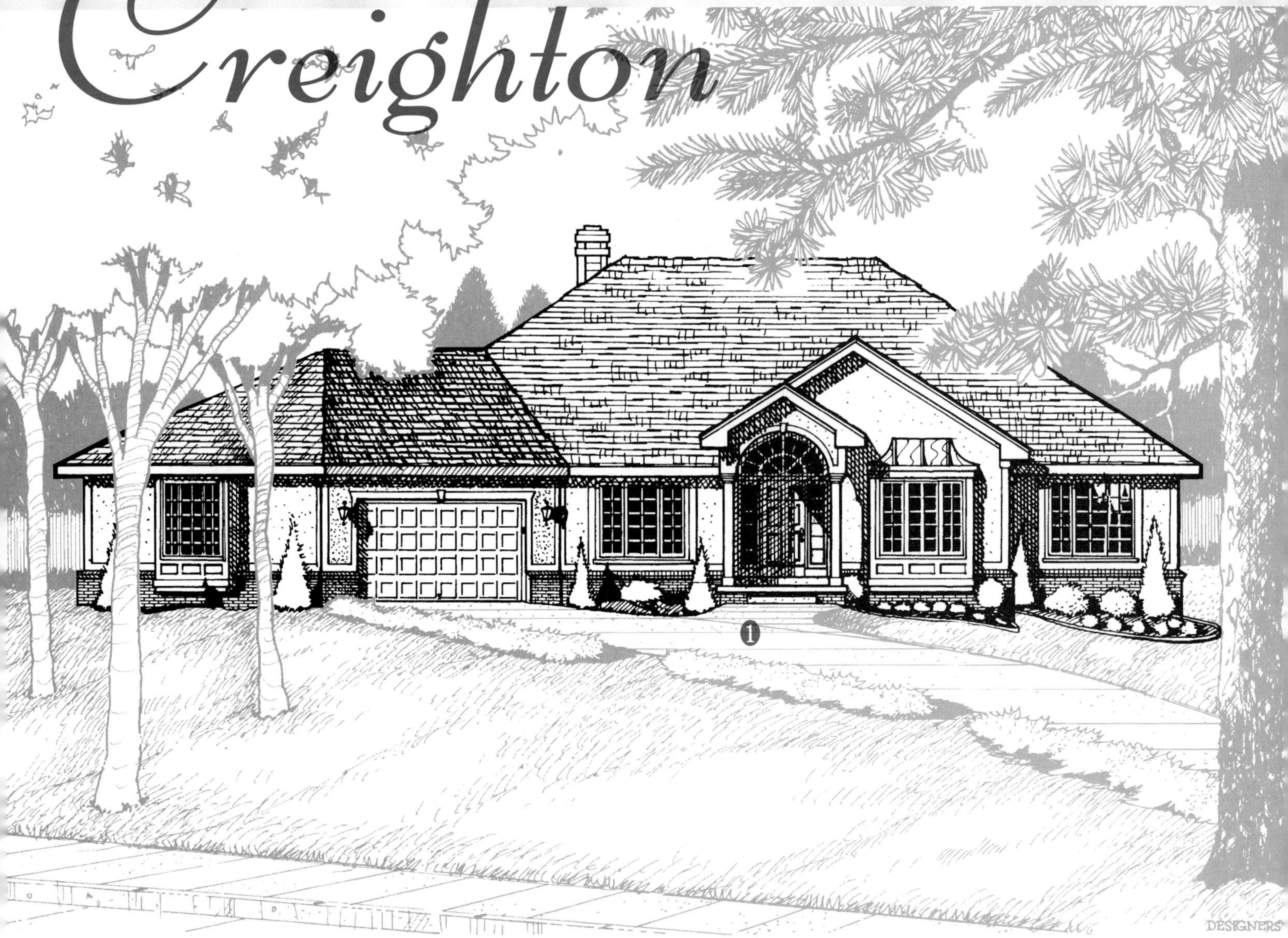

❶ Attractive columns, an angled garage and a stucco veneer dignify this eye-catching one-story home.

❷ A feeling of tranquility rests in the great room featuring a see-through fireplace, entertainment center and French doors to a covered back porch.

❸ The see-thru fireplace creates a comfortable atmosphere for working in the kitchen, which also boasts a walk-in pantry and huge snack bar.

❹ Extra space in the master bedroom provides a place for sitting or work area.

❺ Two covered rear porches encourage relaxation, and offer fun opportunities for outdoor activities.

❻ An angled garage makes the home useable on a narrower lot.

AVAILABLE FOR ALL PLANS

For More Information on our Custom Changes see page 157.

9K-4208

2057 Finished Sq. Ft.
NOTE: 8 ft. main level walls

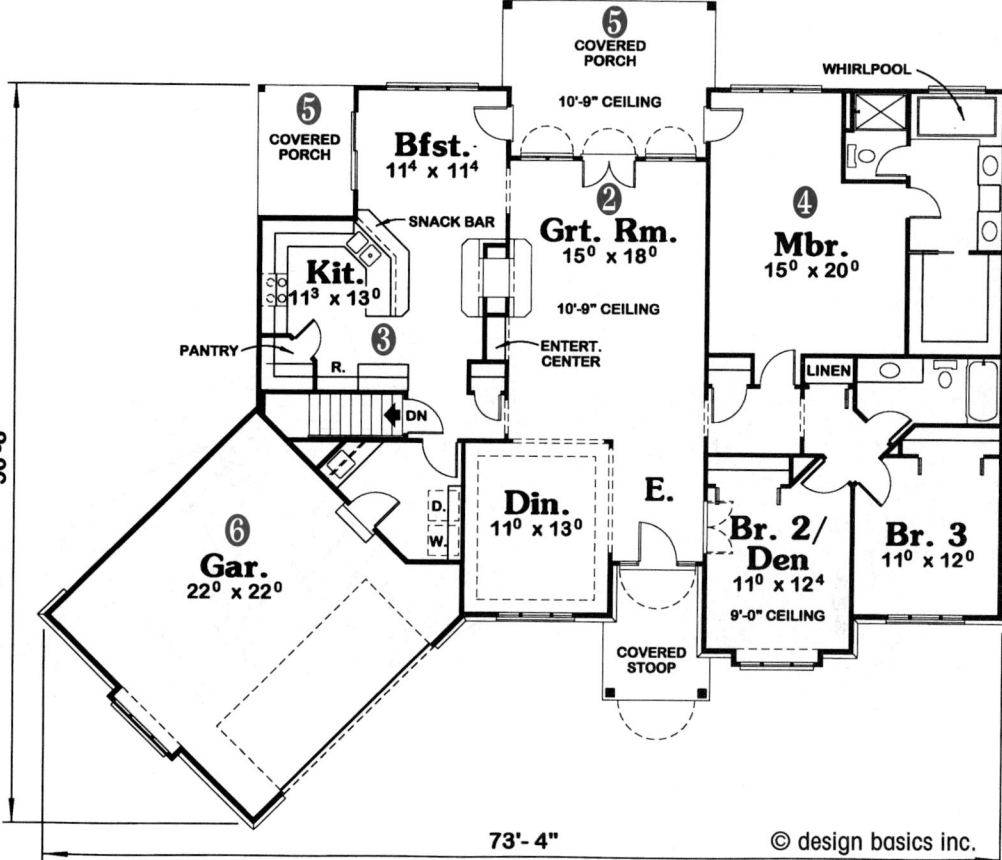

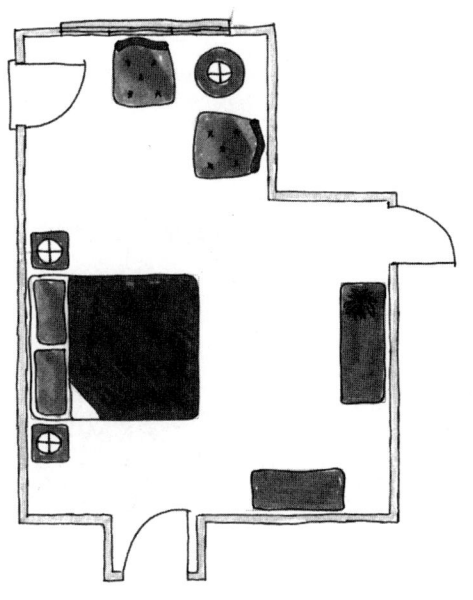

DECORATOR DESIGN TIPS

MASTER SUITE - A small sitting area in the master bedroom provides a great opportunity to add upholstery. Two chairs seem to fill the sitting room the best without overdoing it. Anything larger, such as a loveseat, would overpower the space. The placement of the bed works best on the left side of the room so that a long path from the lower door to the upper left door isn't created. The bed placement also breaks up the space in the bedroom, helping to define the two areas.

TO ORDER THIS PLAN CALL
1-800-947-7526

design basics inc
HOME PLAN DESIGN SERVICE

Cameron

❶ A Prairie influence brings refreshing symmetry to the front elevation.

❷ Perfect for a walk-out lot situation, a stairway in the great room leads to the lower level and is open to two-story-high windows with a view to the back.

❸ A three-sided stone fireplace brings warmth to the spacious kitchen, dinette and great room.

❹ The master suite provides ample closet space and twin lavs across from a whirlpool tub.

❺ Separated for privacy, two secondary bedrooms share a full bath.

❻ Depending on the need, a den or dining room can be located just inside the entry.

ALL PLANS COPYRIGHTED

For More Information on our Copyrights see page 154.

Nostalgia

9K-5036 PRICE CODE 21

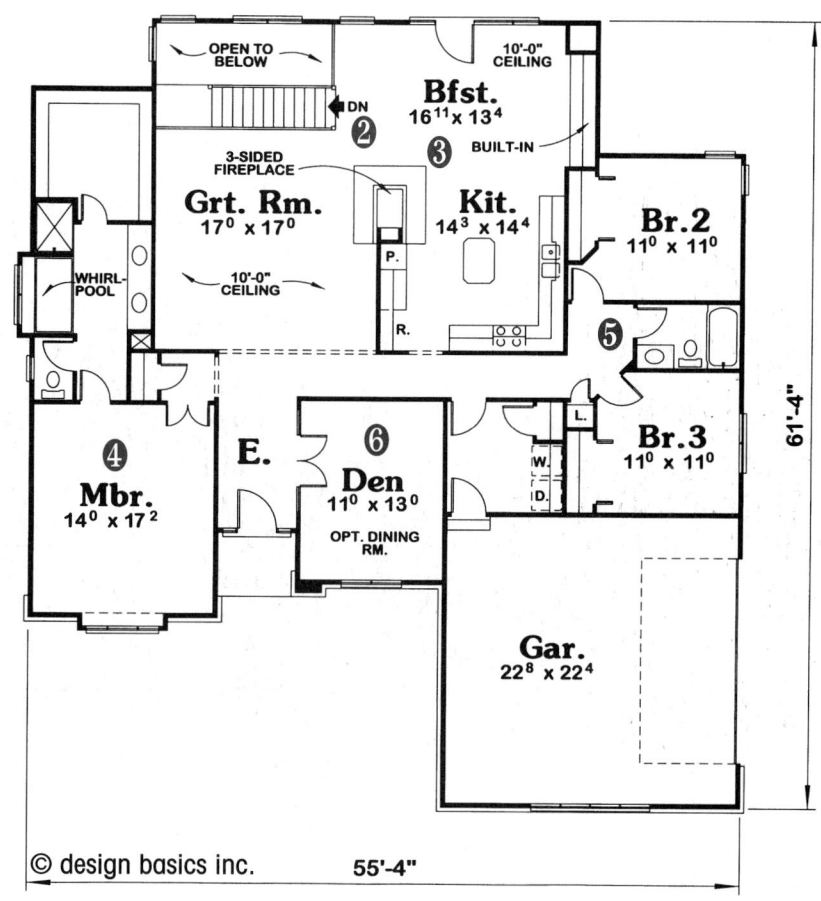

2167 Finished Sq. Ft.

NOTE: 9 ft. main level walls

INTERIOR VIEW

GREAT ROOM - The great room views a stone-sided fireplace which also warms the kitchen and breakfast area. At the rear of the great room, an open balcony showcases a lower level atrium highlighting two-story, floor-to-ceiling windows.

TO ORDER THIS PLAN CALL
1-800-947-7526

design basics inc.
HOME PLAN DESIGN SERVICE

Nostalgia

Holden

❶ The entry opens immediately to a dining room and a great room, both offering ample space for entertaining.

❷ Secluded down a hall, is a private office providing the option of becoming a fourth bedroom.

❸ The kitchen and breakfast area open spaciously to the great room, and have a convenient island, planning desk and pantry.

❹ Perfect for individual desires, bedroom 3 could easily convert into a formal living room.

❺ The master suite is also privately situated in the left wing and has a large walk-in closet, dual lavs and a compartmental stool and shower.

❻ Plenty of storage space in the garage forms the perfect work alcove.

AVAILABLE FOR ALL PLANS

Roof Construction Package

For More Information on our Roof Construction Package see page 158.

9K-4998 PRICE CODE 22

2227 Finished Sq. Ft.
NOTE: 9 ft. main level walls

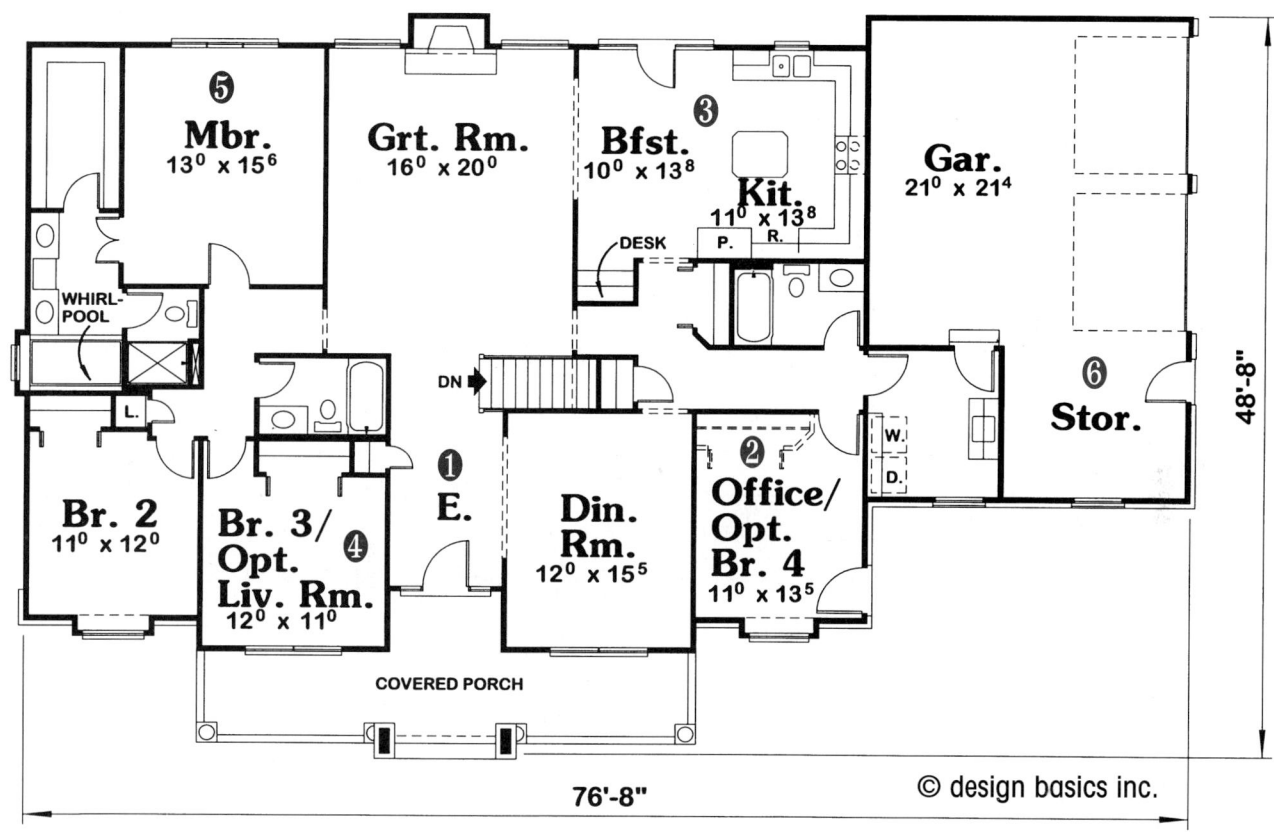

EXTERIOR HIGHLIGHT

The focal point on this home's front elevation, the porch was designed with a unique combination of brick and wood columns. The effect brings an unpretentious, yet polished look to the home.

TO ORDER THIS PLAN CALL
1-800-947-7526

design basics inc.
HOME PLAN DESIGN SERVICE

Nostalgia

Enfield

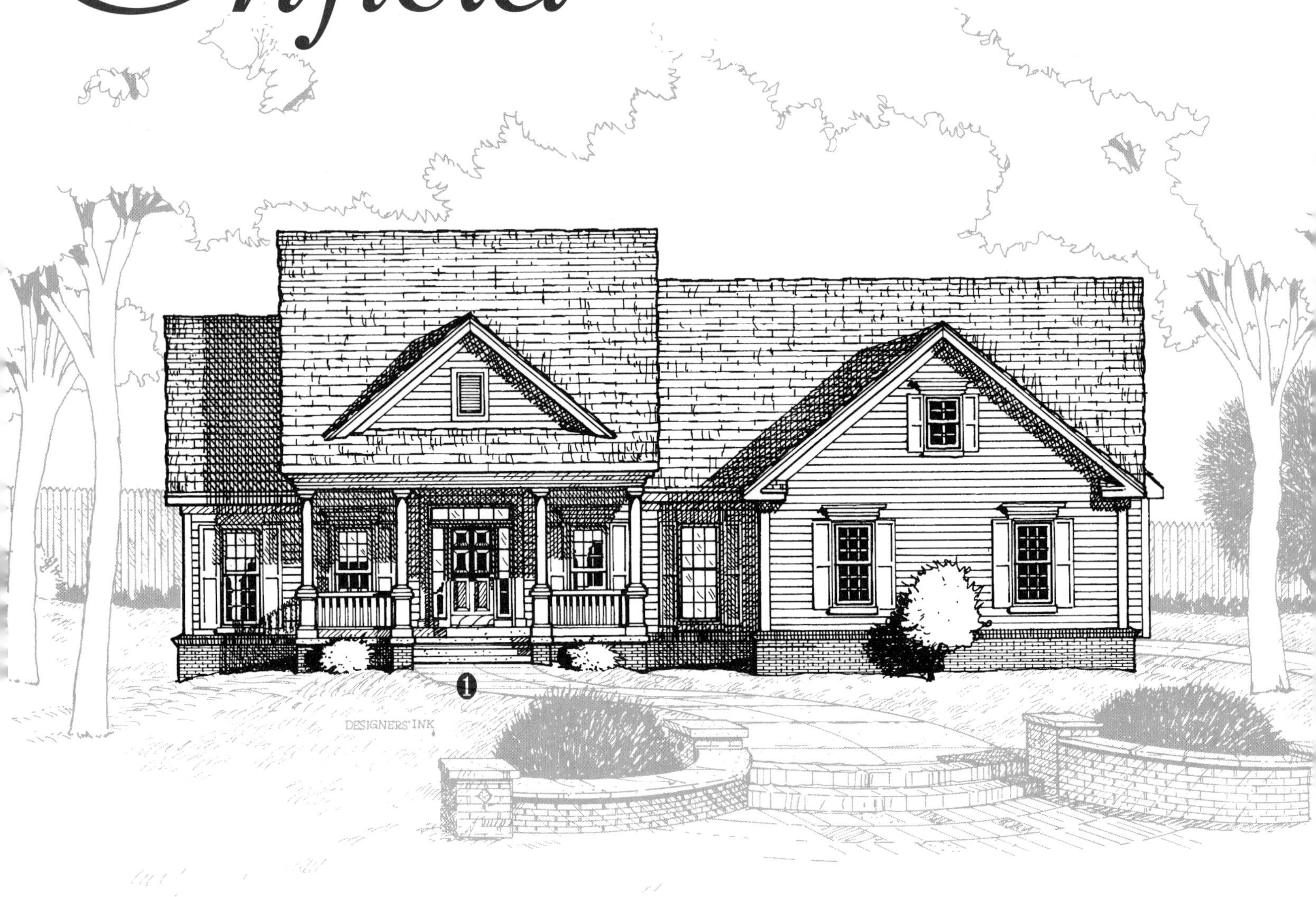

❶ The serene nature of this front elevation will complement almost any neighborhood.

❷ An attic with two long dormers adds ambiance and romance to this home.

❸ Set at an angle, the see-thru fireplace warms both the great room and hearth room.

❹ The kitchen and dinette extend the cozy atmosphere of the hearth room.

❺ Both the dining room and the garage have streamlined access to the kitchen.

❻ A built-in desk and walk-in closet accommodate the second bedroom, conveniently separated from the master suite.

AVAILABLE FOR ALL PLANS

For More Information on Reverse Plans see page 158.

9K -5141 PRICE CODE 22

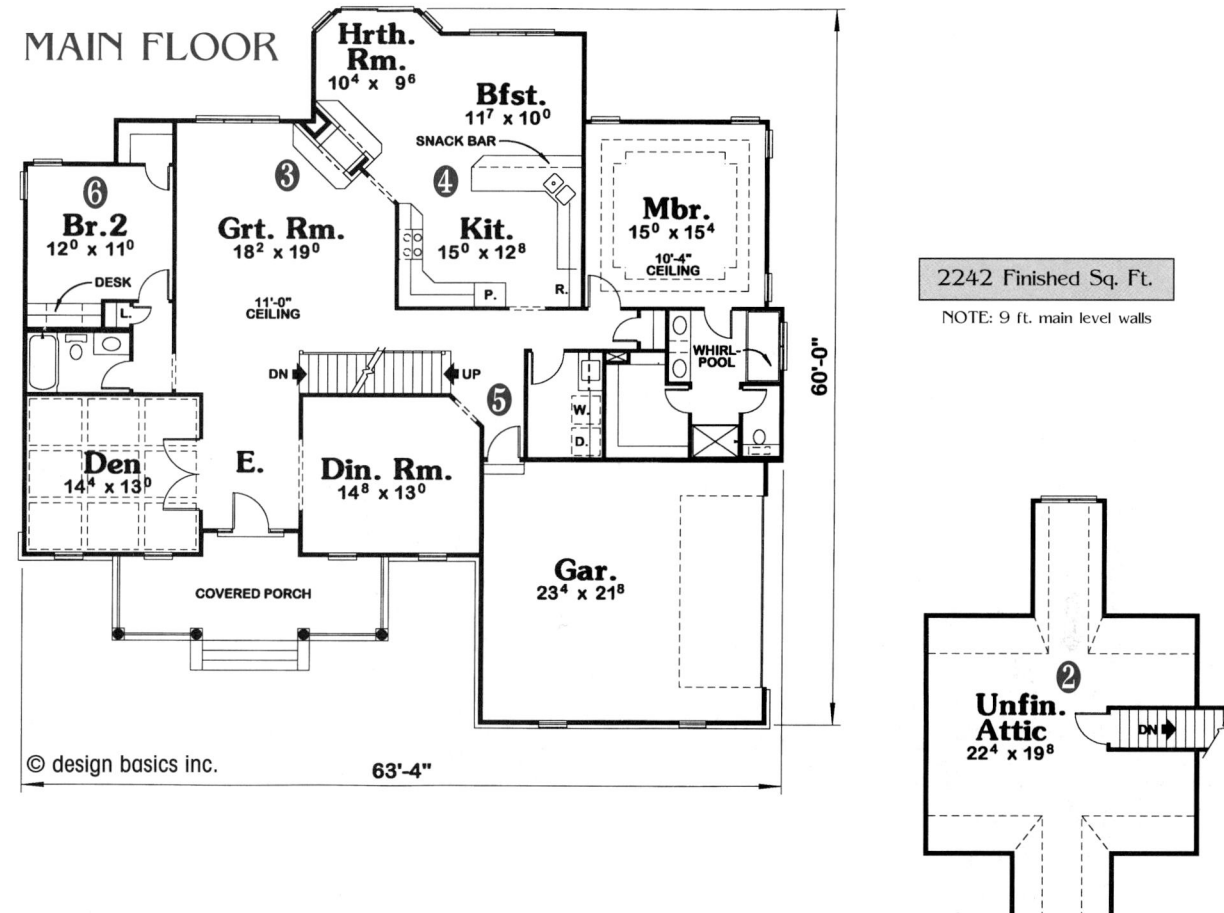

MAIN FLOOR

- Hrth. Rm. 10⁴ x 9⁶
- Bfst. 11⁷ x 10⁰
- Br. 2 12⁰ x 11⁰
- Grt. Rm. 18² x 19⁰
- Kit. 15⁰ x 12⁸
- Mbr. 15⁰ x 15⁴ (10'-4" CEILING)
- 11'-0" CEILING
- Den 14⁴ x 13⁰
- Din. Rm. 14⁸ x 13⁰
- Gar. 23⁴ x 21⁸
- COVERED PORCH
- 63'-4"
- 60'-0"
- © design basics inc.

2242 Finished Sq. Ft.
NOTE: 9 ft. main level walls

ATTIC FLOOR

Unfin. Attic 22⁴ x 19⁸

Unfinished Attic Adds 613 Sq. Ft.

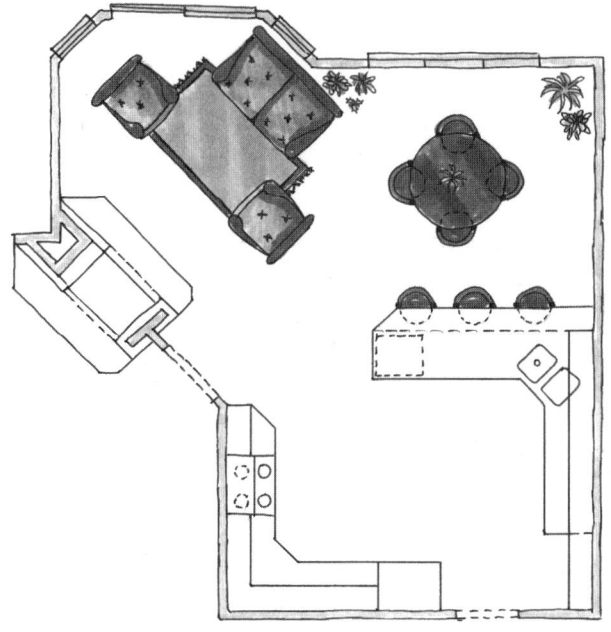

DECORATOR DESIGN TIPS

KITCHEN/HEARTH ROOM - The furniture arrangement allows for easy entertainment and conversation in the hearth room. An area rug pulls all of the upholstery together and unifies the arrangement. Placing the furniture parallel to the fireplace emphasizes its unique angle.

TO ORDER THIS PLAN CALL
1-800-947-7526

design basics inc.
HOME PLAN DESIGN SERVICE

Nostalgia

Saybrooke

❶ The tapered columns, panel shutters and beautiful arched window treatments of this design offer an influential first impression.

❷ Just off the entry, the dining room features double doors that link to the kitchen for serving ease.

❸ The kitchen, with an island and snack bar, serves the breakfast area and great room.

❹ An 11-foot-high ceiling and raised-hearth fireplace distinguish the great room.

❺ Bedrooms 2 and 3 are located in the left wing of the home, and share a Hollywood bath.

❻ Bedroom 4 – a perfect guest suite – easily converts into a den with double doors off the entry.

AVAILABLE FOR ALL PLANS

For More Information on Parade Home Packages see page 158.

Nostalgia

9K-5003 PRICE CODE 27

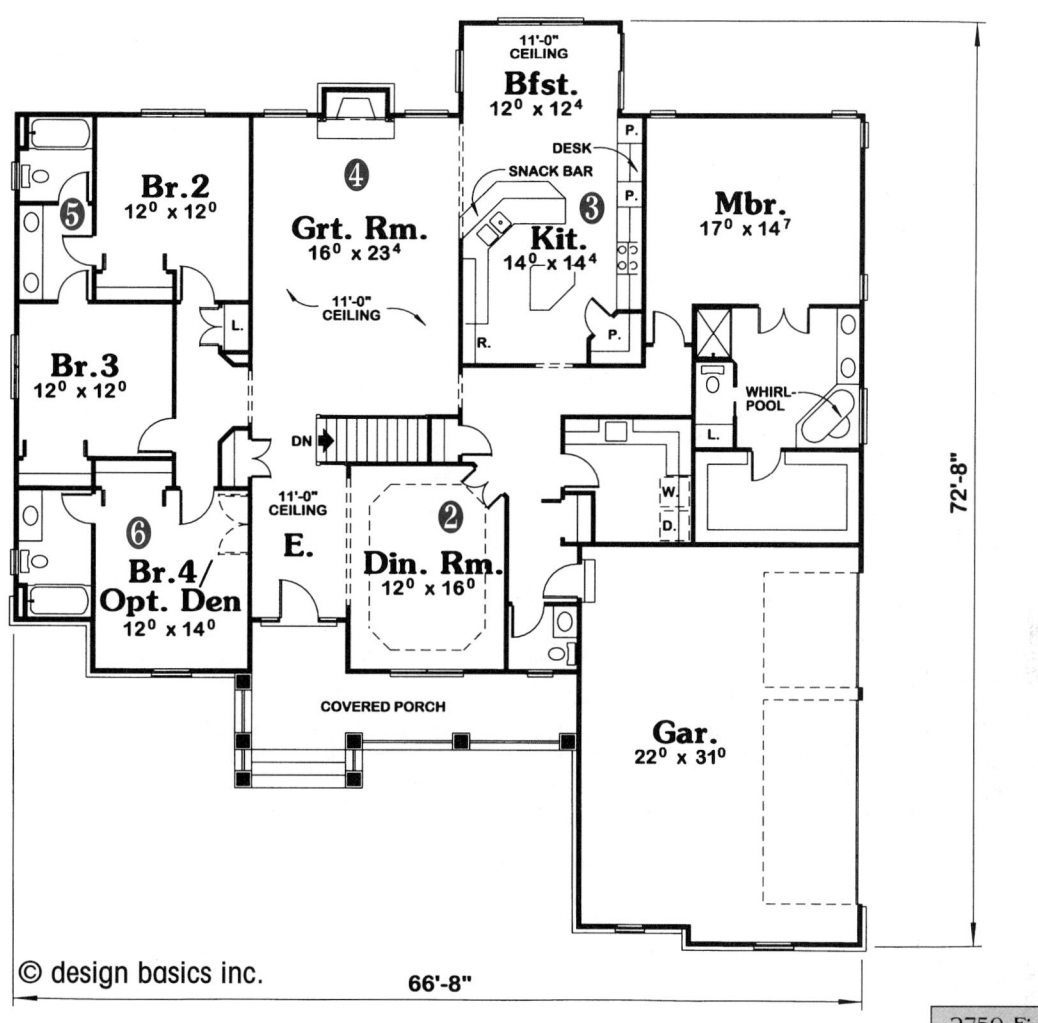

2750 Finished Sq. Ft.
NOTE: 9 ft. main level walls

INTERIOR VIEW

MASTER BATH - A view of the master bath reveals a corner whirlpool tub and spacious dressing area to accompany a large walk-in closet.

TO ORDER THIS PLAN CALL
1-800-947-7526

In the **Nostalgia** *Collection you will find...*

SIDE-LOAD GARAGES

"Probably one of the most difficult things to work around in home design is the garage. Since it is large to begin with, and getting larger all of the time, designers like ourselves do everything we can to 'de-emphasize' its presence. The majority of the homes in this collection feature side-load garages, in part, to help replicate the architectural styles of homes before there were garages. But doing so also creates an easier option to change the garage to a front-load entry than vice versa."

WORK SPACE

"With the popularity of 'do-it-yourself' home improvement, we as designers have to ask ourselves where the buyer will put his work bench or lawn equipment, when designing the garage. We tried as much as we possibly could to design alcoves and obvious storage areas into the garages in this collection. This will, in many cases, allow buyers and builders to include a garden center or work bench in the construction of the home."

1½-story Homes

Plan Index

Plan #	Plan Name	Sq. Ft.	Page #
5151	Sedona	1755	50-51
5160	Tecoma	1762	52-53
4133	Marcell	1772	54-55
5079	Cumberland	1851	56-57
4646	Kirkwood	1853	58-59
5159	Blaire	2118	60-61
5131	Chambers	2143	62-63
5161	Auburn	2167	64-65
5149	Camrose	2190	66-67
5136	Stanfield	2221	68-69
5148	Bowden	2339	70-71
4082	Kenneth	2351	72-73
5162	Calidore	2393	74-75
5150	Magrath	2421	76-77
5158	Carey	2512	78-79
5146	Ellsworth	2536	80-81
4081	Hanna	2576	82-83
4134	Schuyler	2613	84-85
5178	Rowena	2637	86-87
5210	Colette	2681	88-89
5157	Reston	2738	90-91
4641	Nicole	2781	92-93
5185	Wayland	2820	94-95
5105	Mahoning	2826	96-97
5000	Middleboro	2989	98-99
4144	Marlow	3040	100-101
4089	Eleanor	3103	102-103
5142	Landreth	3480	104-105

Sedona

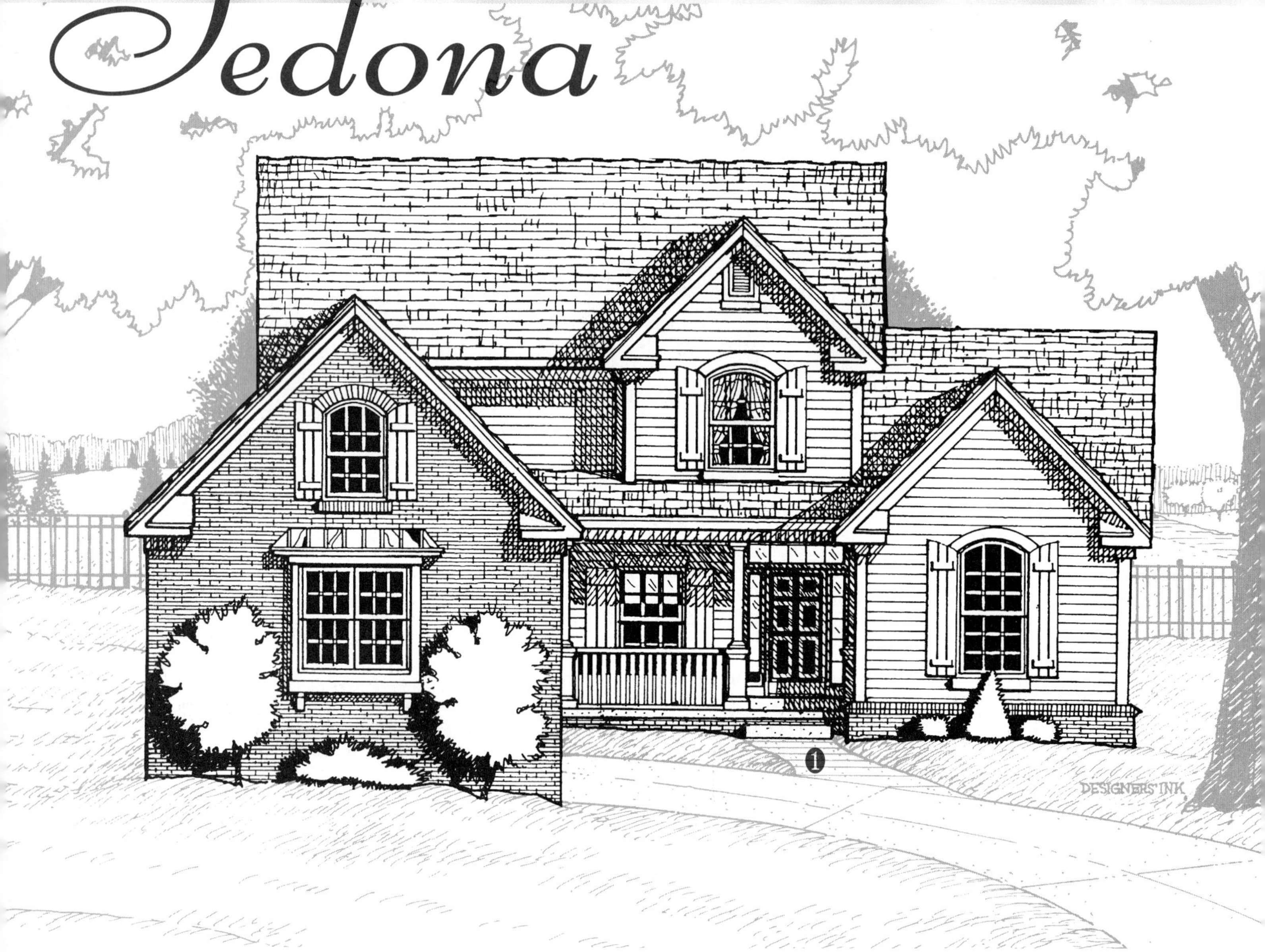

❶ Charismatic details on this facade will welcome you home again and again.

❷ An interior side-load garage is perfect for a narrow lot situation.

❸ The laundry room offers plenty of counter space to fold clothes and is roomy enough to accommodate entry from the garage.

❹ A sloped ceiling adds interesting appeal to the fireplace and windows in the great room.

❺ The garage easily has room for a work area and shelving for tools.

❻ Unfinished storage on the second floor could complement the secondary bedrooms as a play area.

AVAILABLE FOR ALL PLANS

For More Information on our Custom Changes see page 157.

9K-5151 PRICE CODE 17

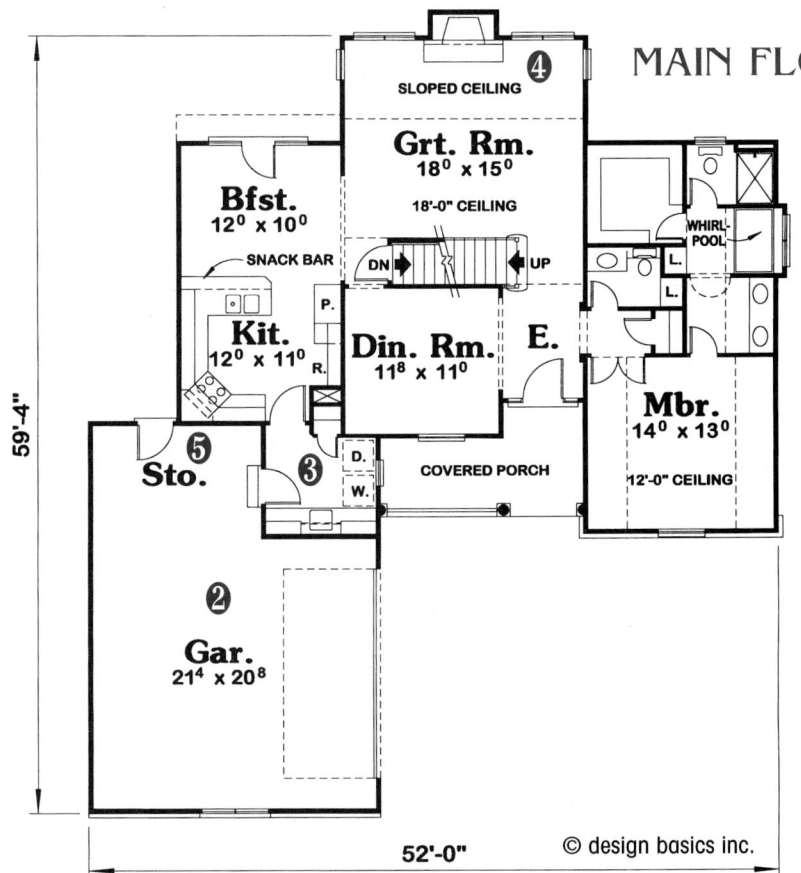

MAIN FLOOR

Main	1331 Sq. Ft.
Second	424 Sq. Ft.
Total	1755 Sq. Ft.

NOTE: 9 ft. main level walls

SECOND FLOOR

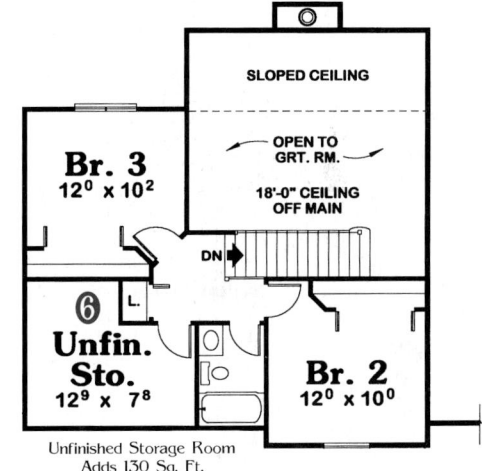

Unfinished Storage Room Adds 130 Sq. Ft.

EXTERIOR HIGHLIGHT

The addition of sidelights and a transom to the front door of this home makes it feel substantial in the entry. The porch is capped off with Doric columns on a square column base.

TO ORDER THIS PLAN CALL
1-800-947-7526

Nostalgia

Tecoma

❶ Separated from the second floor, the master suite provides a walk-in closet, whirlpool tub and dual-lav vanity.

❷ Elegant upon entry, the dining room shows off a lovely window to the front.

❸ Patio doors in the breakfast area lead to a natural place for a deck.

❹ Tall windows in the corners of the great room bring in an abundance of light to the volume space.

❺ Informal meals are easily served on the large snack bar in the kitchen.

❻ A large linen closet on the second floor is great for storing toys or games.

ALL PLANS COPYRIGHTED

For More Information on our Copyrights see page 154.

9K-5160 PRICE CODE 17

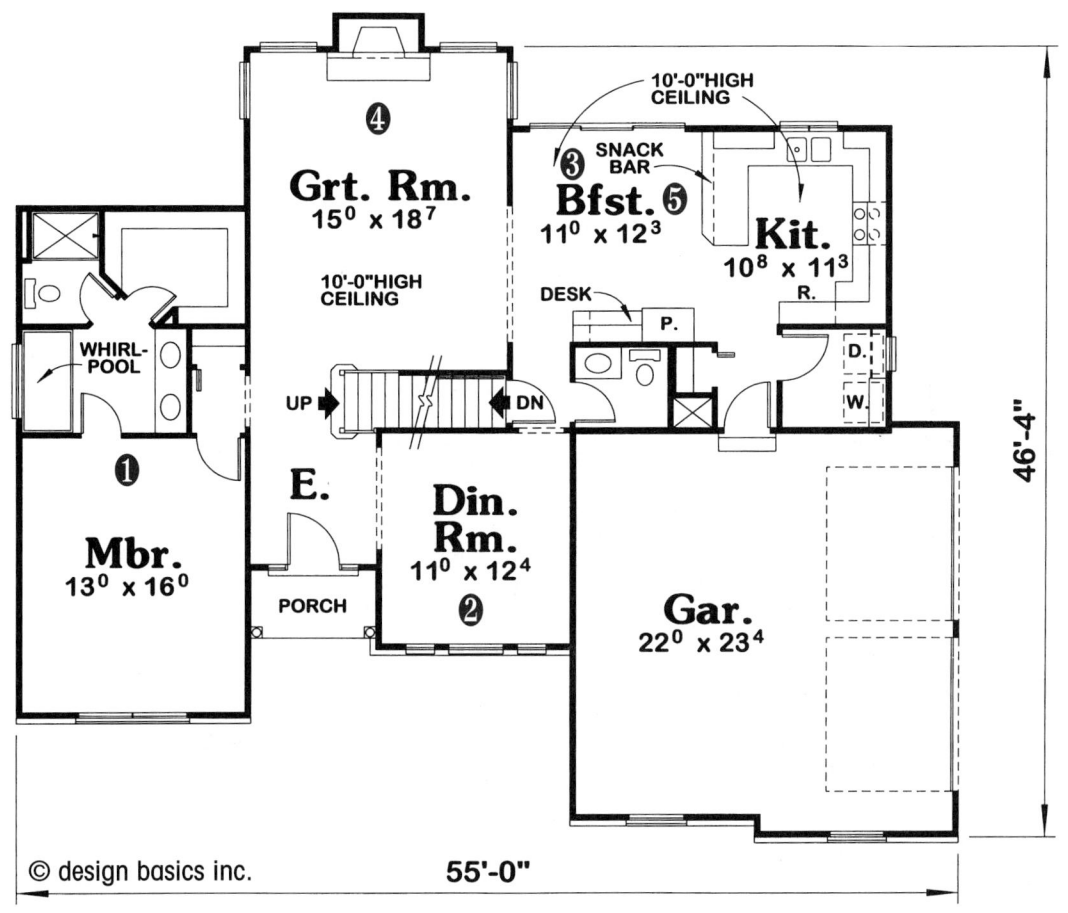

MAIN FLOOR

Main	1363 Sq. Ft.
Second	399 Sq. Ft.
Total	1762 Sq. Ft.

NOTE: 9 ft. main level walls

SECOND FLOOR

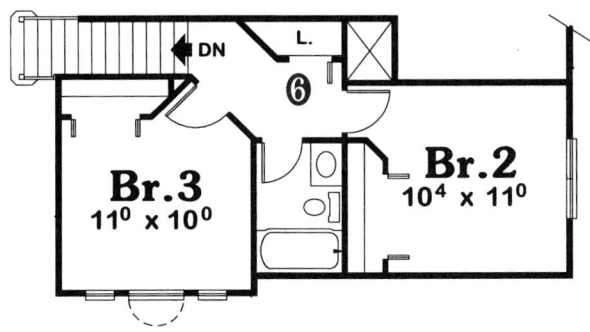

EXTERIOR HIGHLIGHT

It's the subtle detailing on this entry – dentil moulding that offsets a triple window and square side columns framing the entry – that will make the home enjoyed long after it is built.

TO ORDER THIS PLAN CALL
1-800-947-7526

Marcell

❶ Handsome detailing and unique windows are hallmarks on the front elevation of this design.

❷ In the entry, a U-shaped staircase with a window leads to a second-floor balcony, two bedrooms and a full bath.

❸ Triple-arch windows in the front and rear of the great room create an impressive view.

❹ An island counter in the kitchen is within steps of the stove and sink, making it convenient for preparing meals.

❺ A compartmental master bath provides a well-planned, convenient dressing area and vanity space.

❻ Spacious secondary bedrooms easily grant room for a desk or toy chest.

AVAILABLE FOR ALL PLANS

For More Information on Reverse Plans see page 158.

Nostalgia

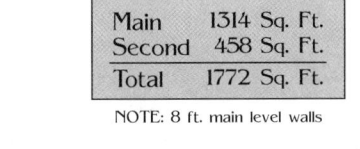

MAIN FLOOR

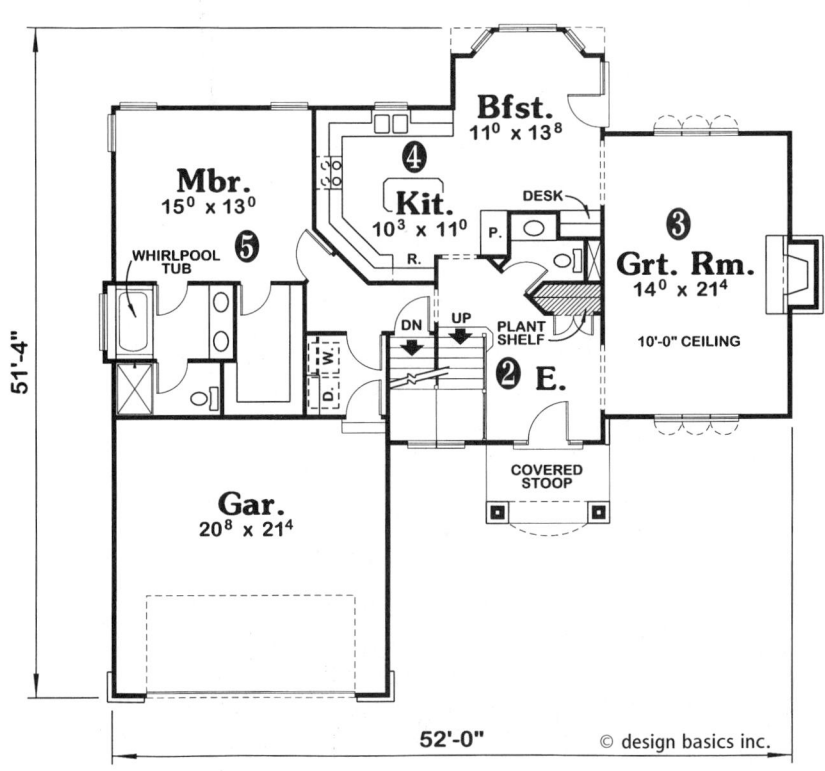

Main	1314 Sq. Ft.
Second	458 Sq. Ft.
Total	1772 Sq. Ft.

NOTE: 8 ft. main level walls

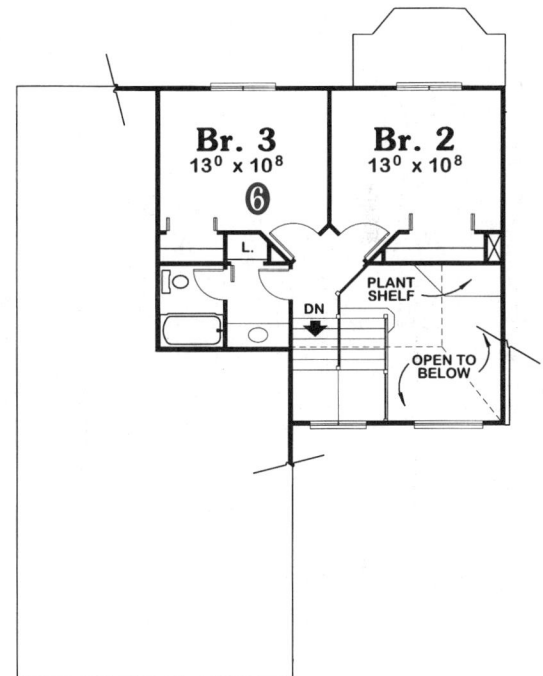

SECOND FLOOR

EXTERIOR HIGHLIGHT

A large transom over the front door on this home helps bring a sense of balance to the striking windows on either side. A brick covered stoop helps draw the eye to this window giving it just the right amount of emphasis on the front elevation.

TO ORDER THIS PLAN CALL
1-800-947-7526

Cumberland

❶ This sophisticated facade invites further inspection of its simultaneously informal styling.

❷ Walls designed at 9-feet in height enhances the spaciousness of all main-level rooms.

❸ A rear-entry staircase steers traffic away from the formal dining room and entry.

❹ A hard-surfaced walkway connects the dining room to the kitchen.

❺ A walk-in closet illuminated with a window and his and her vanities adorn the master bath.

❻ Two bedrooms on the second floor are secluded from main-floor activity.

AVAILABLE FOR ALL PLANS

Roof Construction Package

For More Information on our Roof Construction Package see page 158.

Nostalgia

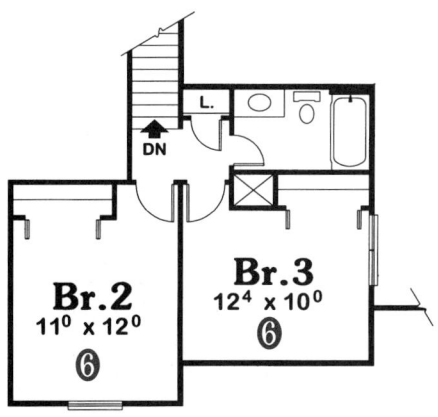

9K-5079 PRICE CODE 18

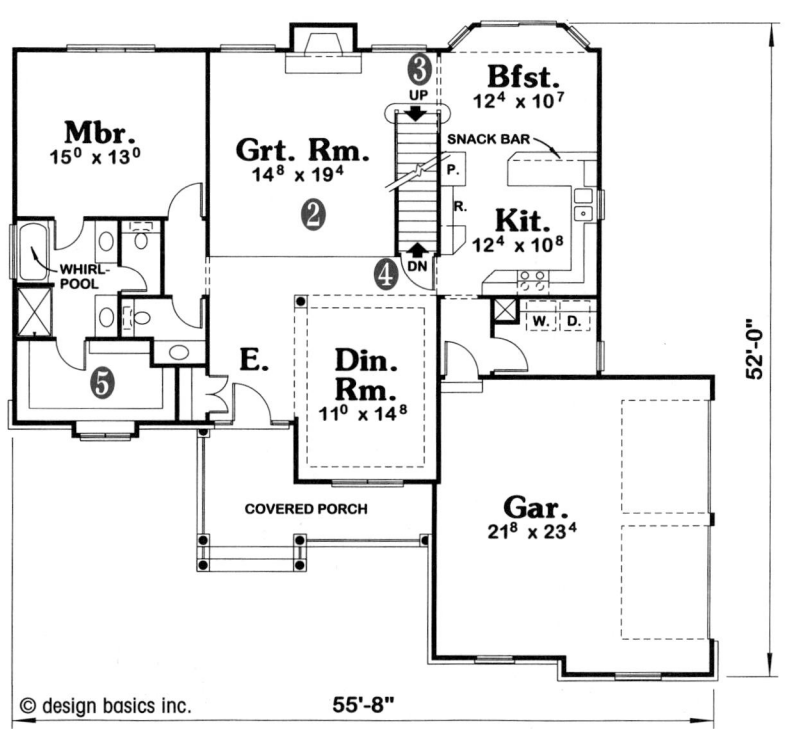

MAIN FLOOR

SECOND FLOOR

Main	1426 Sq. Ft.
Second	425 Sq. Ft.
Total	1851 Sq. Ft.

NOTE: 9 ft. main level walls

EXTERIOR HIGHLIGHT

Detailing, such as crown moulding on a pediment and batten board shutters on a second-story window, are a part of the understated appeal designed into this home.

TO ORDER THIS PLAN CALL
1-800-947-7526

Nostalgia

Kirkwood

❶ A covered porch with a quaint flower box highlights this home's clean facade.

❷ Inside, a wide entry leads to a stairway with a unique vista of the great room from its midway landing.

❸ An informal kitchen uniquely located to the front of the home.

❹ The master suite features a dual-sink vanity, whirlpool tub, large walk-in closet and an elegant window to the front.

❺ Walk-in closets in two secondary bedrooms provide more room for storage.

❻ An alcove in the garage provides a convenient place for tools and lawn equipment.

AVAILABLE FOR ALL PLANS

For More Information on Parade Home Packages see page 158.

Nostalgia

9K -4646 PRICE 18 CODE

MAIN FLOOR

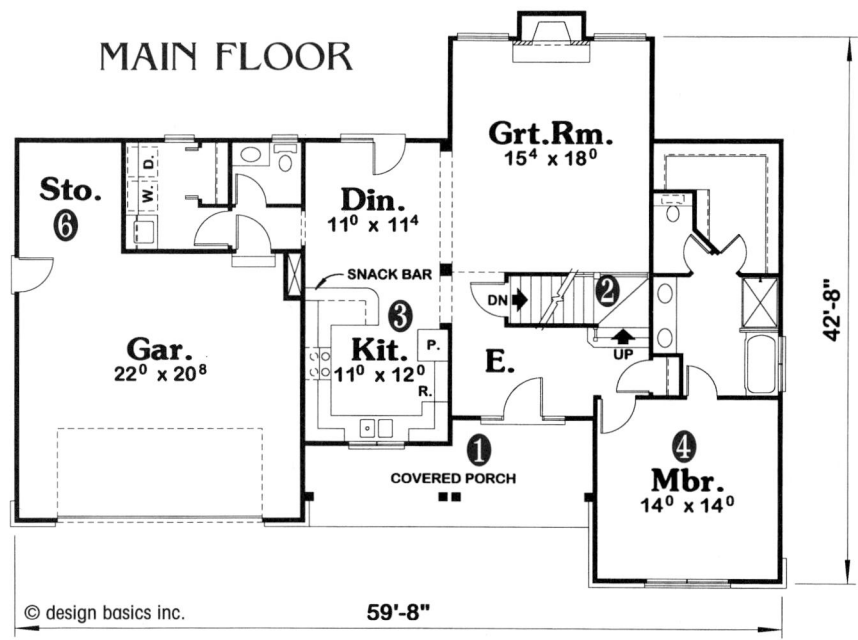

Main	1285 Sq. Ft.
Second	568 Sq. Ft.
Total	1853 Sq. Ft.

NOTE: 8 ft. main level walls

SECOND FLOOR

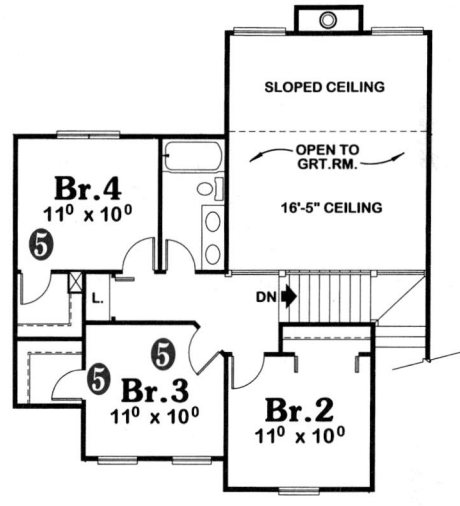

INTERIOR VIEW

GREAT ROOM/KITCHEN - Dropped soffits add definition to the views of the breakfast area and kitchen from the great room. Shown here with formal furniture, the dining area of this home can also function informally.

TO ORDER THIS PLAN CALL
1-800-947-7526

design basics inc.
HOME PLAN DESIGN SERVICE

Nostalgia

Blaire

❶ A row of three windows capped with shutters draws attention to this home's simple beauty.

❷ The practical family area at the rear of the home highlights a large great room that is open to the kitchen and breakfast area.

❸ Accompanying the master suite is a large walk-in closet and whirlpool tub across from a dual-lav vanity.

❹ A T-shaped stairway makes the second-floor accessible from either the front or rear of the home.

❺ Bedroom 2 offers a walk-in closet that could be used for storage space.

❻ Additional storage space is also offered through an unfinished bonus room above the garage.

ALL PLANS COPYRIGHTED

For More Information on our Copyrights see page 154.

9K -5159 PRICE CODE 21

MAIN FLOOR

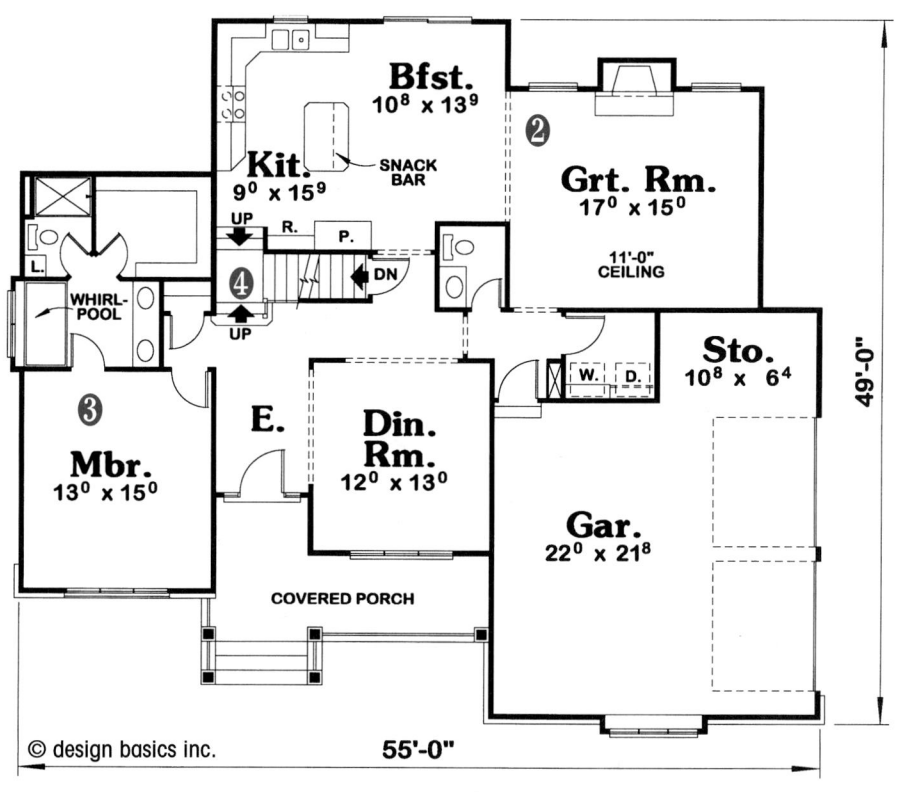

Main	1453 Sq. Ft.
Second	665 Sq. Ft.
Total	2118 Sq. Ft.

NOTE: 9 ft. main level walls

EXTERIOR HIGHLIGHT

A transom and sidelights surrounding the front door and Doric columns framing a portico, make this home reminiscent of Greek Revival architecture. Balanced by a triplet of windows to either side, this classic entry exudes a refreshing welcome.

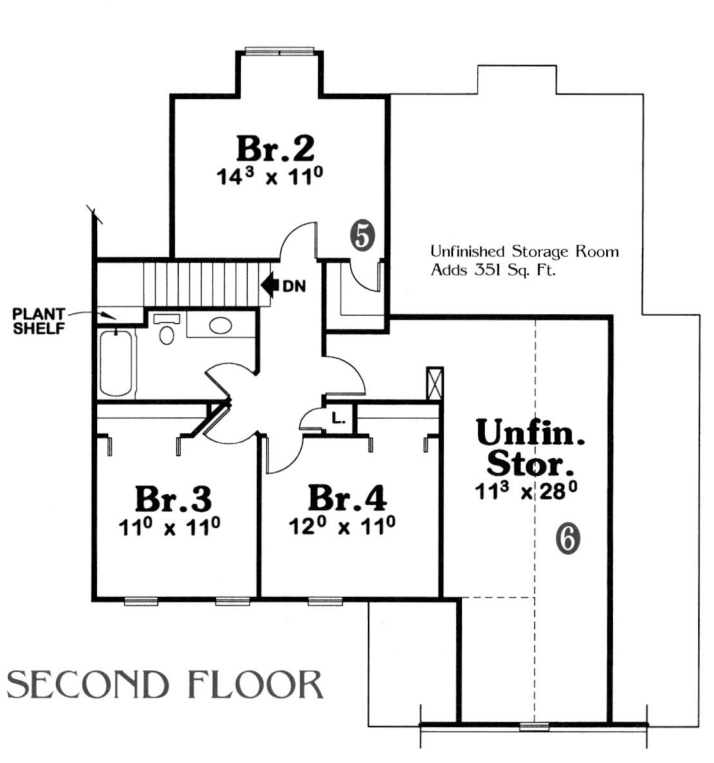

SECOND FLOOR

TO ORDER THIS PLAN CALL
1-800-947-7526

design basics inc.
HOME PLAN DESIGN SERVICE

Nostalgia

Chambers

❶ A classical pediment frames the entry and porch on this home and anchors the front elevation.

❷ A singular, free-standing column brings a hint of timelessness to the dining room.

❸ A corner fireplace encased with two sides of windows illuminates the great room.

❹ The kitchen is brightened with plenty of light from the breakfast area and great room.

❺ A second-floor loft overlooks the dinette and creates the perfect family computer center.

❻ An unfinished bonus room offers flexibility as a fourth bedroom, exercise room or storage for seasonal items.

AVAILABLE FOR ALL PLANS

For More Information on Reverse Plans see page 158.

Nostalgia

9K -5131 PRICE CODE 21

MAIN FLOOR

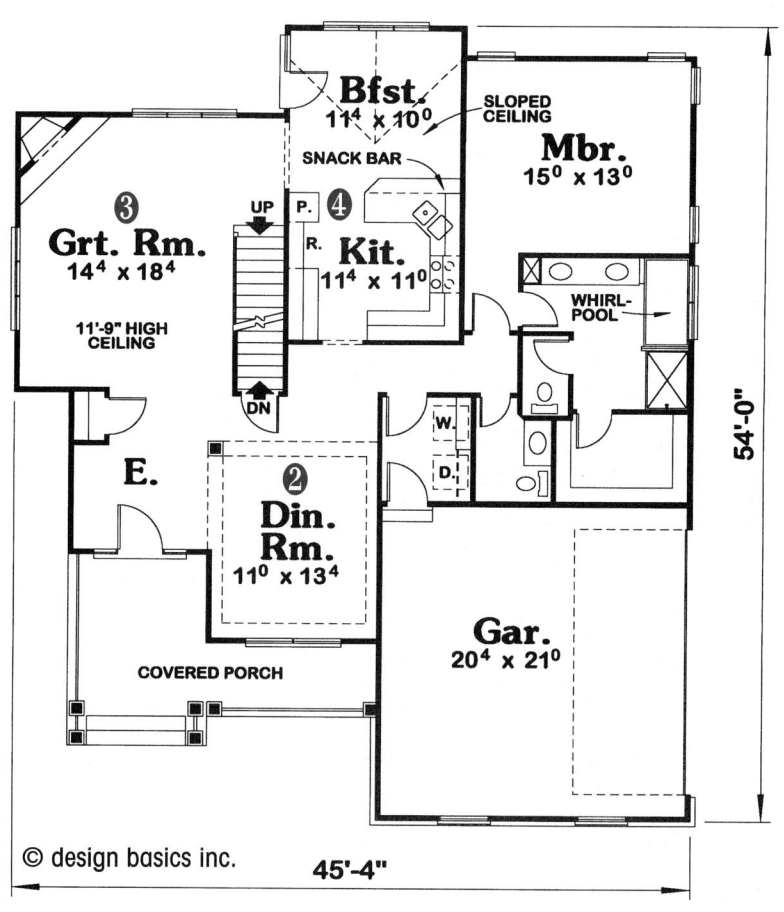

Main	1457 Sq. Ft.
Second	686 Sq. Ft.
Total	2143 Sq. Ft.

NOTE: 9 ft. main level walls

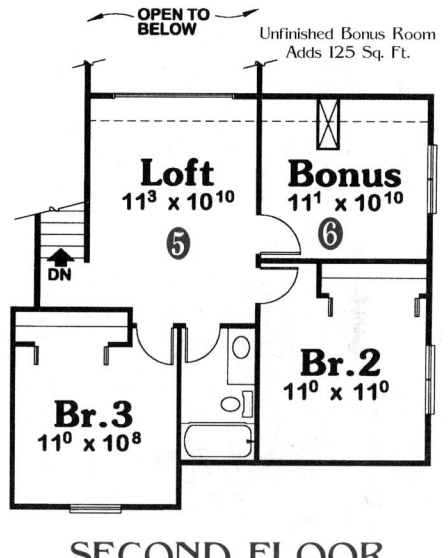

SECOND FLOOR

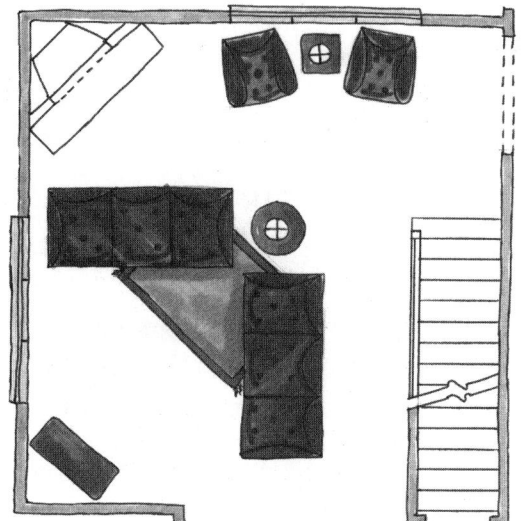

DECORATOR DESIGN TIPS

GREAT ROOM - If including an entertainment unit in this room, the sofas are pulled to the lower half of the room and placed in an "L" shape around the TV unit. A secondary seating area is placed behind the sofas, next to the fireplace, for those who want a more private area. If this room does not require a TV unit, the sofas could flip the opposite way to face the fireplace, while staying in an "L" shape. If the upholstery gets spread too far apart, an ineffective combination is created and isn't conducive for entertaining and conversation.

TO ORDER THIS PLAN CALL
1-800-947-7526

Nostalgia

Auburn

❶ This uncomplicated elevation is a welcome site and coincides with the need to simplify today's lifestyles.

❷ An optional home office, hobby room or extra bedroom, the study increases the flexibility of this design.

❸ The kitchen is strategically located near many living areas, as well as the laundry room and garage.

❹ A second, smaller closet in the master suite is perfect for storing seasonal items and clothing.

❺ A fireplace and tall windows will add to memorable events in the great room.

❻ Three second-floor bedrooms will serve relatives for special occasions.

AVAILABLE FOR ALL PLANS

For More Information on our Roof Construction Package see page 158.

9K-5161   PRICE CODE 21

DECORATOR DESIGN TIPS

STUDY - In a quaint study such as this, it is important not to fill it with too much furniture or pieces that are too large. Smaller chairs will not overpower the space and thus, create a cozy place for reading and working on a computer.

MAIN FLOOR

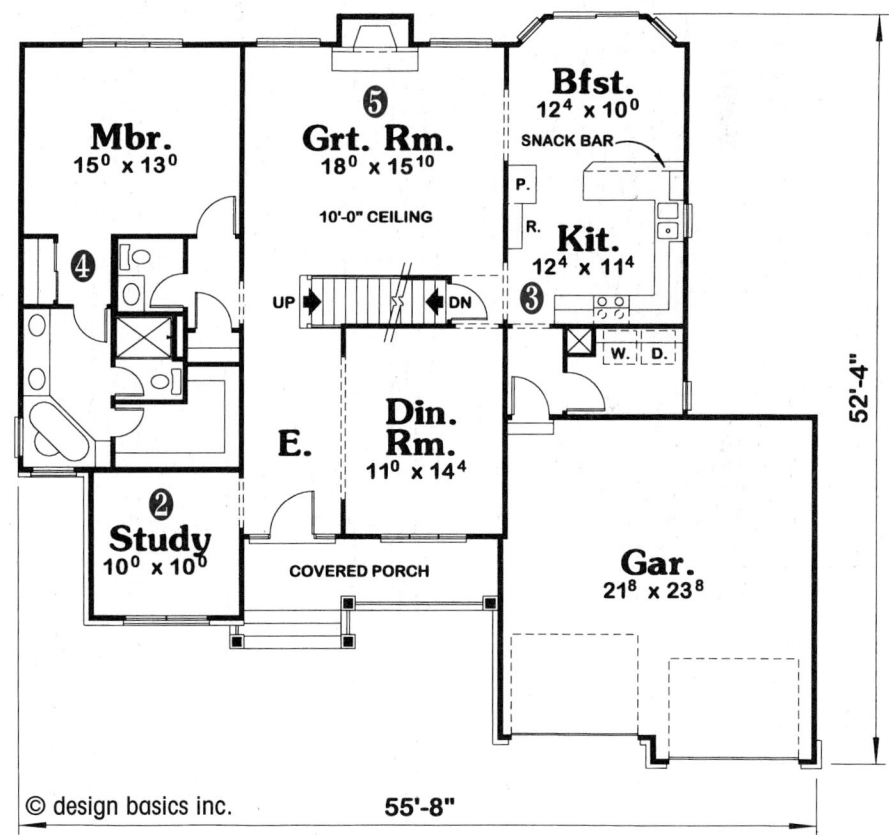

Main	1569 Sq. Ft.
Second	598 Sq. Ft.
Total	2167 Sq. Ft.

NOTE: 9 ft. main level walls

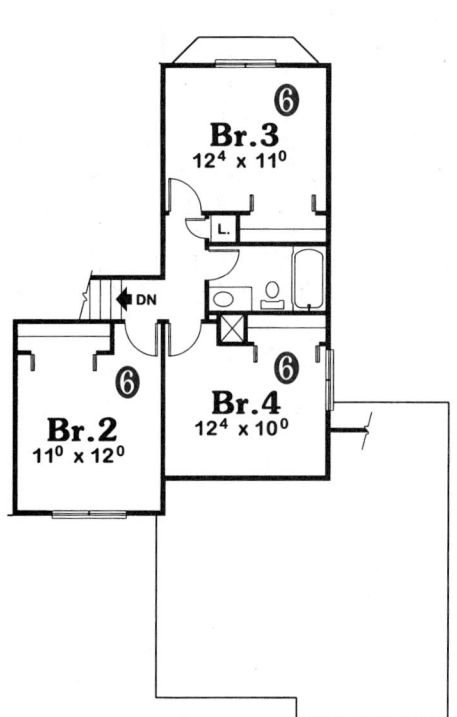

SECOND FLOOR

TO ORDER THIS PLAN CALL
1-800-947-7526

design basics inc.
HOME PLAN DESIGN SERVICE

Nostalgia

Camrose

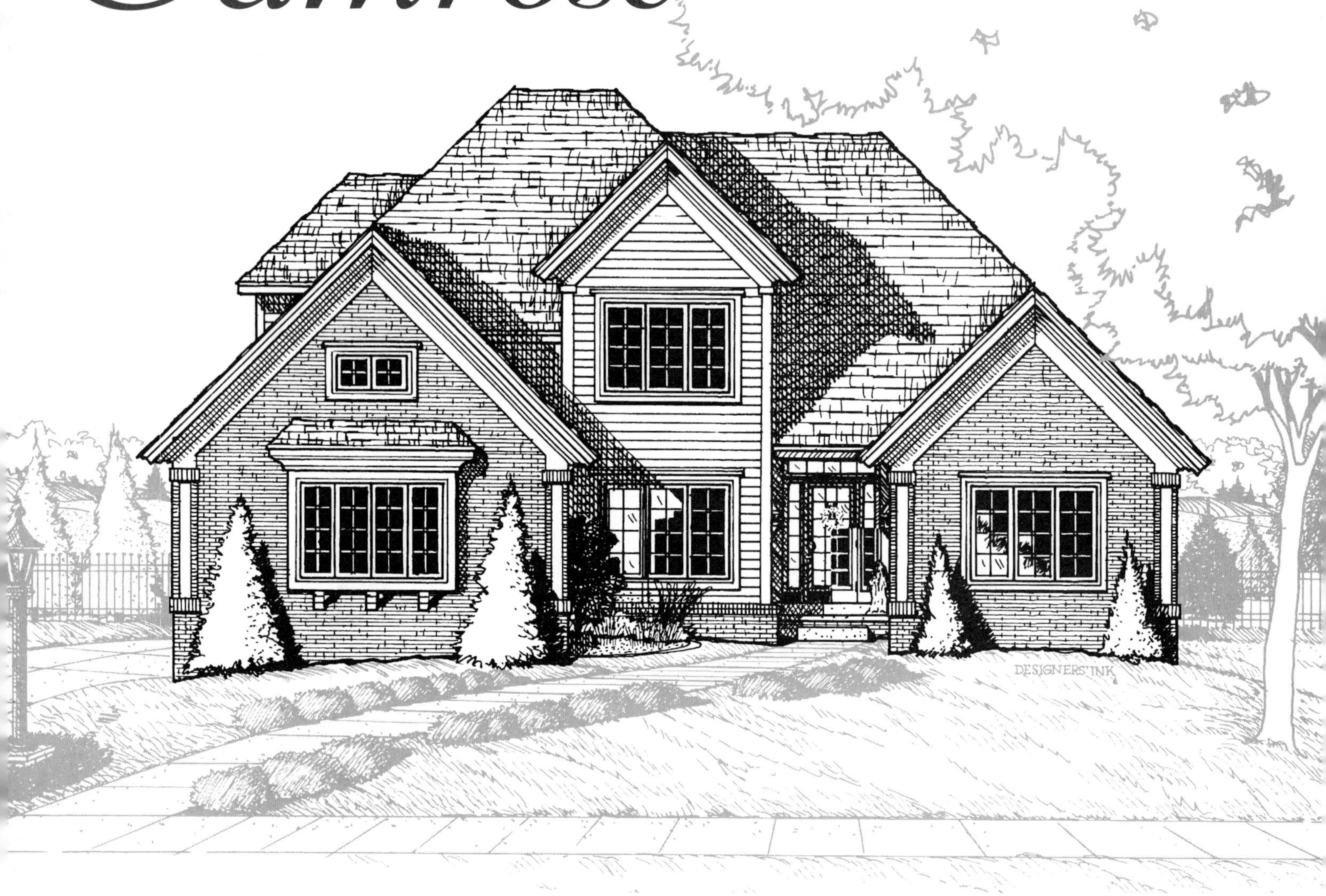

❶ Triple-wide windows illuminate both the exterior and interior of this home.

❷ Built-in bookshelves add to the practicality of studying and working in the library.

❸ Bayed windows in the breakfast area provide a beautiful frame for viewing the back.

❹ When family comes to visit, three bedrooms are located on the second floor.

❺ A spacious master suite tempts one to relax in its corner whirlpool tub.

❻ The garage provides a place for storing lawn and garden equipment.

AVAILABLE FOR ALL PLANS

For More Information on Parade Home Packages see page 158.

9K-5149　PRICE CODE 21

Main	1624 Sq. Ft.
Second	566 Sq. Ft.
Total	2190 Sq. Ft.

NOTE: 9 ft. main level walls

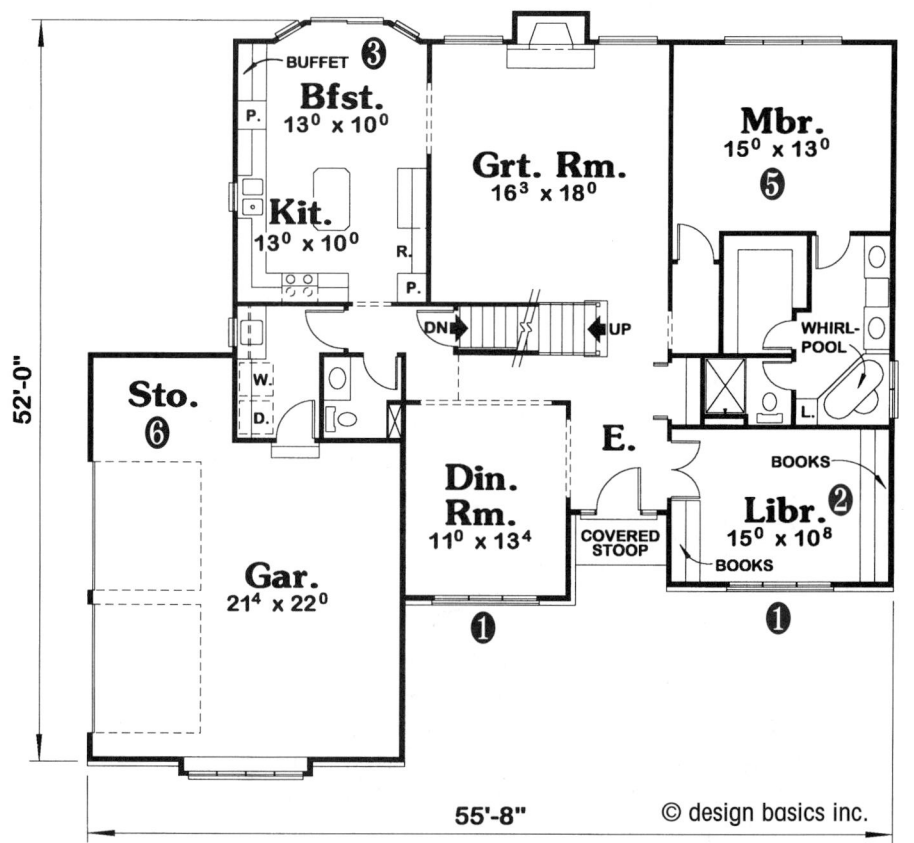

MAIN FLOOR

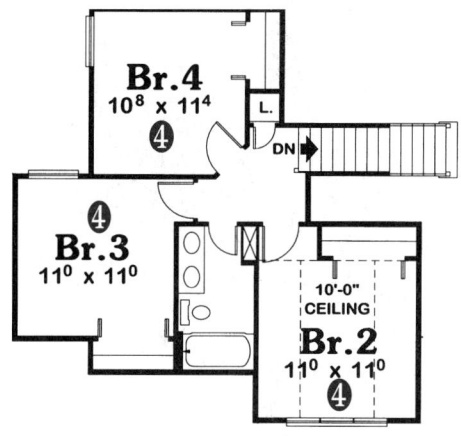

SECOND FLOOR

EXTERIOR HIGHLIGHT

A classic mixture of brick and siding makes this home appealing in any part of the country. This unique home was also designed to be appealing whether finished completely in brick or siding.

TO ORDER THIS PLAN CALL
1-800-947-7526

design basics inc
HOME PLAN DESIGN SERVICE

Nostalgia

Stanfield

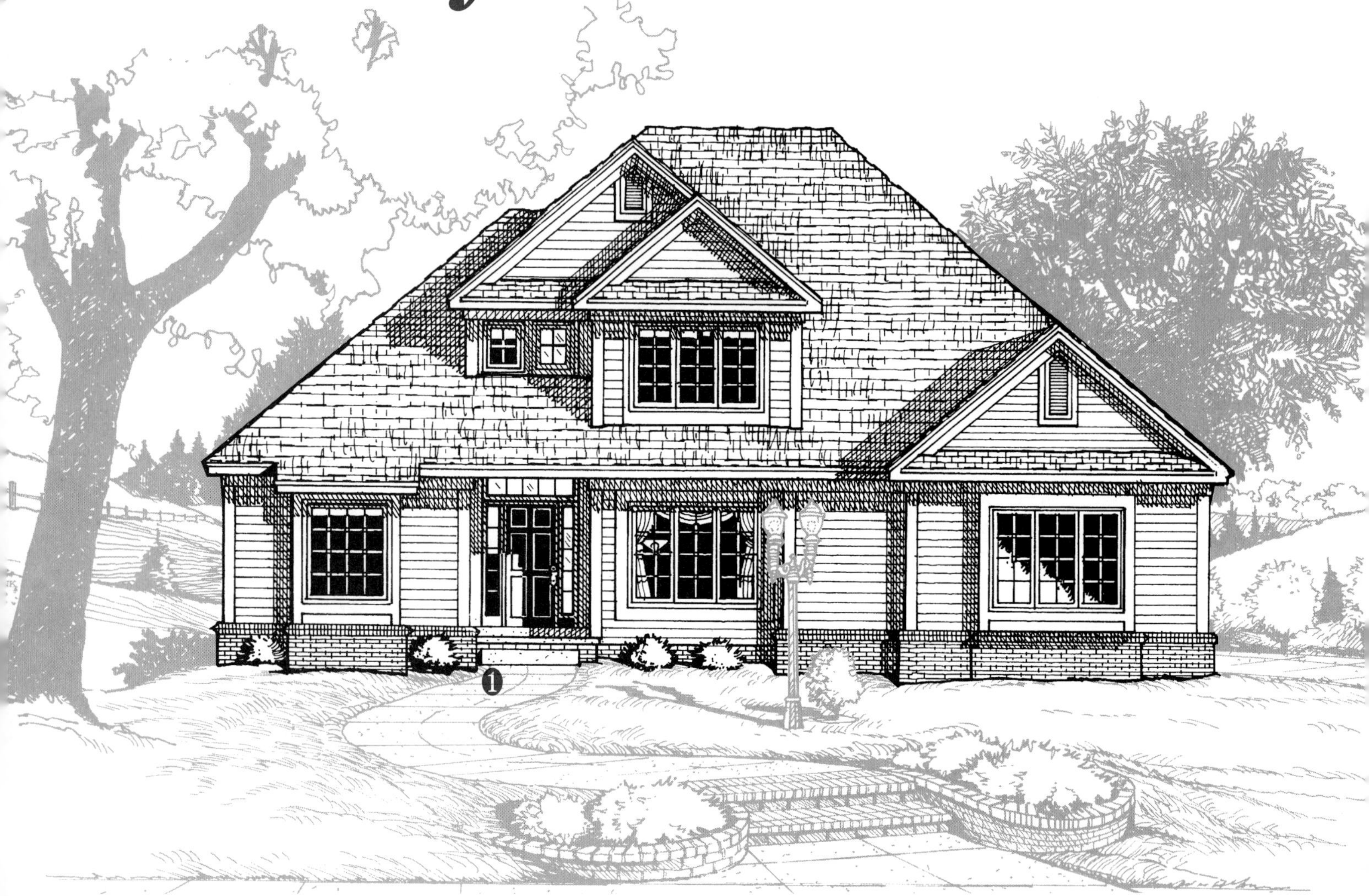

❶ Different combinations of windows contribute to the overall distinction of this dignified home.

❷ Rewarding today's home buyer, double doors open to the master suite with an optional sitting room that's great for working in the evenings.

❸ Conveniently within the master suite's walk-in closet, there's room for a stacked washer and dryer.

❹ The second-floor is provided with its own laundry room to serve bedrooms 2 and 3.

❺ A second-floor loft overlooks the family room and could become a fourth bedroom.

❻ Unfinished storage offers a place to keep the children's items while away at college.

AVAILABLE FOR ALL PLANS

For More Information on our Custom Changes see page 157.

9K -5136 PRICE CODE 22

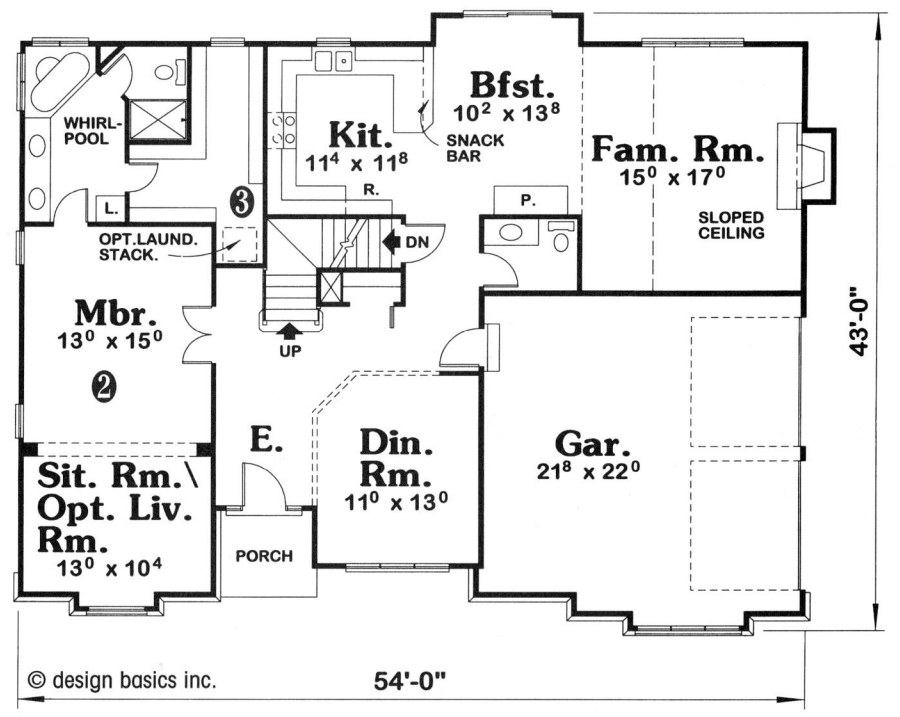

MAIN FLOOR

Main	1589 Sq. Ft.
Second	632 Sq. Ft.
Total	2221 Sq. Ft.

NOTE: 9 ft. main level walls

EXTERIOR HIGHLIGHT

A recessed stoop was designed on this home to give dimension and interest to the strong symmetry on the front elevation. Corner boards add a clean, finished appeal to the entry.

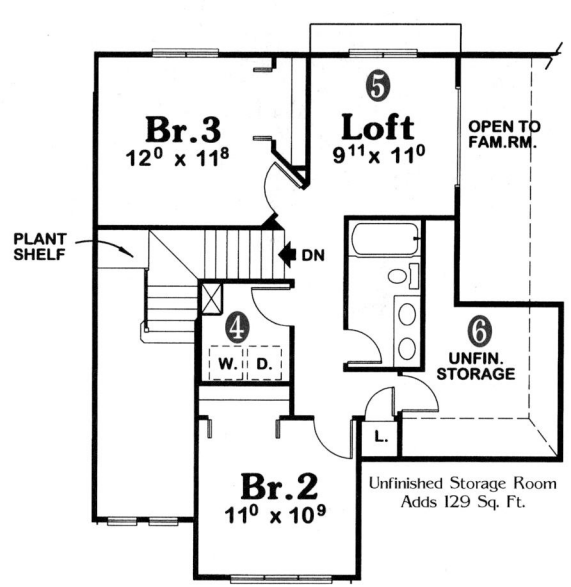

SECOND FLOOR

TO ORDER THIS PLAN CALL
1-800-947-7526

design basics inc.
HOME PLAN DESIGN SERVICE

Nostalgia

Bowden

❶ Brackets and the absence of the railing bring an open-air quality a this front porch.

❷ Privately located, the study is a great place for a home-based business.

❸ Double doors open to the master suite with a bath featuring a large walk-in closet, corner whirlpool tub and separate shower.

❹ The dinette and kitchen function together for day-to-day use and offer a planning desk and island counter.

❺ Within steps of the kitchen, the dining room extends this home's livability.

❻ Unfinished storage on the second floor offers options for expanding living and sleeping areas.

ALL PLANS COPYRIGHTED

For More Information on our Copyrights see page 154.

9K -5148 PRICE CODE 23

MAIN FLOOR

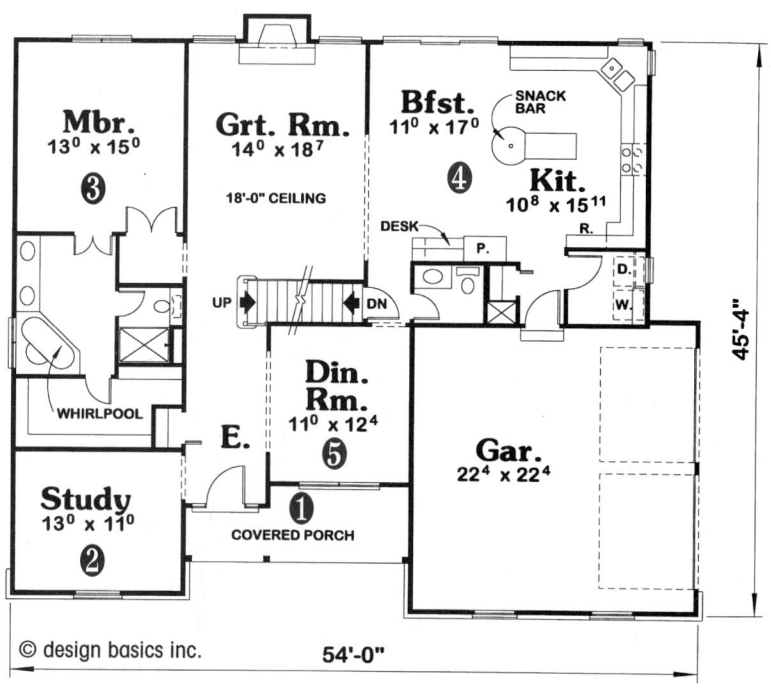

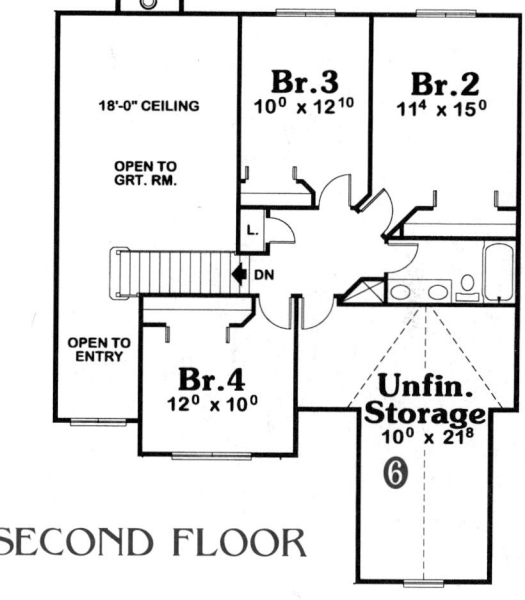

SECOND FLOOR

Main	1665 Sq. Ft.
Second	674 Sq. Ft.
Total	2339 Sq. Ft.

NOTE: 9 ft. main level walls

Unfinished Storage Room Adds 293 Sq. Ft.

EXTERIOR HIGHLIGHT

The brackets on the front porch of this home are consistent with the French Cottage detailing on the exterior windows. Updating this charming look is the oversized double window on the porch and a multi-paned front door.

TO ORDER THIS PLAN CALL
1-800-947-7526

design basics inc.
HOME PLAN DESIGN SERVICE

Kenneth

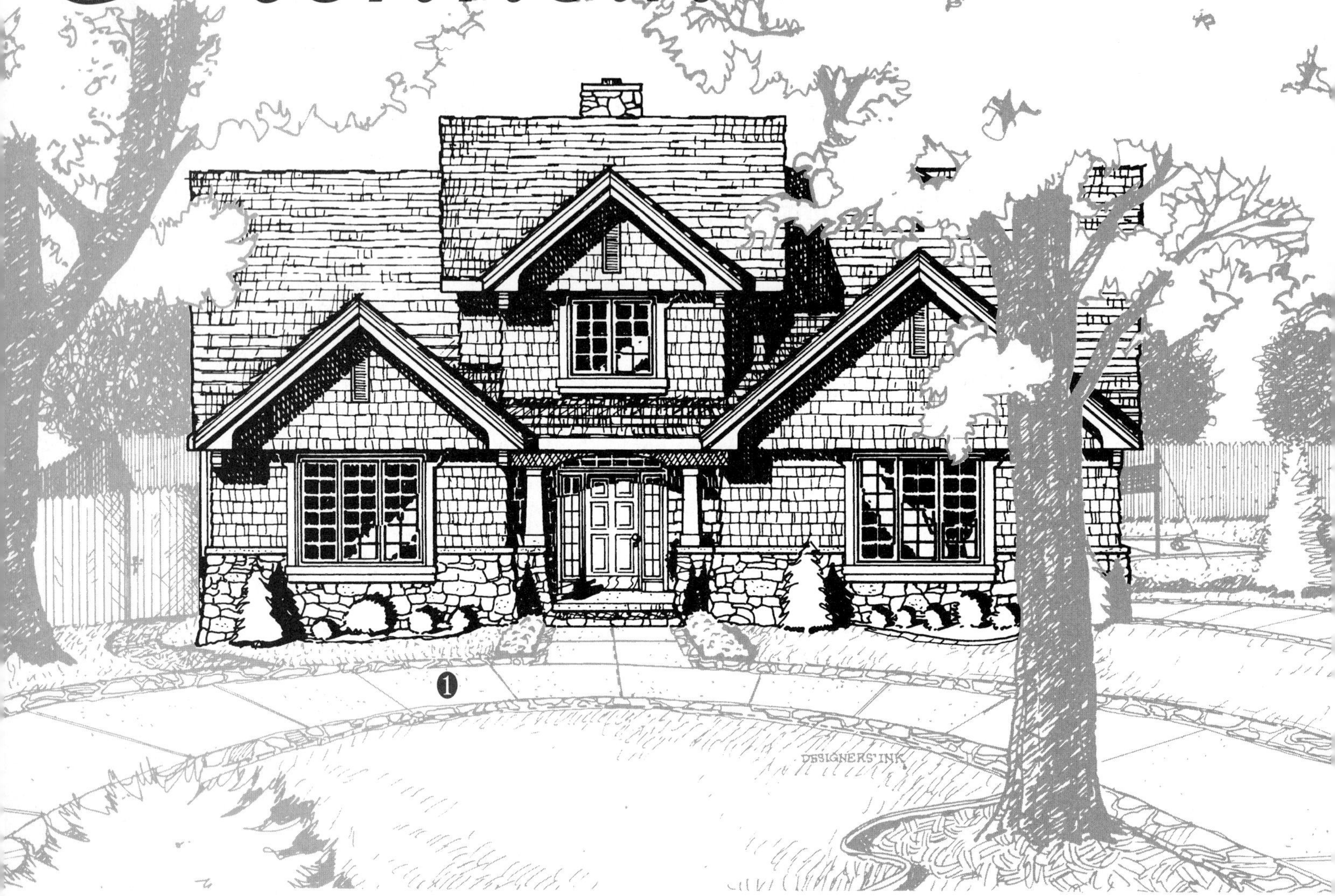

❶ The cozy mix of cobblestone and shake siding of this home brings to life the romance of an era long past.

❷ A valley cathedral ceiling and stunning windows highlight the great room.

❸ The large kitchen features an island counter with a snack bar and quick access to a rear stairway.

❹ Located at the top of the stairwell, a loft with bookshelves makes the perfect place for reading or studying, or even a unique fourth bedroom.

❺ An immense walk-in closet with a built-in dresser, whirlpool tub and dual-sink vanity are enclosed behind French doors adding intimacy to the master suite.

AVAILABLE FOR ALL PLANS

For More Information on Reverse Plans see page 158.

9K-4082 PRICE CODE 23

MAIN FLOOR

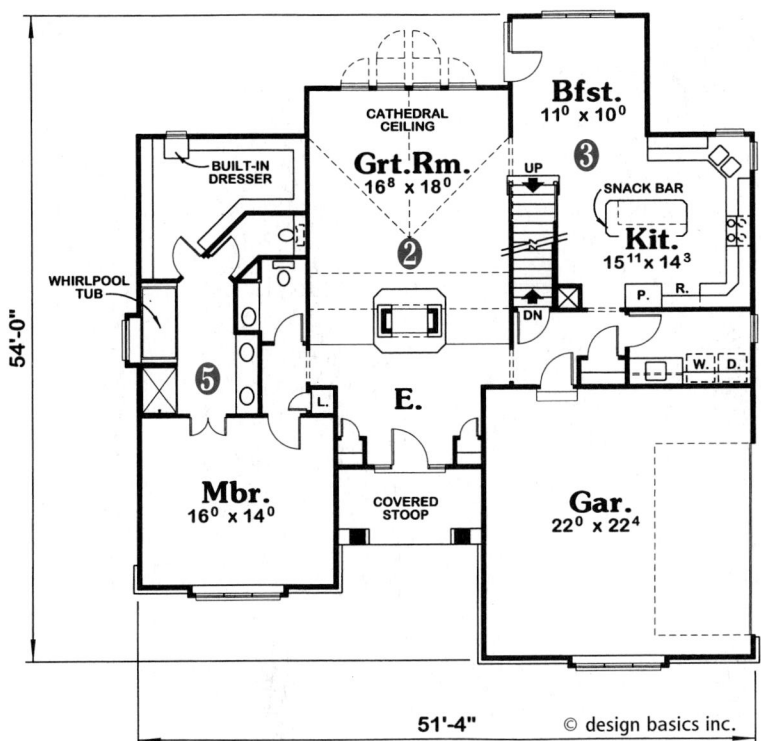

Main 1640 Sq. Ft.
Second 711 Sq. Ft.
Total 2351 Sq. Ft.

NOTE: 9 ft. main level walls

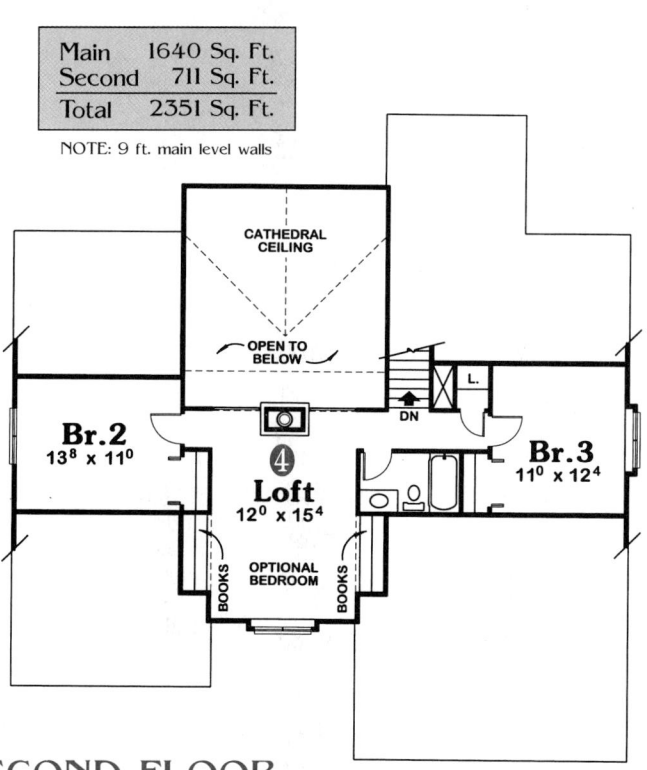

SECOND FLOOR

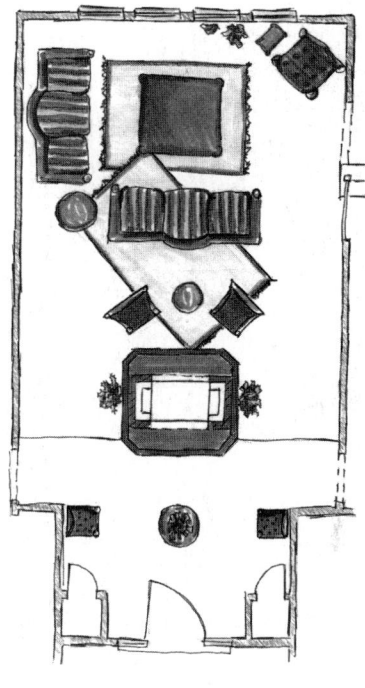

DECORATOR DESIGN TIPS

GREAT ROOM - While this home's freestanding fireplace makes furniture placement a challenge, it also establishes an opportunity for creative arrangements. A conversation area is created in the great room by placing two sofas in an "L" shape combination. Two chairs make an intimate space to enjoy the fireplace. In larger entryways like this one, a point of interest, such as a table with a floral arrangement, works well to break up the space and add special detail. Keep in mind not to overwhelm the space with furniture that is too large and bothers traffic patterns.

TO ORDER THIS PLAN CALL
1-800-947-7526

Nostalgia

Calidore

❶ An open railing on the stairway and large columns defining the great room are the impressive view upon entering.

❷ The wide-open kitchen serves the breakfast area with built-in buffet.

❸ The large master bedroom has enough room to accommodate a desk or chairs.

❹ A walk-in closet adds storage space to bedroom 4.

❺ Built-in shelves in the rear hall are all beneficial for either the garage or laundry room.

❻ A three-car garage is beneficial for a teenager's car or as a work area.

AVAILABLE FOR ALL PLANS

For More Information on our Roof Construction Package see page 158.

9K -5162 PRICE CODE 23

SECOND FLOOR

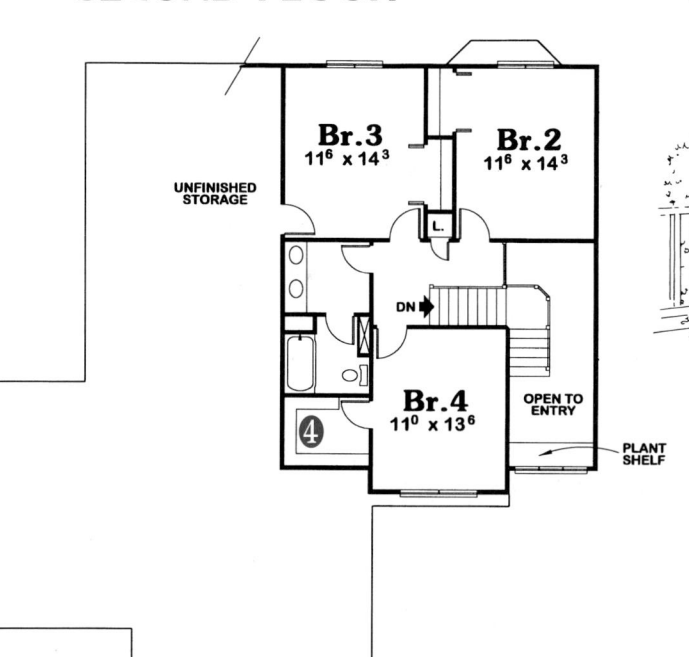

INTERIOR VIEW

GAZEBO PORCH - This home's gazebo porch has plenty of room for outdoor furniture. In pleasant weather, it is a great place to relax or chat with guests.

MAIN FLOOR

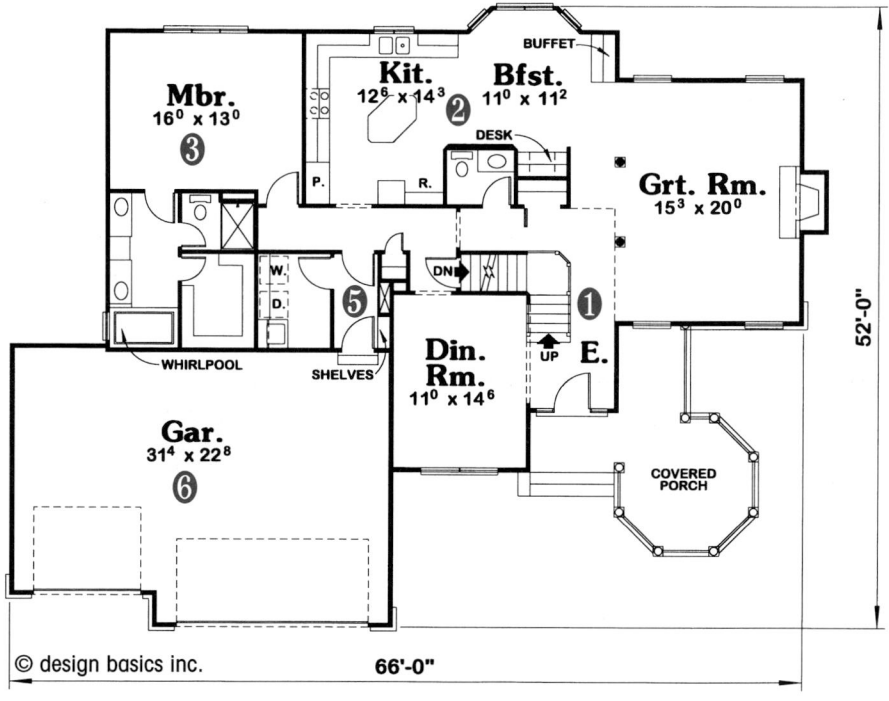

Main	1637 Sq. Ft.
Second	756 Sq. Ft.
Total	2393 Sq. Ft.

NOTE: 9 ft. main level walls

TO ORDER THIS PLAN CALL
1-800-947-7526

design basics inc.
HOME PLAN DESIGN SERVICE

Nostalgia

Magrath

❶ A classic Greek-style entry brings structure to this asymmetrical design.

❷ A study located on the second floor is perfect as a homework area.

❸ Angled walls and a 10-foot ceiling define the dining room and establish its pleasant ambiance.

❹ A hall leads to a private master suite with a large sitting room, great for relaxing or catching up on office work.

❺ Quaint window seats charm bedrooms 2 and 3.

❻ A large bonus room above the garage is beneficial for seasonal storage.

AVAILABLE FOR ALL PLANS

For More Information on Parade Home Packages see page 158.

Nostalgia

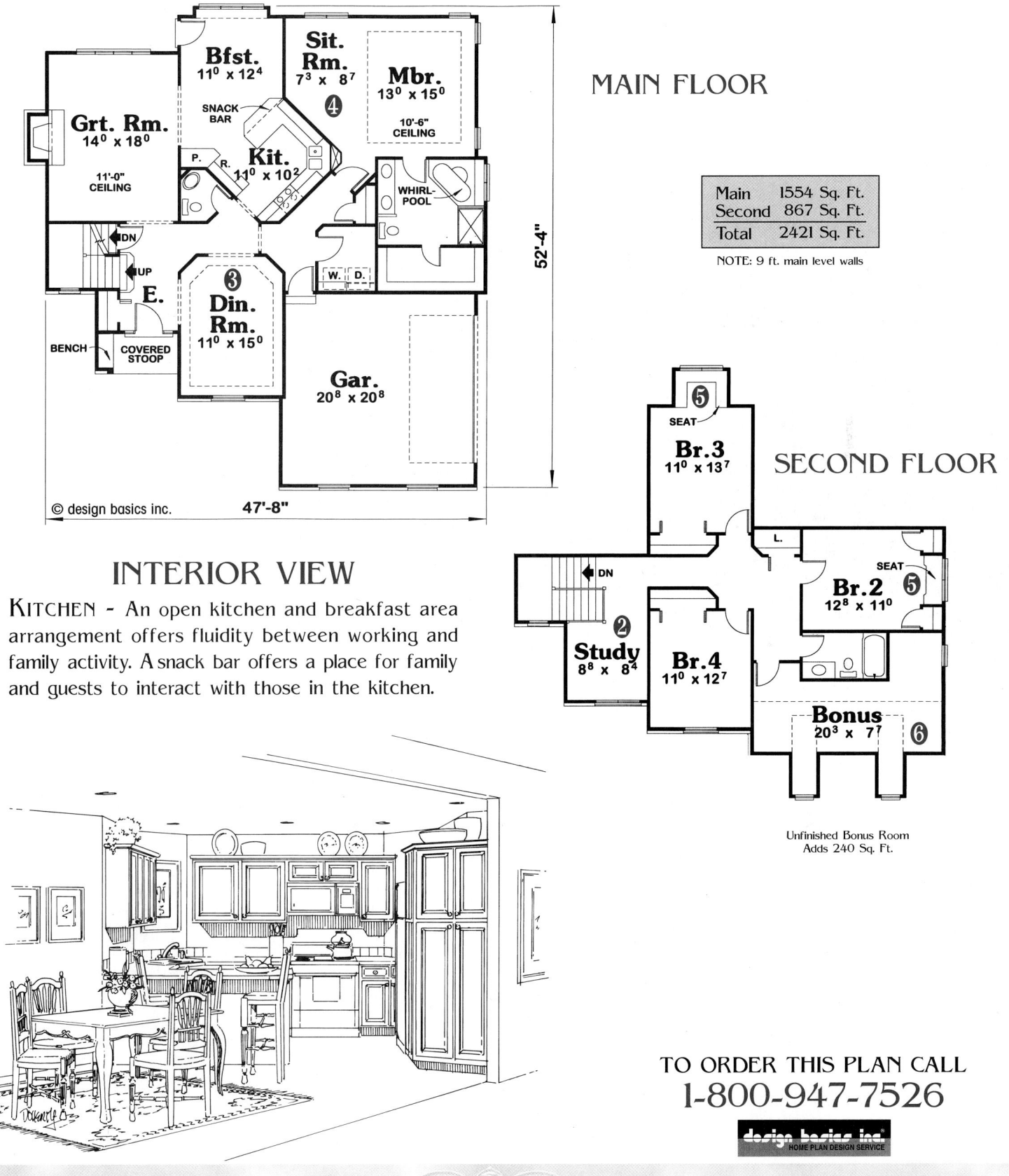

9K -5150 PRICE CODE 24

MAIN FLOOR

Main 1554 Sq. Ft.
Second 867 Sq. Ft.
Total 2421 Sq. Ft.

NOTE: 9 ft. main level walls

SECOND FLOOR

Unfinished Bonus Room Adds 240 Sq. Ft.

INTERIOR VIEW

KITCHEN - An open kitchen and breakfast area arrangement offers fluidity between working and family activity. A snack bar offers a place for family and guests to interact with those in the kitchen.

TO ORDER THIS PLAN CALL
1-800-947-7526

design basics inc.
HOME PLAN DESIGN SERVICE

Nostalgia

Carey

❶ The two-story entry radiates light into the home with a distinctive dormer.

❷ Special hutch space was designed into the elegant bayed dining room.

❸ Double doors reveal the master suite with his and her walk-in closets and a 10-foot vaulted ceiling.

❹ Built-in bookshelves and a fireplace will invite leisure in the hearth room.

❺ Showcased just off the breakfast area, a walk-in pantry and island counter benefit the kitchen.

❻ The stairway features an open railing and balcony that's visible from the great room.

AVAILABLE FOR ALL PLANS

For More Information on Parade Home Packages see page 158.

Nostalgia

9K-5158 PRICE CODE 25

Main	1795 Sq. Ft.
Second	717 Sq. Ft.
Total	2512 Sq. Ft.

NOTE: 9 ft. main level walls

SECOND FLOOR

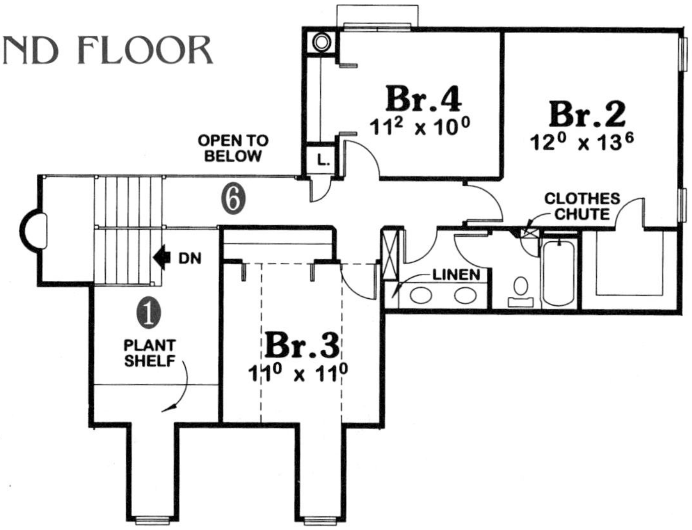

- Br. 4 — $11^2 \times 10^0$
- Br. 2 — $12^0 \times 13^6$
- Br. 3 — $11^0 \times 11^0$
- Open to Below
- Plant Shelf
- Linen
- Clothes Chute

MAIN FLOOR

- Grt. Rm. — $18^0 \times 16^0$ — 18'-0" HIGH CEILING
- Bfst. — $10^8 \times 11^8$
- Kit. — $12^{10} \times 13^4$
- Hrth. Rm. — $14^{10} \times 15^7$ — BOOKS
- Whirlpool
- Din. Rm. — $12^0 \times 15^2$ — HUTCH SPACE
- Mbr. — $13^4 \times 19^6$ — 10'-0" HIGH CEILING
- Gar. — $20^4 \times 21^4$
- Storage
- Covered Porch
- 57'-0" × 51'-0"

© design basics inc.

EXTERIOR HIGHLIGHT

Amidst the prominent beauty of other elements on the facade, an entry such as this can get lost. This porch was designed, not to draw attention away from this home's exterior beauty, but to complement its many features.

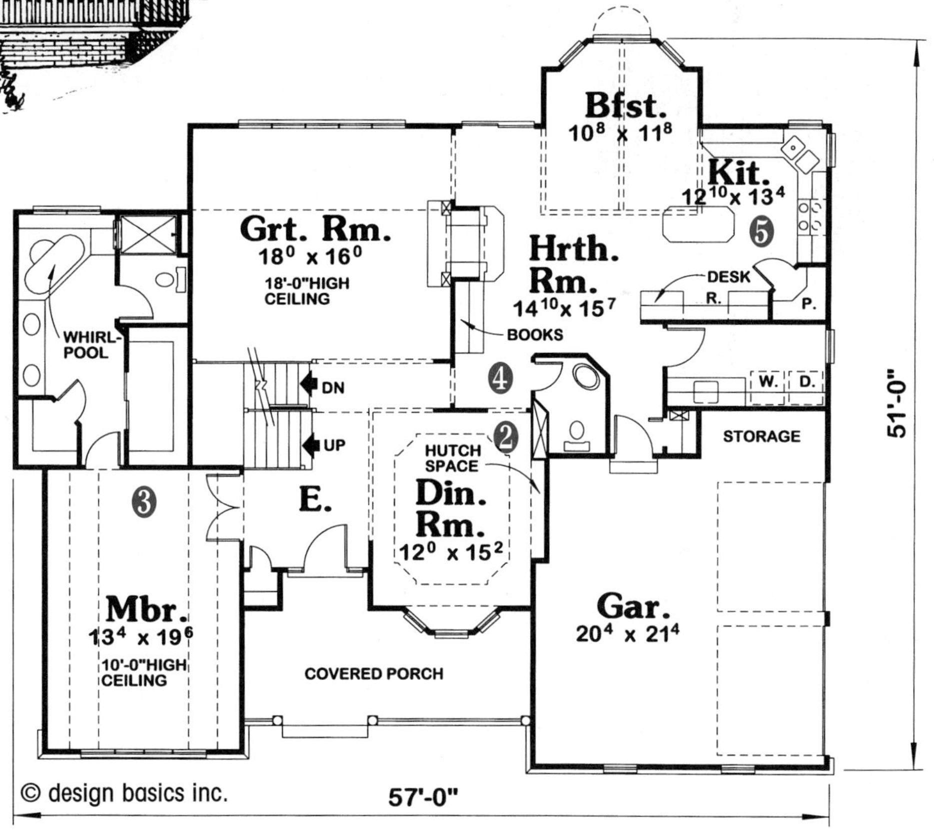

TO ORDER THIS PLAN CALL
1-800-947-7526

Ellsworth

❶ Arched openings frame a central fireplace that becomes the focal point in the entry.

❷ A dropped soffit around the perimeter of the dining room sets off the contrasting ceiling heights between the dining room and entry.

❸ Arched openings frame a walkway between the breakfast area and great room and thus seclude the powder bath.

❹ Walk-in closets are featured in all second-floor bedrooms.

❺ The master suite can access the den via a pocket door.

❻ Extra counter space is provided in the laundry room to assist when hand washing clothing.

AVAILABLE FOR ALL PLANS

For More Information on our Custom Changes see page 157.

9K-5146 PRICE CODE 25

EXTERIOR HIGHLIGHT

A brick archway and double doors are singularly fitting in this entry. The cottage-like appeal of the windows, such as this boxed window with brackets, is updated with an all-brick exterior.

MAIN FLOOR

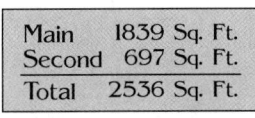

Main 1839 Sq. Ft.
Second 697 Sq. Ft.
Total 2536 Sq. Ft.

NOTE: 9 ft. main level walls

SECOND FLOOR

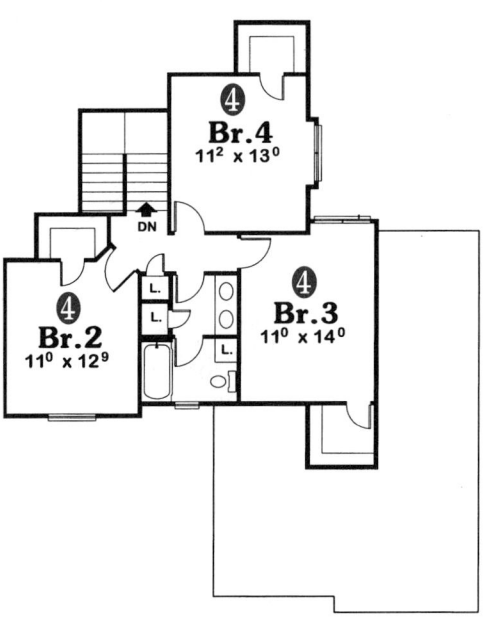

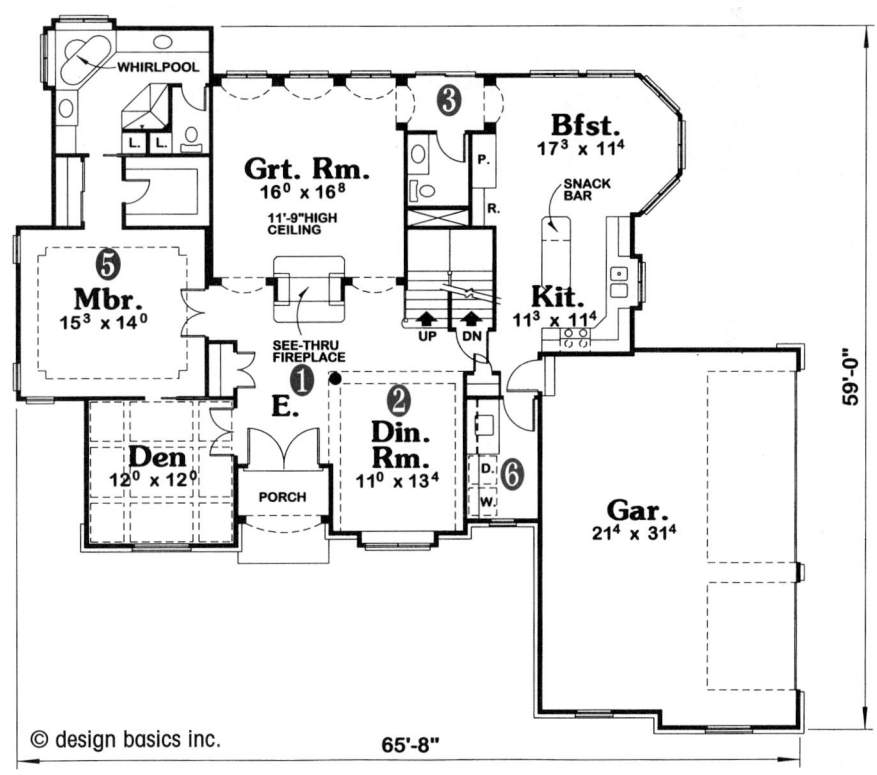

TO ORDER THIS PLAN CALL
1-800-947-7526

design basics inc
HOME PLAN DESIGN SERVICE

Hanna

❶ The discreet Prairie-style influence of this facade will be celebrated wherever it is built.

❷ A see-thru fireplace adds a sense of rugged warmth to the kitchen while making an elegant showpiece in the great room.

❸ Midway up the staircase, double doors lead to the master suite with built-in bookcases, his and her walk-in closets, a barrel-vault ceiling and oval whirlpool tub.

❹ On the second floor, a computer loft with a built-in desk overlooks the impressive great room.

❺ Bedroom 2 has bookshelves on either side of a triple-wide window and could easily be converted to a study.

ALL PLANS COPYRIGHTED

For More Information on our Copyrights see page 154.

Nostalgia

9K -4081 PRICE CODE 25

INTERIOR VIEW

DINING ROOM - Twin curio cabinets make a great place to display pottery or antique dishes in the spacious dining room. Guests will enjoy the decorative triple window which frames a view to the front.

MAIN FLOOR

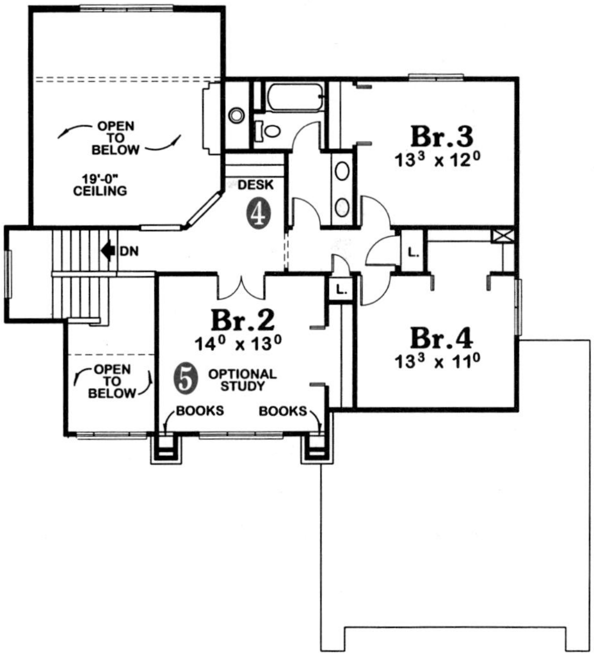

Main	1735 Sq. Ft.
Second	841 Sq. Ft.
Total	2576 Sq. Ft.

NOTE: 9 ft. main level walls

- Grt. Rm. 16⁰ x 17¹⁰ — 19'-0" CEILING, CATHEDRAL CEILING, ENTERT. CENTER
- Bfst. 10⁸ x 16⁰ — SNACK BAR
- Kit. 11⁰ x 12⁰
- WHIRLPOOL TUB
- Mbr. 14⁰ x 15² — 10'-4" CEILING, BOOKS
- E.
- Din. 14⁰ x 13⁰ — CURIO CURIO
- STOOP
- Gar. 22⁰ x 23⁰
- P. R., W. D.

54'-0" × 58'-8"

© design basics inc.

SECOND FLOOR

- Br.3 13³ x 12⁰
- Br.2 14⁰ x 13⁰ — OPTIONAL STUDY, BOOKS BOOKS
- Br.4 13³ x 11⁰
- OPEN TO BELOW — 19'-0" CEILING
- DESK
- DN
- OPEN TO BELOW

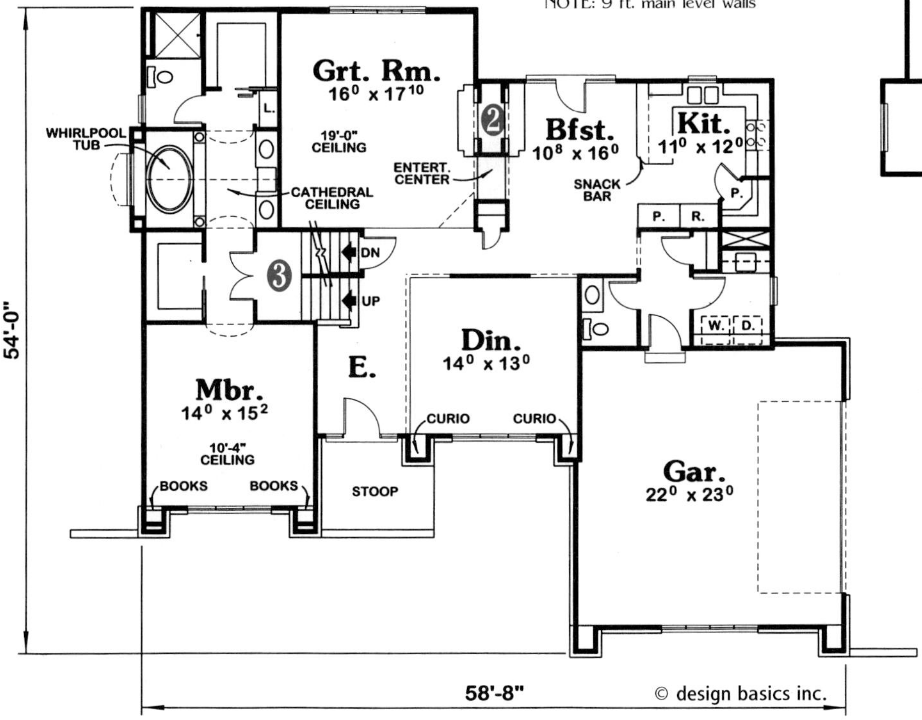

TO ORDER THIS PLAN CALL
1-800-947-7526

design basics inc.
HOME PLAN DESIGN SERVICE

Nostalgia 83

Schuyler

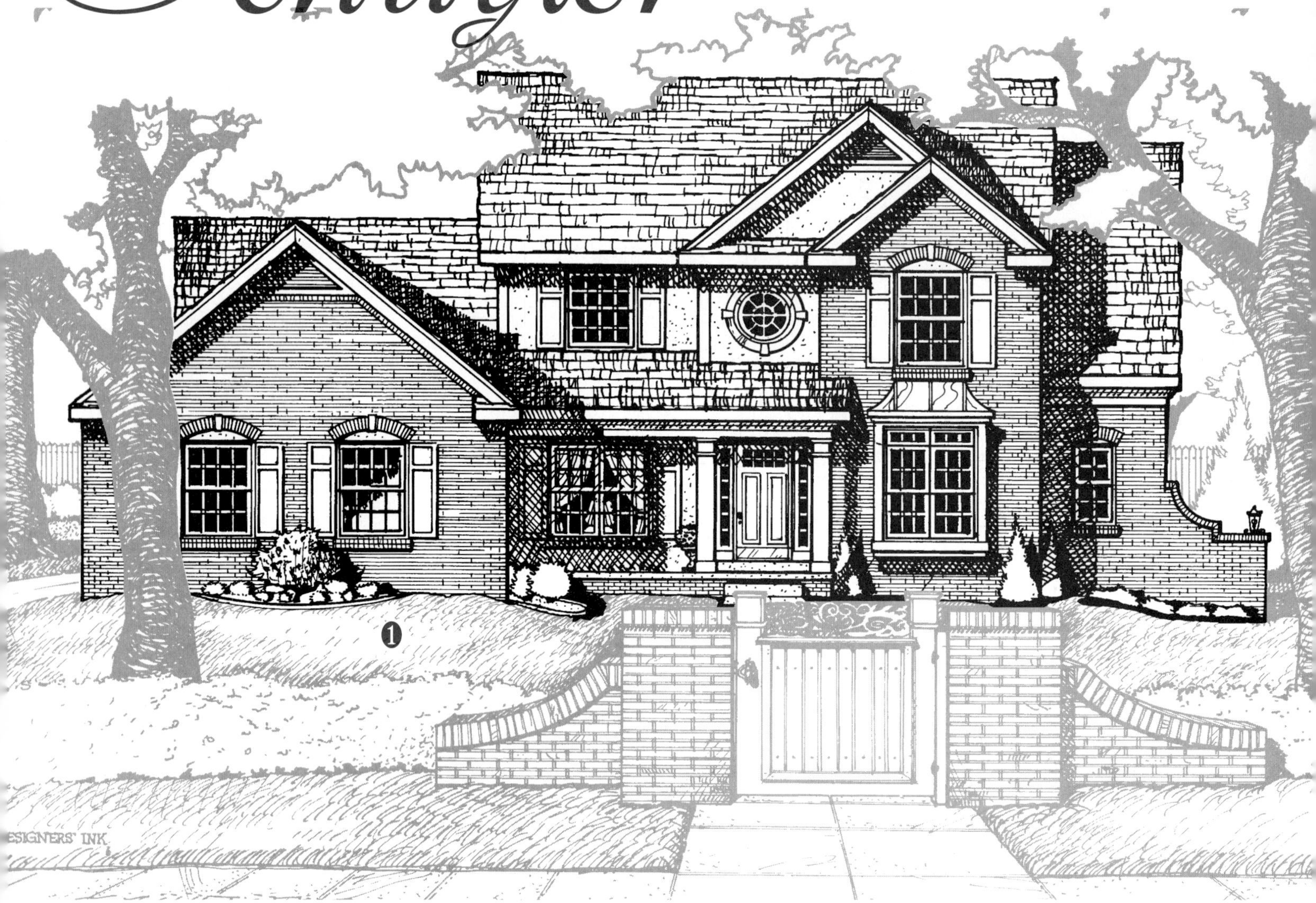

❶ Timeless details in unique proportions give this design its eclectic edge.

❷ Adding glamour to the entry, the dining room features a hutch space.

❸ When entertaining, the den with double doors makes a wonderful companion to the dining room.

❹ Bayed windows brighten the breakfast area which is open to the kitchen with a peninsula snack bar.

❺ Eleven-foot-high ceilings in the master bedroom and great room bring a sense of openness to daily living.

❻ An unfinished storage space offers the potential for a hobby room or exercise area.

AVAILABLE FOR ALL PLANS

For More Information on Reverse Plans see page 158.

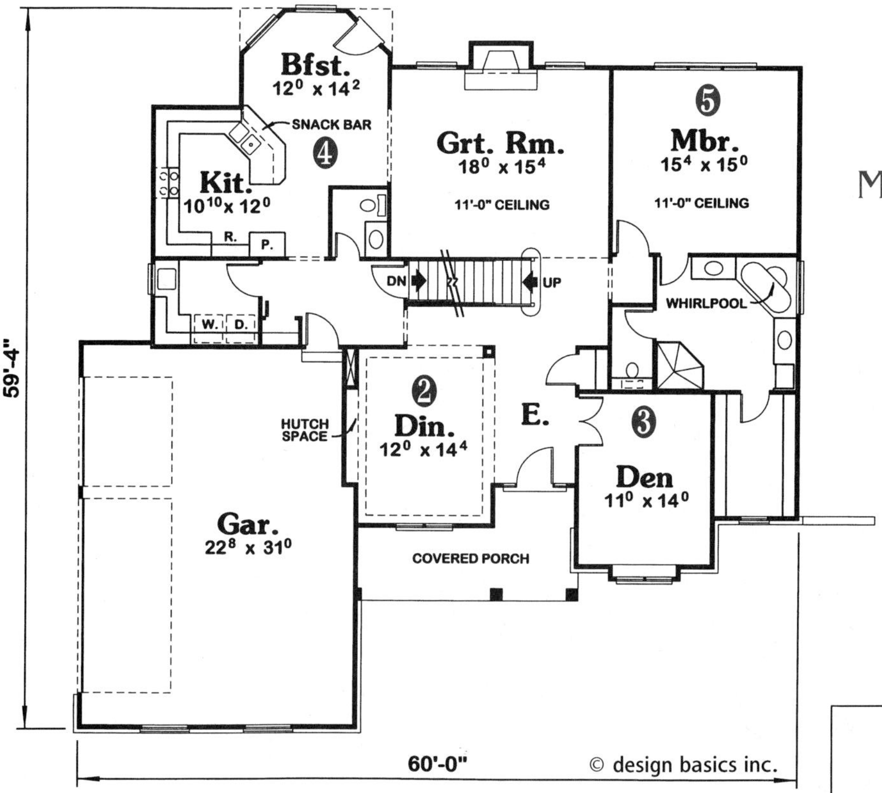

9K-4134 PRICE CODE 26

MAIN FLOOR

- Bfst. 12⁰ x 14²
- SNACK BAR ④
- Kit. 10¹⁰ x 12⁰
- Grt. Rm. 18⁰ x 15⁴ — 11'-0" CEILING
- Mbr. 15⁴ x 15⁰ — 11'-0" CEILING ⑤
- WHIRLPOOL
- Din. 12⁰ x 14⁴ ②
- HUTCH SPACE
- Den 11⁰ x 14⁰ ③
- E.
- Gar. 22⁸ x 31⁰
- COVERED PORCH
- 59'-4"
- 60'-0"
- © design basics inc.

Main	1847 Sq. Ft.
Second	766 Sq. Ft.
Total	2613 Sq. Ft.

NOTE: 9 ft. main level walls

SECOND FLOOR

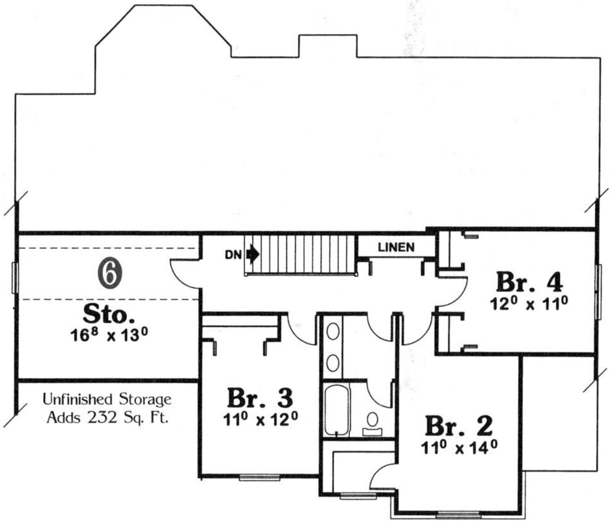

- Sto. 16⁸ x 13⁰ ⑥
- Unfinished Storage Adds 232 Sq. Ft.
- Br. 3 — 11⁰ x 12⁰
- Br. 4 — 12⁰ x 11⁰
- Br. 2 — 11⁰ x 14⁰
- LINEN

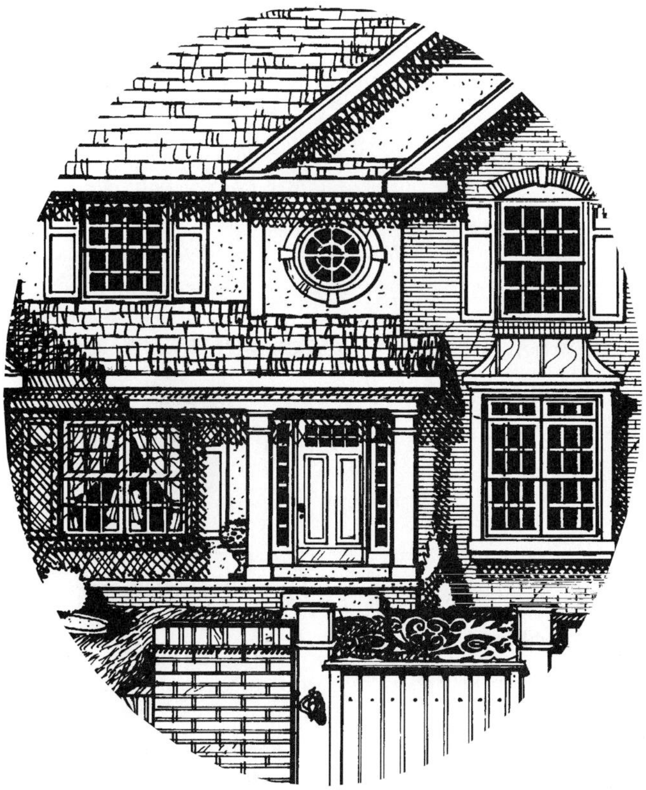

EXTERIOR HIGHLIGHT

A porthole window set under a double gable end naturally draws attention to the entry below. Sturdy columns were designed to announce the beautiful front door adorned with a transom and sidelights.

TO ORDER THIS PLAN CALL
1-800-947-7526

Nostalgia

Rowena

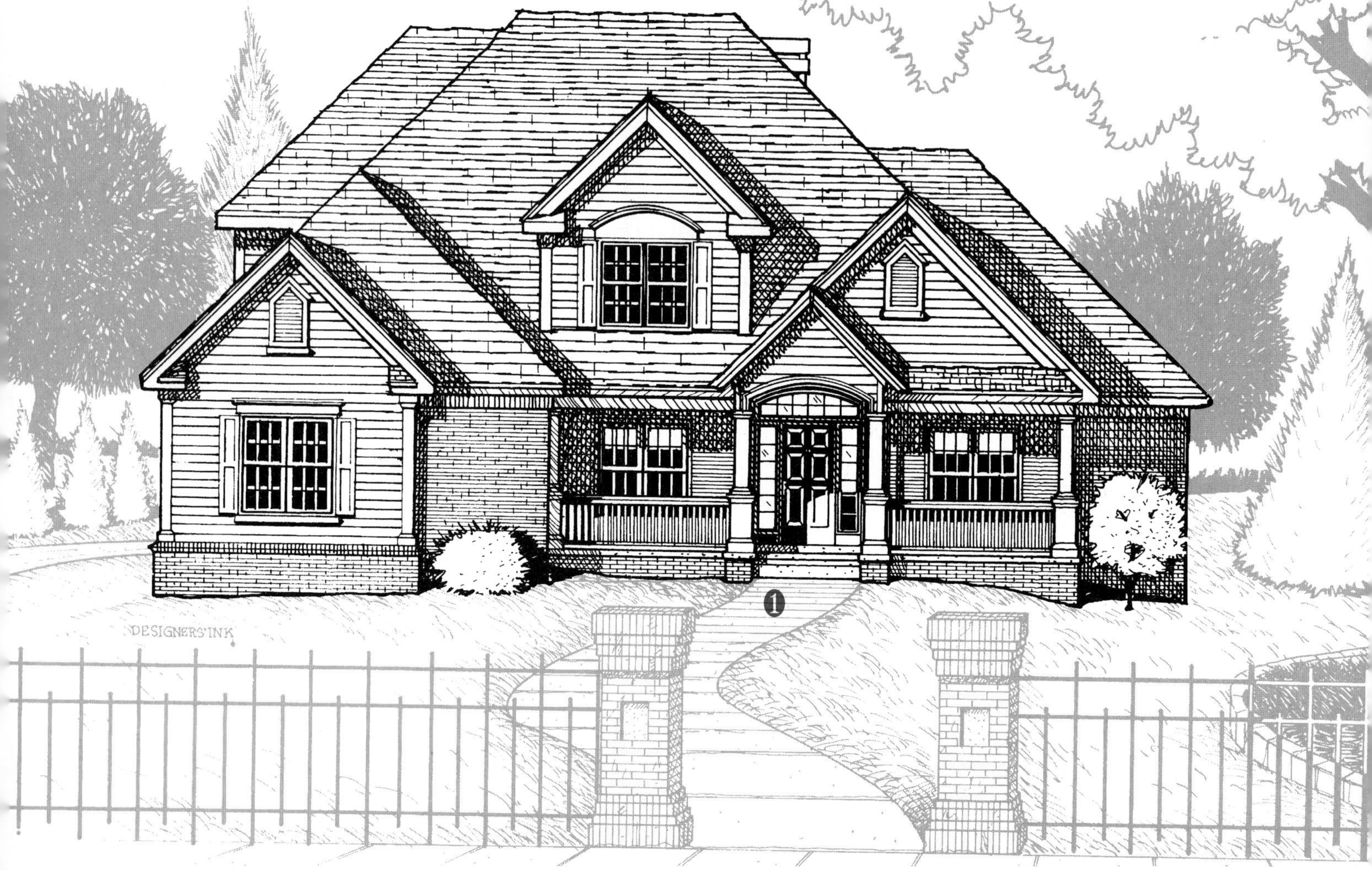

❶ This pleasant elevation offers a warm welcome through elements such as its front porch and use of siding and brick.

❷ Formal rooms polish the entry and offer views past the front porch.

❸ Three sides of windows bring a cheerful atmosphere to the breakfast area, as well as the kitchen.

❹ Triple windows and a built-in bookshelf add luster to the master bedroom.

❺ All three second-floor bedrooms feature walk-in closets.

❻ Unfinished storage on the second floor is beneficial for keeping seasonal items or storing kids items while away at college.

AVAILABLE FOR ALL PLANS

For More Information on our Roof Construction Package see page 158.

Nostalgia

9K -5178 PRICE CODE 26

MAIN FLOOR

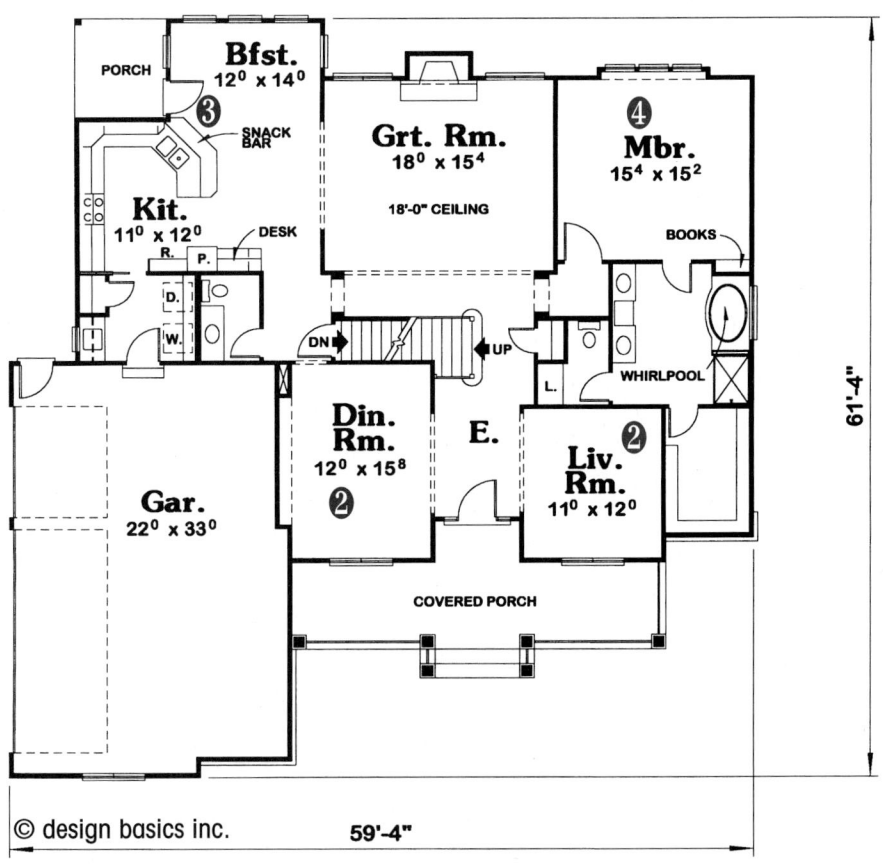

Main	1870 Sq. Ft.
Second	767 Sq. Ft.
Total	2637 Sq. Ft.

NOTE: 9 ft. main level walls

DECORATOR DESIGN TIPS

BEDROOM 3 - This bedroom's unique shape sets up the perfect opportunity for upholstery to be added to its decor. Two chairs work the best in the angled alcove since they are smaller and can be manipulated easier than a larger piece, such as a loveseat.

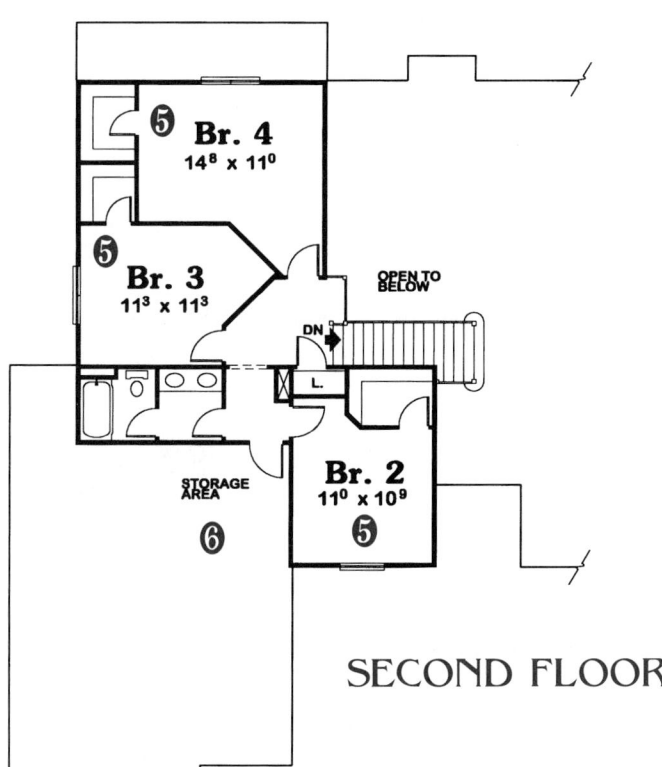

SECOND FLOOR

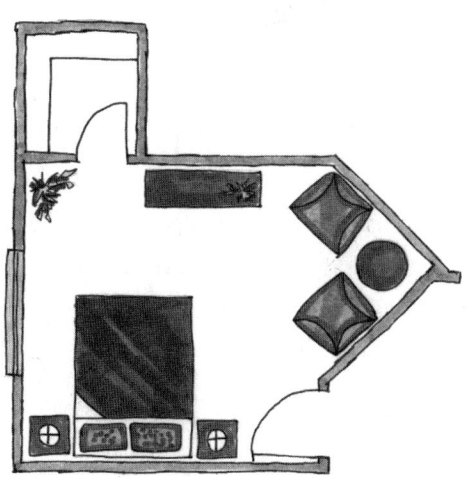

TO ORDER THIS PLAN CALL
1-800-947-7526

Nostalgia

Colette

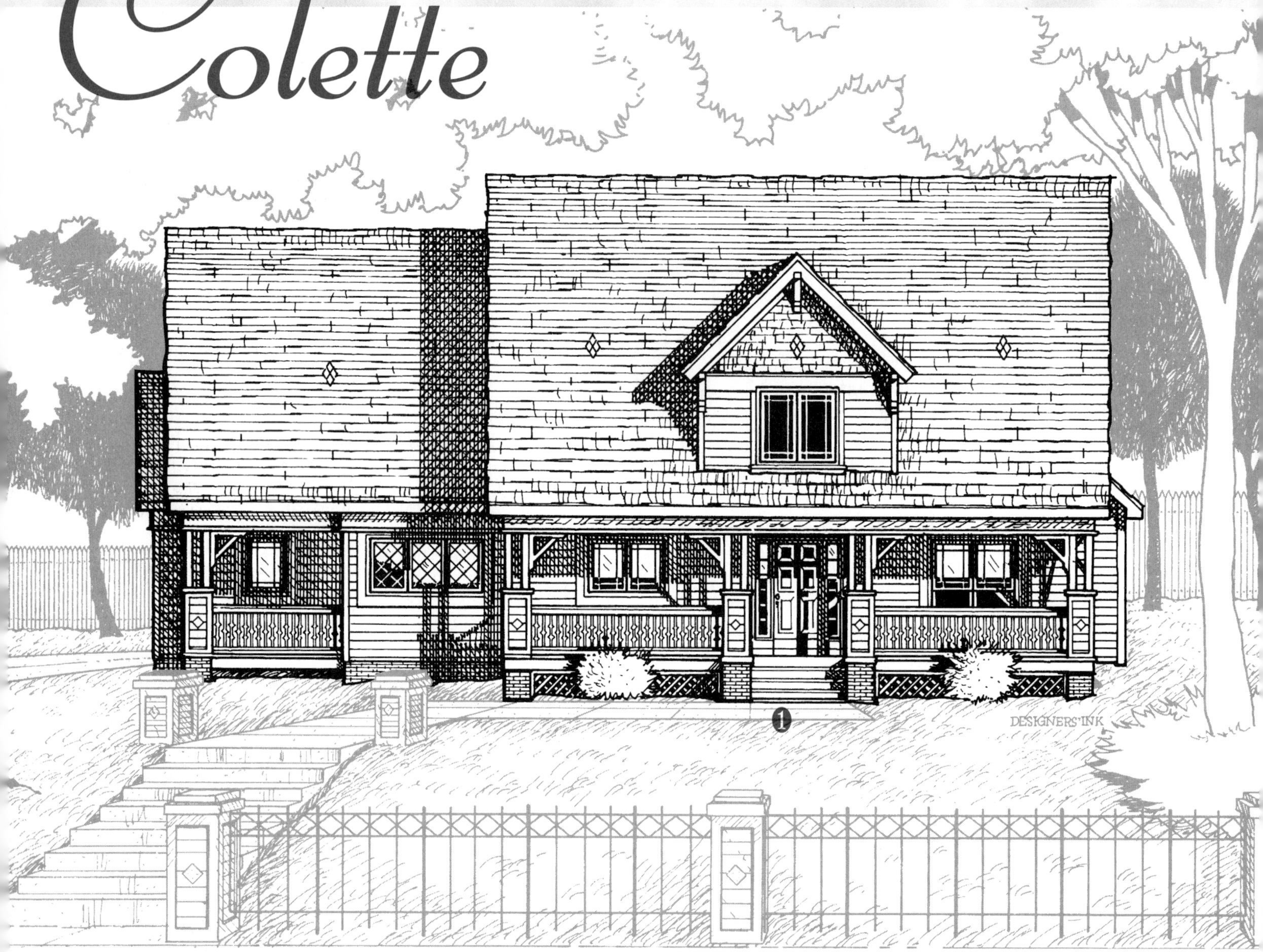

❶ This home's steep roof, two front porches and diamond-muntin windows lend the feel of a cottage by the sea.

❷ The airiness of the kitchen is enhanced with openings to the second-floor, entry and dinette.

❸ A built-in buffet and two half railings warmly welcome passersby into the dining room.

❹ A tall ceiling in the great room is further dramatized when viewed from an open railing on second floor.

❺ A computer area on the second floor accompanies the second-floor bedrooms as a homework area.

❻ A large storage area accessed from the mid-level staircase landing offers a place for a playroom.

AVAILABLE FOR ALL PLANS

For More Information on our Custom Changes see page 157.

9K -5210 PRICE CODE 26

INTERIOR VIEW

SECOND - FLOOR CORRIDOR - The upstairs landing offers a view of the comfortable kitchen. Sloped ceilings and a plant shelf add beauty and drama to this charming vista.

SECOND FLOOR

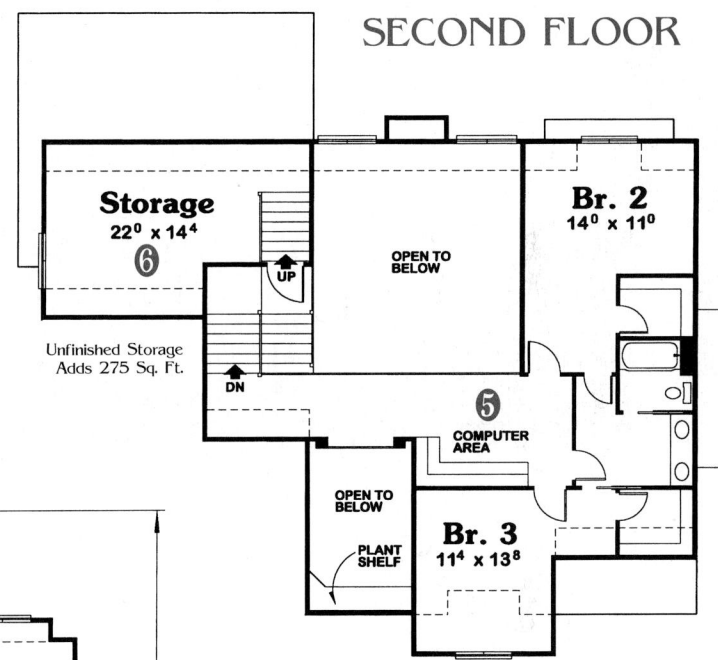

Unfinished Storage Adds 275 Sq. Ft.

Main	1823 Sq. Ft.
Second	858 Sq. Ft.
Total	2681 Sq. Ft.

NOTE: 9 ft. main level walls

MAIN FLOOR

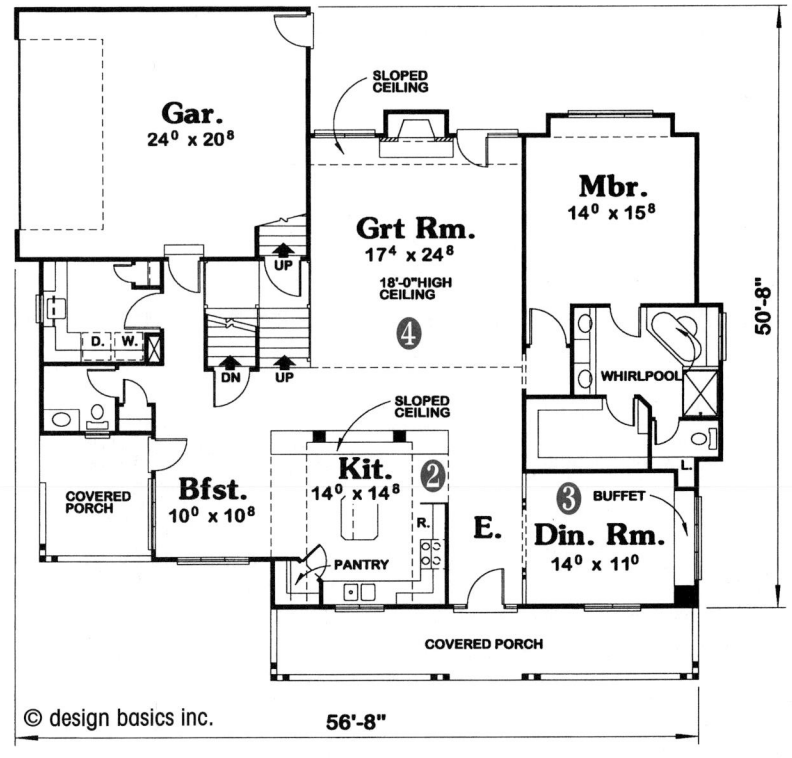

© design basics inc.

TO ORDER THIS PLAN CALL
1-800-947-7526

design basics inc.
HOME PLAN DESIGN SERVICE

Nostalgia

Reston

❶ This uncomplicated elevation complements the effortless floor plan inside.

❷ The master suite is a haven worth retreating to with its private sitting area offering a cozy window sill and built-in bookshelves.

❸ A corner whirlpool tub and compartmented shower offer escape in the master bath.

❹ A fireplace in the family room welcomes those in the kitchen and breakfast area.

❺ Bedroom 4 makes a wonderful guest suite offering its own bath.

❻ A large bonus room is beneficial for storage or if living space is desired.

ALL PLANS COPYRIGHTED

For More Information on our Copyrights see page 154.

9K -5157 PRICE CODE 27

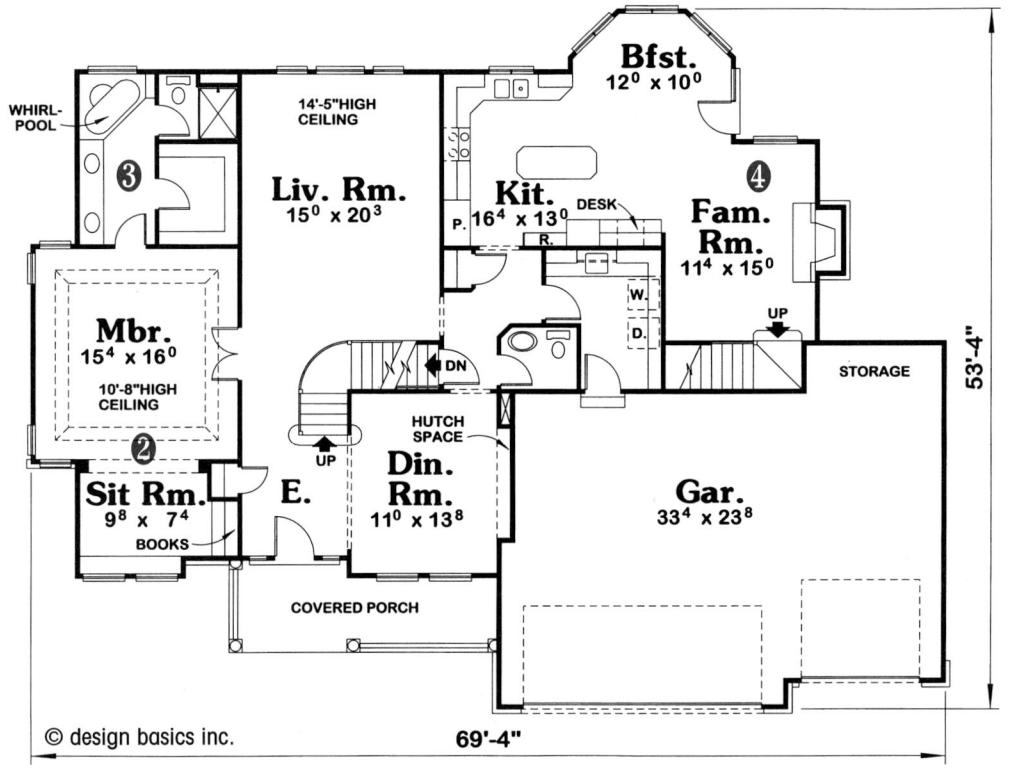

Main	1901 Sq. Ft.
Second	837 Sq. Ft.
Total	2738 Sq. Ft.

NOTE: 9 ft. main level walls

MAIN FLOOR

EXTERIOR HIGHLIGHT

Incorporating large sidelights makes the front door on this home feel more like a window - naturally fitting among the numerous windows on the front elevation.

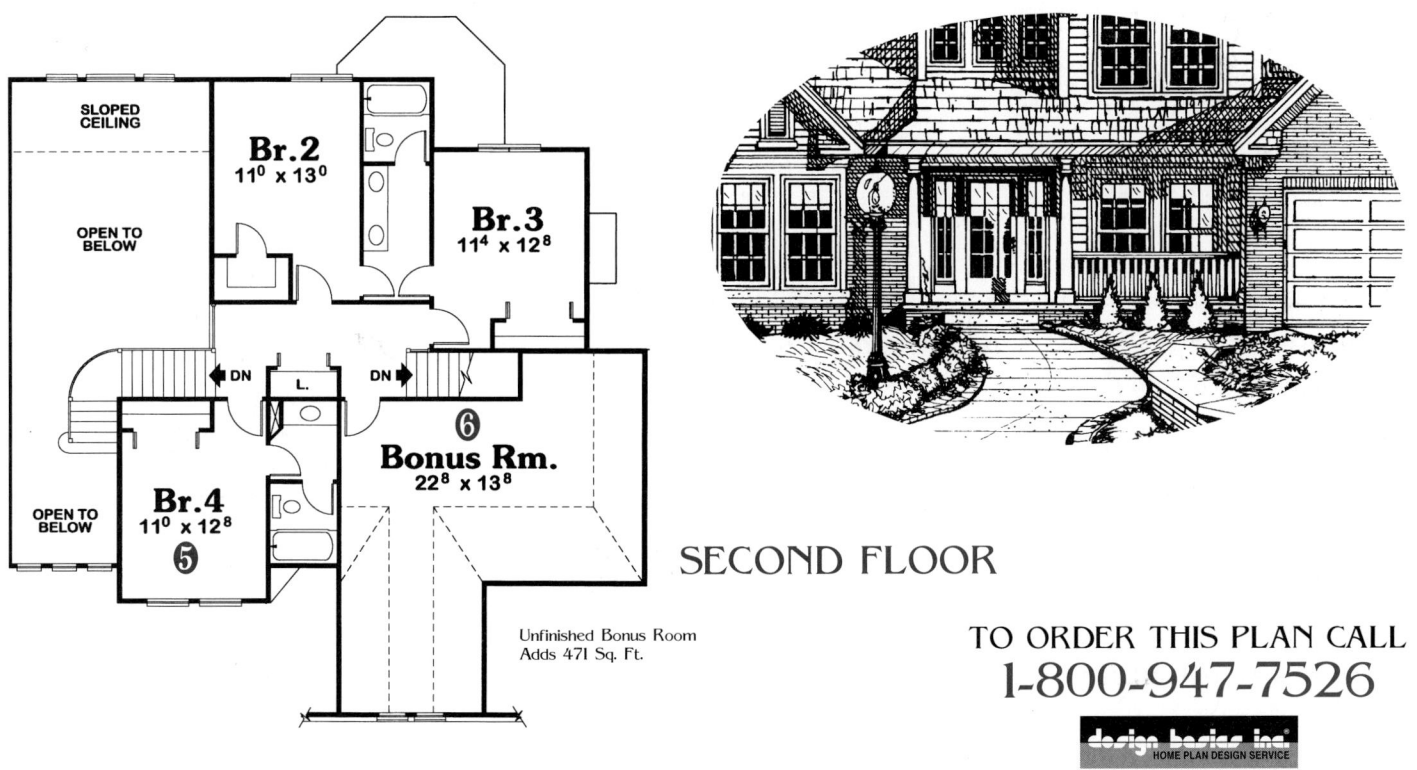

SECOND FLOOR

Unfinished Bonus Room Adds 471 Sq. Ft.

TO ORDER THIS PLAN CALL
1-800-947-7526

design basics inc
HOME PLAN DESIGN SERVICE

Nostalgia

Nicole

❶ The Cape Cod influence of this design is apparent with its reminiscent shutters and twin dormers.

❷ A great room has a sloped two-story ceiling and raised-hearth fireplace framed by windows.

❸ A rear staircase is practical for heavy traffic not wanted in view of the formal entry and dining room.

❹ An island cooktop combined with considerable counter space makes the kitchen accommodating and efficient.

❺ The second-floor corridor has a dramatic view of the great room from the railing balcony.

❻ A Hollywood bath connects bedrooms 3 and 4, both highlighted with alcove window seats.

AVAILABLE FOR ALL PLANS

For More Information on our Roof Construction Package see page 158.

9K-4641 PRICE CODE 27

MAIN FLOOR

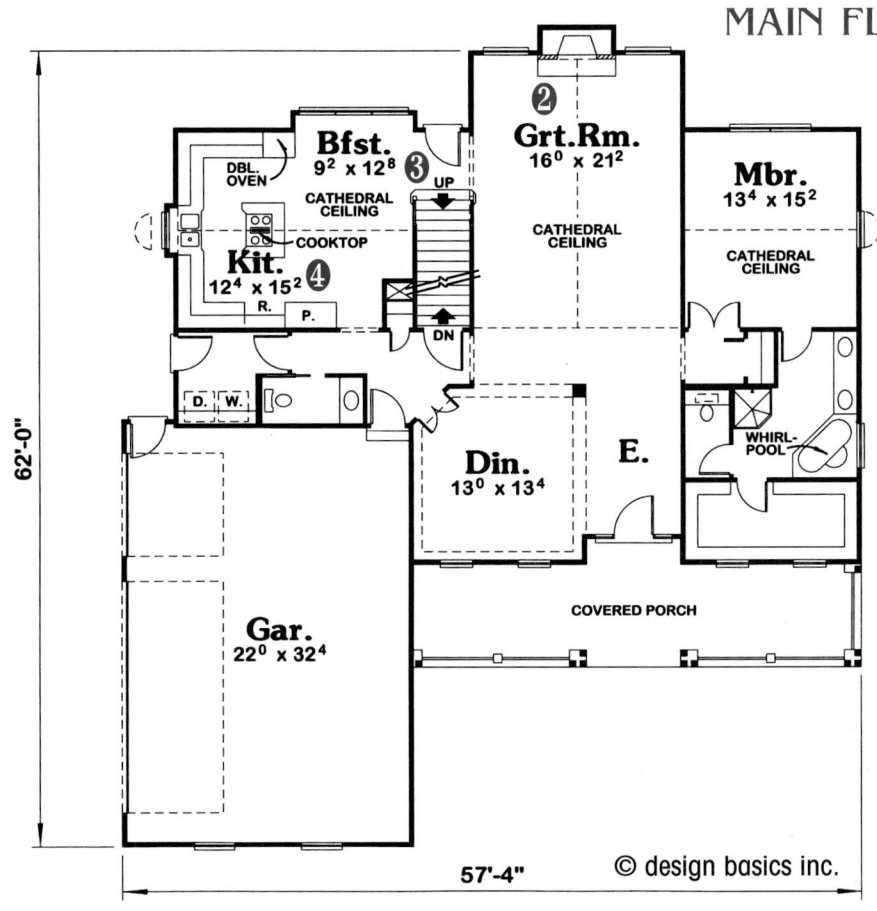

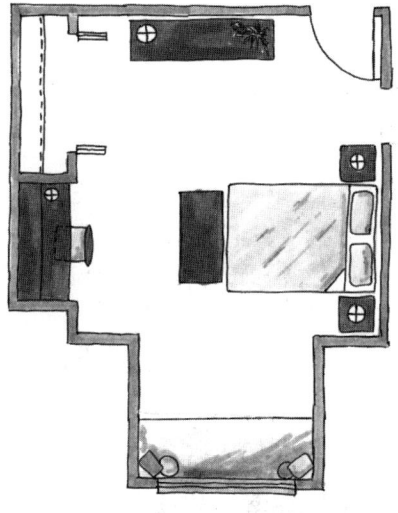

DECORATOR DESIGN TIPS

BEDROOM 3 - A large window seat in this bedroom is filled with big pillows to create a comfortable place for a nap or studying. The bed fits perfectly on the right wall and gives good balance to the window seat. Its placement also avoids a long walkway inside the room.

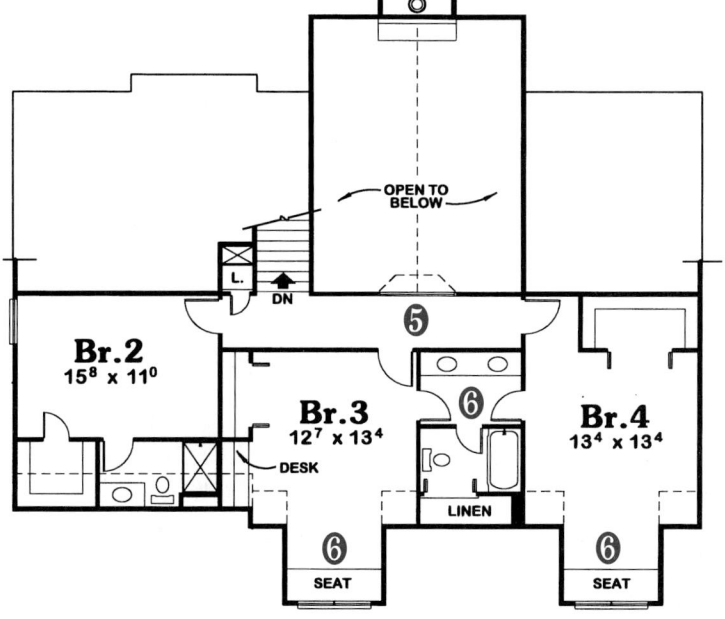

Main	1717 Sq. Ft.
Second	1064 Sq. Ft.
Total	2781 Sq. Ft.

NOTE: 9 ft. main level walls

SECOND FLOOR

TO ORDER THIS PLAN CALL
1-800-947-7526

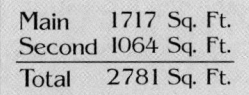

Nostalgia

Wayland

❶ This farmhouse beauty is replete with brick on its front porch and a third-story attic with quaint dormers.

❷ A dropped-soffit perimeter adorns the dining room with double doors accessing the kitchen.

❸ A large kitchen adjoins the breakfast area with quaint window seat built into a bayed window.

❹ The deserving master suite offers a private sitting area and large master bath that's accommodating as a dressing area.

❺ Out of direct view, the garage is accessible to the stairway and a large laundry room.

❻ The second-floor corridor has a dramatic view of the great room and leads to three bedrooms.

AVAILABLE FOR ALL PLANS

For More Information on Reverse Plans see page 158.

Nostalgia

9K -5185 PRICE CODE 28

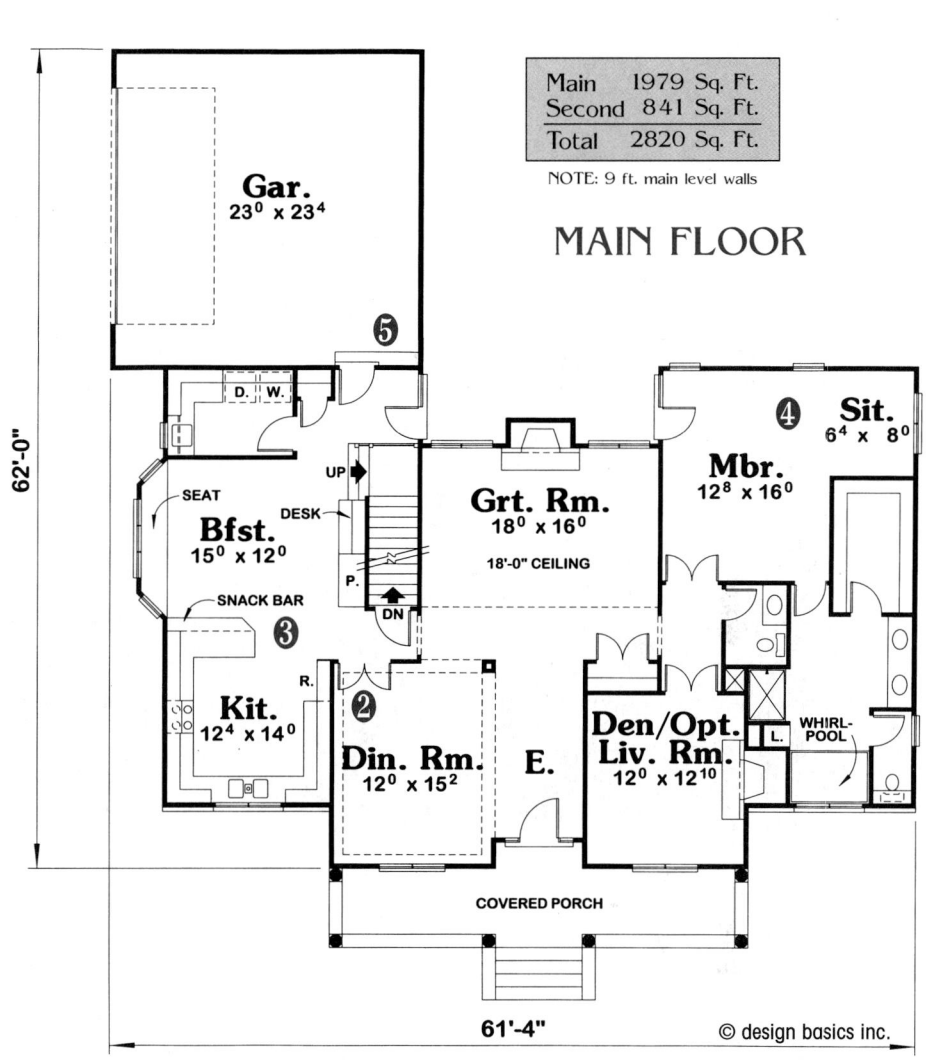

Main 1979 Sq. Ft.
Second 841 Sq. Ft.
Total 2820 Sq. Ft.

NOTE: 9 ft. main level walls

MAIN FLOOR

Unfinished Attic Adds 455 Sq. Ft.

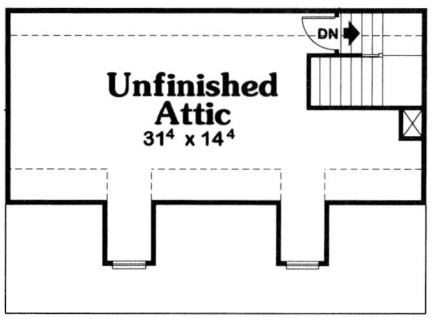

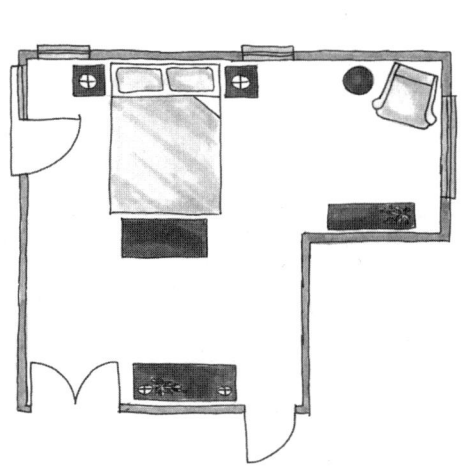

DECORATOR DESIGN TIPS

MASTER BEDROOM - This large bedroom contains a small nook that welcomes a chair and TV wall unit. This private setting makes a nice get-away for parents.

SECOND FLOOR

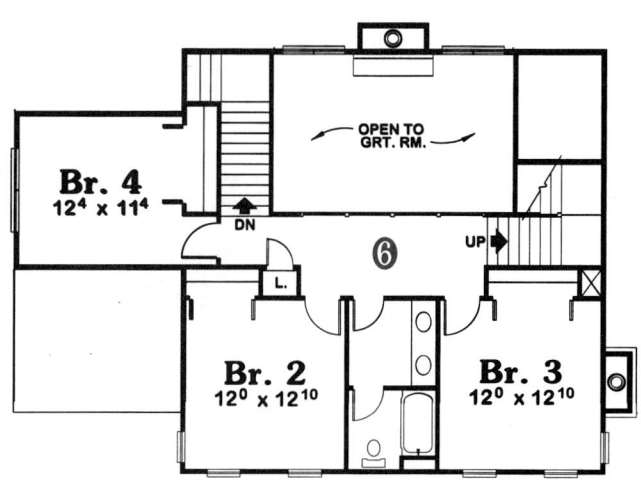

TO ORDER THIS PLAN CALL
1-800-947-7526

design basics inc.
HOME PLAN DESIGN SERVICE

Mahoning

❶ A sunny haven to relax in, the sunroom off the breakfast area features three sides of glass.

❷ A huge walk-in pantry and island cooktop in the kitchen free counter space for preparing meals.

❸ Unfinished storage space creates the opportunity for a second-floor bonus room.

❹ All three second-floor bedrooms have walk-in closets and private access to full baths.

❺ Double doors seclude a privately located den with sloped ceiling.

❻ A built-in work bench in the garage is handy for outdoor projects.

AVAILABLE FOR ALL PLANS

For More Information on Parade Home Packages see page 158.

9K-5105 PRICE CODE 28

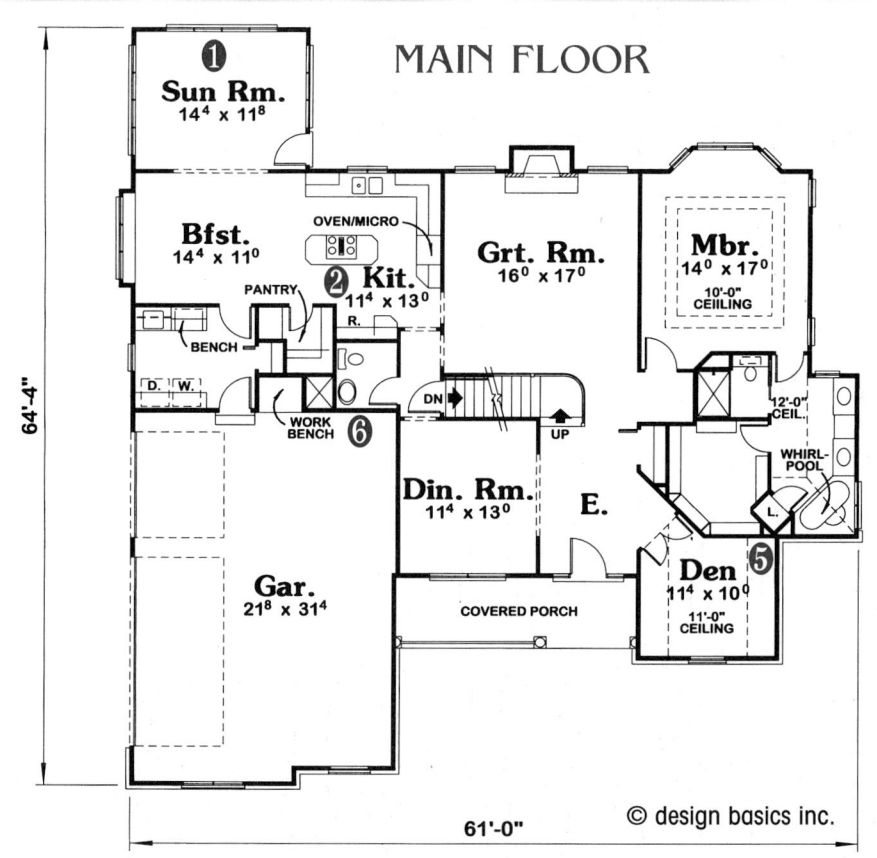

MAIN FLOOR

Main	1979 Sq. Ft.
Second	847 Sq. Ft.
Total	2826 Sq. Ft.

NOTE: 9 ft. main level walls

INTERIOR VIEW

Laundry Room - A built-in bench complements this room by offering a place to remove muddy apparel when entering from the garage. A soaking sink and hanging rod add to the functionality of the room.

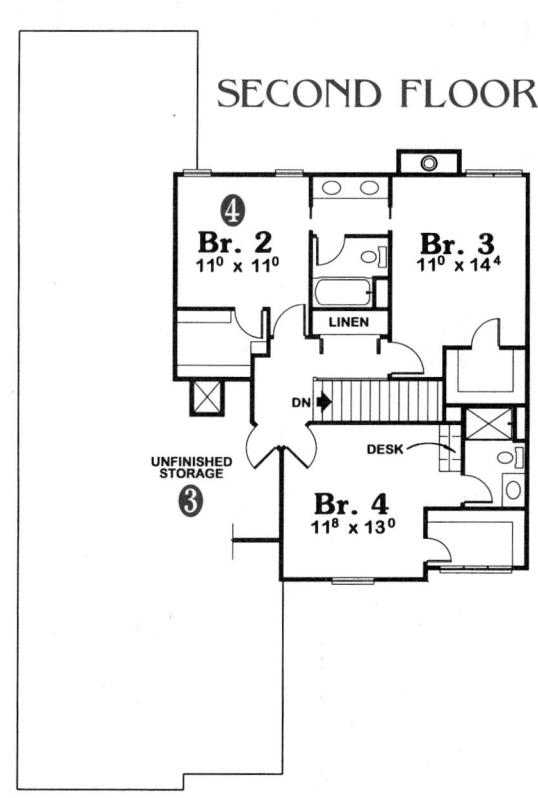

SECOND FLOOR

TO ORDER THIS PLAN CALL
1-800-947-7526

Nostalgia

Middleboro

❶ Toned-down window treatments and sturdy columns bring warmth to the front elevation.

❷ French doors leading to the master bath reveal a large walk-in closet with ample storage space.

❸ The three-car, side-load garage has the perfect place for a built-in work bench.

❹ Whether an exercise room or study, the storage room caters to the individual needs of any family.

❺ Each second-floor bedroom has convenient access to a full bath and offers a walk-in closet.

❻ 10-foot main level walls provide an old-home openness to main level rooms.

AVAILABLE FOR ALL PLANS

For More Information on our Custom Changes see page 157.

Nostalgia

9K-5000
PRICE CODE 29

MAIN FLOOR

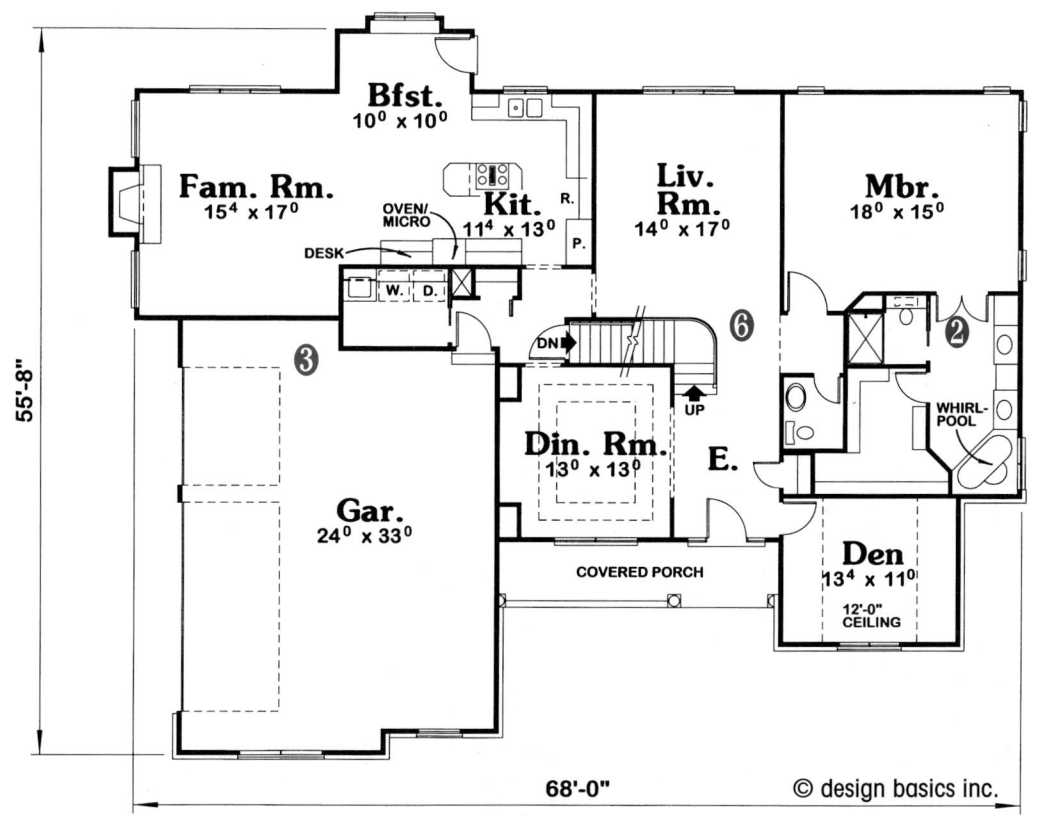

Main	2072 Sq. Ft.
Second	917 Sq. Ft.
Total	2989 Sq. Ft.

NOTE: 10 ft. main level walls

SECOND FLOOR

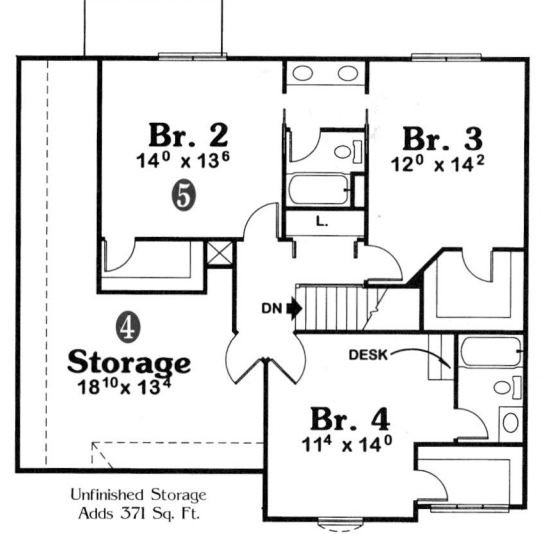

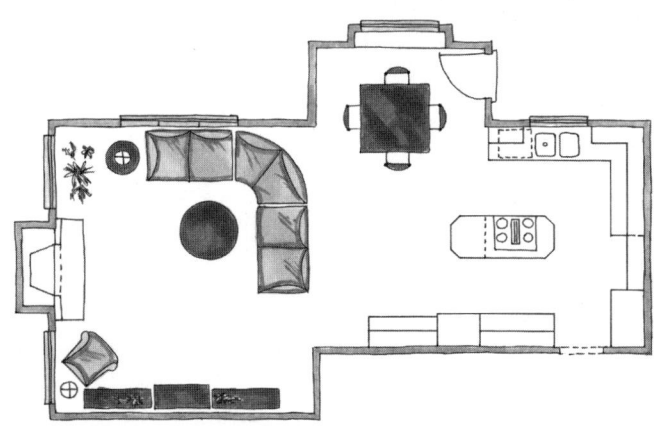

DECORATOR DESIGN TIPS

KITCHEN/FAMILY ROOM - In a space as large and open as this, it works well to position a sectional (or two sofas) in the family area to create room separation. While defining each room, it also creates a great arrangement for TV viewing and fireplace enjoyment. Choosing a square dining table emphasizes the shape of the breakfast area. The sharp corners of its shape contrast nicely with the soft curves of the sectional.

TO ORDER THIS PLAN CALL
1-800-947-7526

Marlow

❶ A plant shelf and arched transom window decorate the entry of this appealing home.

❷ A fireplace and cathedral ceiling are highlights in the den, located just inside the entry.

❸ A tall window grouping offers a dramatic view from the great room, with double doors leading outside.

❹ French doors seclude the dining room from the informal area of the home.

❺ The warm hearth room is a natural place to relax just off the sunny breakfast area.

❻ The gourmet kitchen includes a unique double island, walk-in pantry and plenty of counter space.

ALL PLANS COPYRIGHTED

For More Information on our Copyrights see page 154.

9K -4144 PRICE CODE 30

MAIN FLOOR

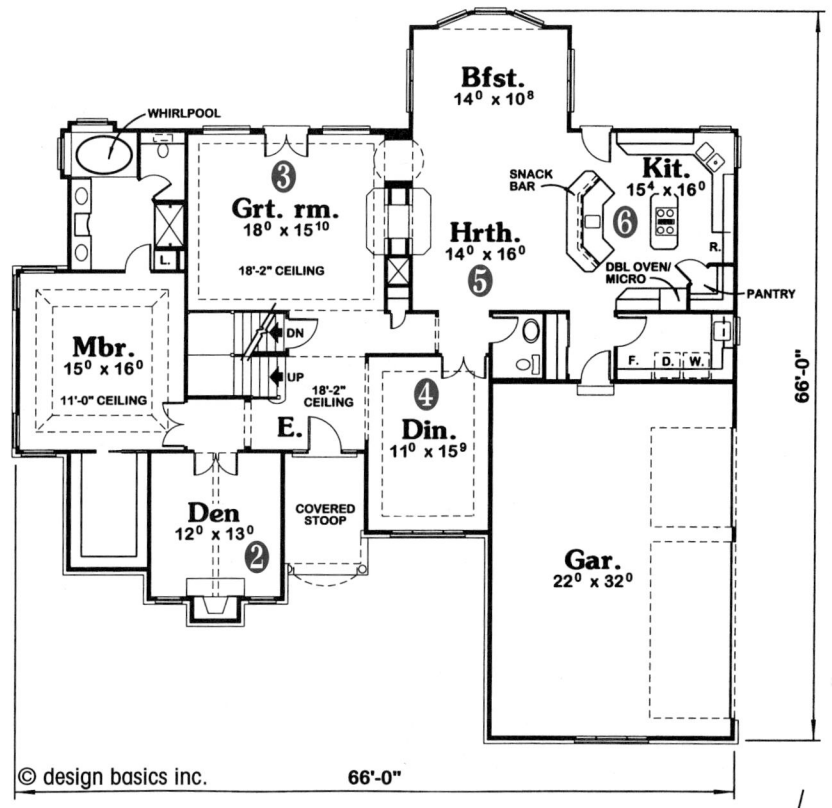

Main	2215 Sq. Ft.
Second	825 Sq. Ft.
Total	3040 Sq. Ft.

NOTE: 9 ft. main level walls

SECOND FLOOR

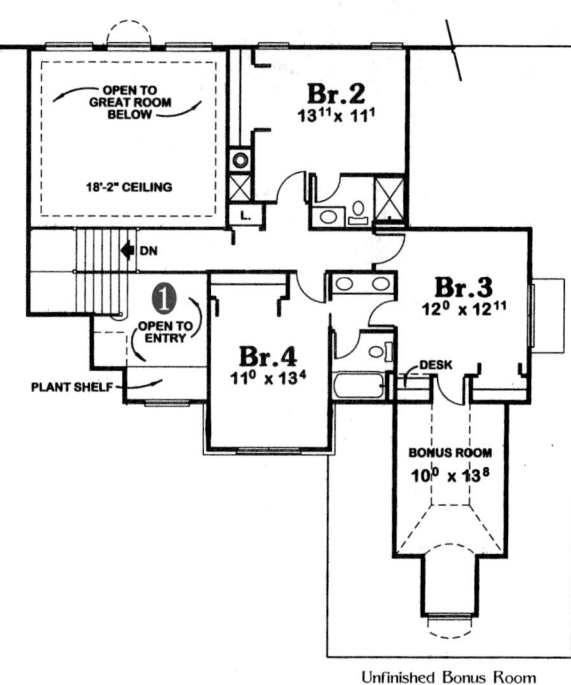

Unfinished Bonus Room Adds 186 Sq. Ft.

INTERIOR VIEW

HEARTH ROOM – From this room, beautiful double-hung windows capture the nostalgic feel of the kitchen and breakfast area.

TO ORDER THIS PLAN CALL
1-800-947-7526

design basics inc.
HOME PLAN DESIGN SERVICE

Nostalgia
101

Eleanor

❶ A Georgian influence gives this design a sense of timelessness and prominence.

❷ Coat closets and formal rooms flank the entry, making this area convenient for entertaining.

❸ An informal family area at the rear of the home features a bayed breakfast area, snack bar and raised hearth fireplace.

❹ His and her closets, built-in dressers and a luxurious whirlpool tub enhanced by bayed windows highlight a pampering master suite.

❺ All second-floor bedrooms provide access to walk-in closets — great for the storage of toys.

❻ Bedroom 4 easily converts into a study and showcases a gorgeous balcony that views the family room.

AVAILABLE FOR ALL PLANS

For More Information on Reverse Plans see page 158.

Nostalgia
102

9K -4089 PRICE CODE 31

MAIN FLOOR

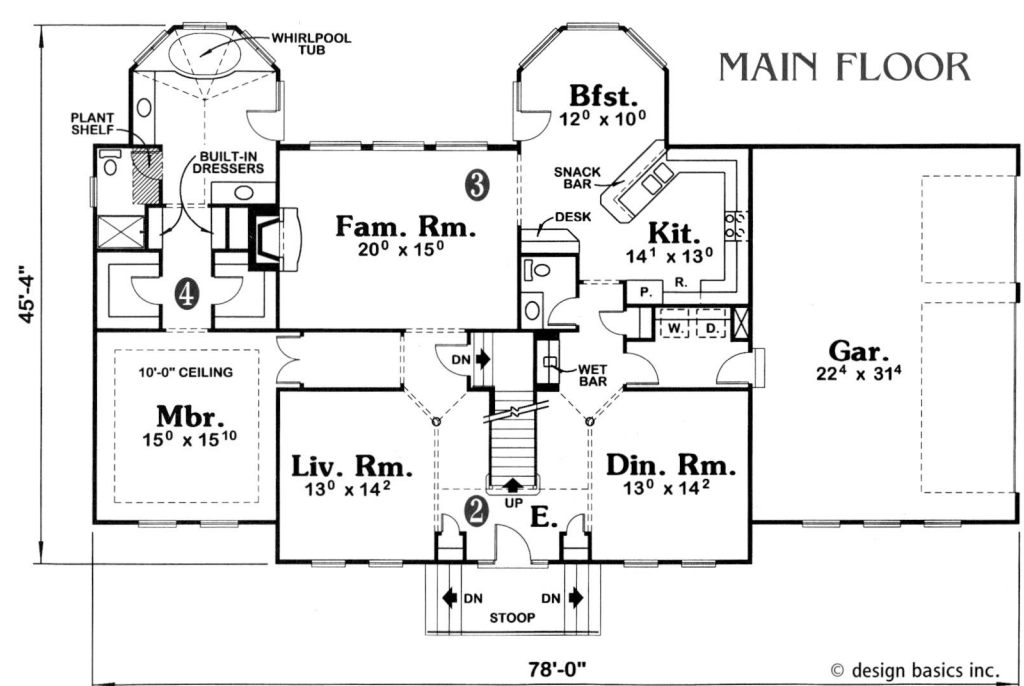

Main 2130 Sq. Ft.
Second 973 Sq. Ft.
Total 3103 Sq. Ft.

NOTE: 9 ft. main level walls

© design basics inc.

SECOND FLOOR

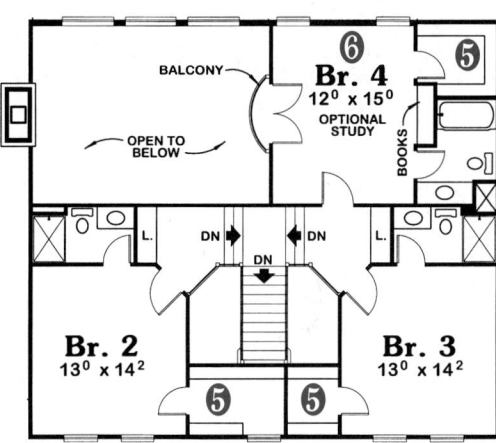

INTERIOR VIEW

MASTER BATH - This master bath offers a spa atmosphere with a sloped ceiling and large plant ledge. Bayed windows and atrium doors leading to the outside bring in an abundance of natural light.

TO ORDER THIS PLAN CALL
1-800-947-7526

design basics inc.
HOME PLAN DESIGN SERVICE

Nostalgia
103

Landreth

❶ A bayed window and gazebo on the front of this home create a friendly impression upon first view.

❷ An elevated entry views the dining room past an open hand railing.

❸ French doors are centered in the great room and lead outside.

❹ The functional kitchen has a large island with cooktop and snack bar and views the breakfast area via three arched openings.

❺ Twin entertainment centers encase the fireplace in the family room, which also has atrium-door access to the outdoors.

❻ A loft on the second floor works well as a computer center and features double doors that open to view the two-story family room.

AVAILABLE FOR ALL PLANS

Roof Construction Package

For More Information on our Roof Construction Package see page 158.

9K-5142 PRICE CODE 34

MAIN FLOOR

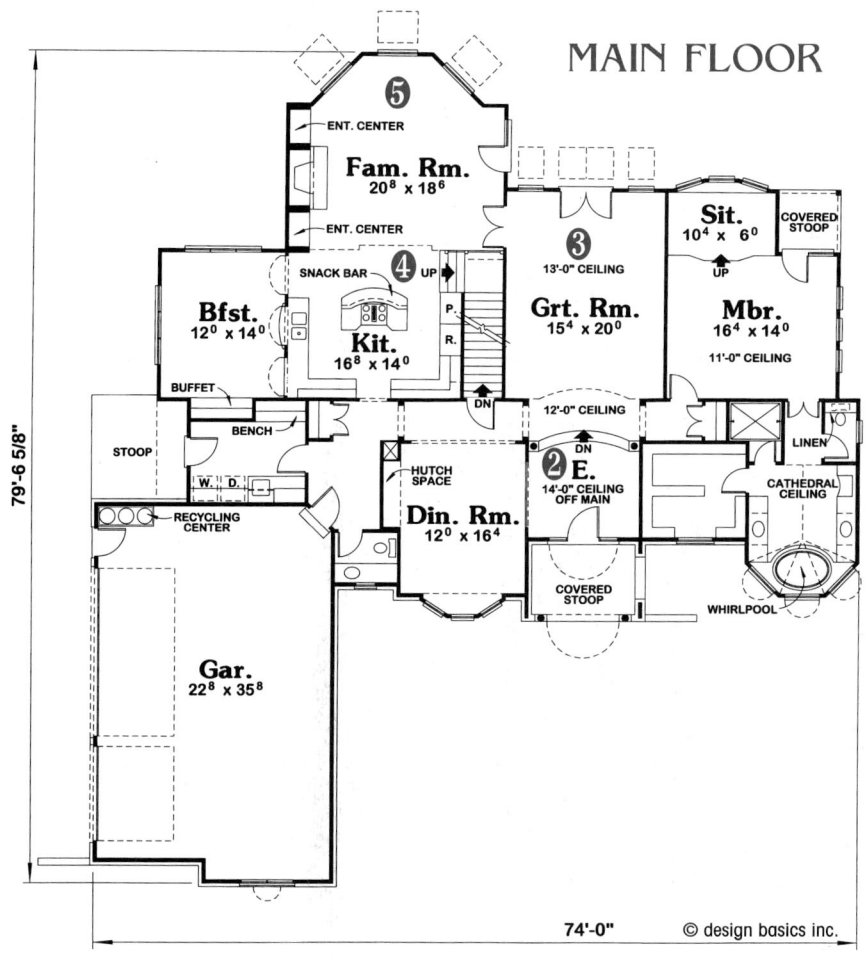

SECOND FLOOR

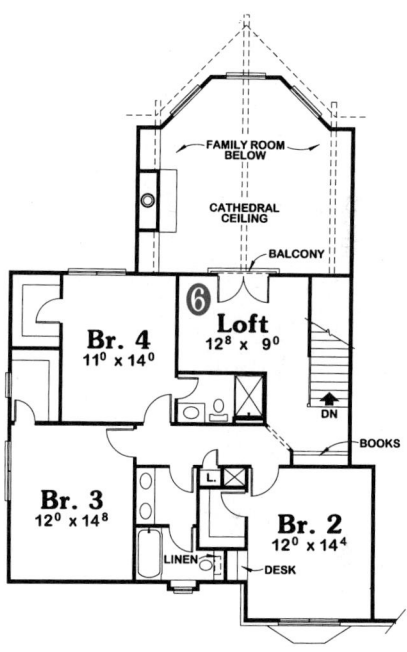

Main	2461 Sq. Ft.
Second	1019 Sq. Ft.
Total	3480 Sq. Ft.

NOTE: 9 ft. main level walls

INTERIOR VIEW

LOFT – This second-floor room offers a striking view of the family room with cathedral ceiling. For more privacy while working, a set of French doors closes off the open balcony.

TO ORDER THIS PLAN CALL
1-800-947-7526

Nostalgia

In the **Nostalgia** *Collection you will find...*

FLEXIBLE ROOMS

"Because the same design may work equally well for an empty-nester *and* family, we've incorporated the use of a variety of flexible rooms in these home plans. While a room may be called out as a bedroom, we've designed it in such a way to suggest that it could be used as an office, exercise room or hobby room. These spaces can really serve a variety of functions and greatly benefit the homes' resale value."

ECONOMIC USE OF SPACE

"Home buyers are continually looking for larger and larger storage areas. They're also looking for the most economical home for their dollar. So, in every inch of these homes, we tried to use the space that's available, especially the space directly under the roof. You'll find plenty of bonus rooms, attics, lofts and second-floor bedrooms with dormers to make the rooms more useable. And all but a few of these homes offer nine-foot main level walls. Buyers can use these spaces as they see fit and will also enjoy the aesthetic appeal since many of these areas create charming nooks with quaintly sloped ceilings."

Two-story Homes

Plan Index

Plan #	Plan Name	Sq. Ft.	Page #
4999	Sanders	1628	108-109
4642	Ackerly	1712	110-111
4997	Rocklund	1778	112-113
5084	Cohasset	1893	114-115
5085	Branford	1928	116-117
4949	Darius	1938	118-119
4996	Amesbury	2069	120-121
4952	Caldera	2144	122-123
5002	Rochdale	2224	124-125
4105	Eldon	2282	126-127
4145	Ainsley	2332	128-129
4135	Gerard	2349	130-131
5086	Patagonia	2417	132-133
5049	Norwood	2475	134-135
5132	Castine	2506	136-137
4125	Emery	2523	138-139
5209	Laveen	2531	140-141
4156	Karlynda	2558	142-143
5037	Suffolk	2560	144-145
4106	Calabretta	2613	146-147
4147	Sutter	2642	148-149
5083	Attleboro	2752	150-151
4950	Neville	2808	152-153

Sanders

❶ The covered porch of this home, together with a lovely transom window above the front door, create a desirable front elevation.

❷ Adding to the entry's impressive view of the French doors leading to a secluded den, is the beautiful staircase.

❸ Indented double doors add interest to the den.

❹ Three large windows and a raised-hearth fireplace add character to the already-inviting family room.

❺ Wrapping counters in the kitchen are convenient for the chef of the house, as are a snack bar, lazy Susan and pantry.

❻ The breakfast area resembles a cozy nook with access to the outside.

AVAILABLE FOR ALL PLANS

For More Information on our Custom Changes see page 157.

9K -4999 PRICE CODE **16**

MAIN FLOOR

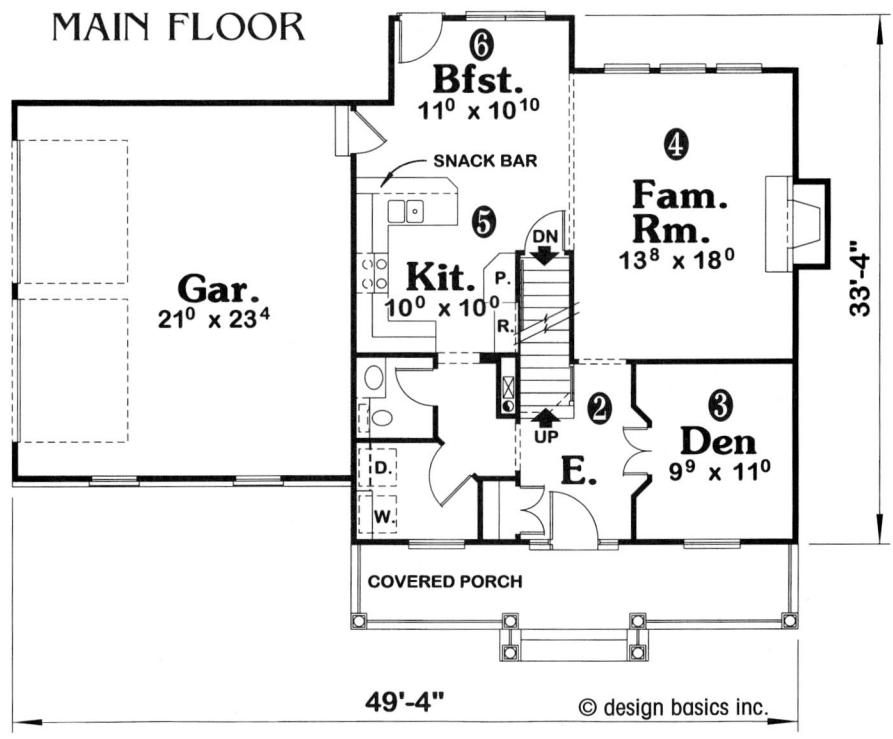

- ⑥ **Bfst.** 11⁰ x 10¹⁰
- SNACK BAR
- ④ **Fam. Rm.** 13⁸ x 18⁰
- **Gar.** 21⁰ x 23⁴
- ⑤ **Kit.** 10⁰ x 10⁰
- P.R.
- DN
- ② UP
- ③ **Den** 9⁹ x 11⁰
- E.
- D. W.
- COVERED PORCH
- 49'-4"
- 33'-4"
- © design basics inc.

Main	874 Sq. Ft.
Second	754 Sq. Ft.
Total	1628 Sq. Ft.

NOTE: 8 ft. main level walls

SECOND FLOOR

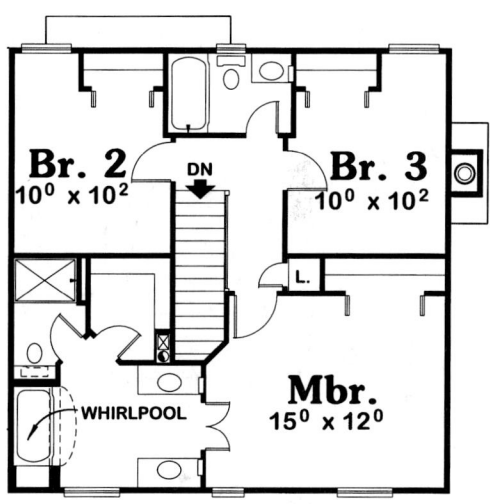

- **Br. 2** 10⁰ x 10²
- **Br. 3** 10⁰ x 10²
- DN
- L.
- **Mbr.** 15⁰ x 12⁰
- WHIRLPOOL

INTERIOR VIEW

MASTER BATH - His and her vanities are exceptional conveniences in this luxurious master bath. A relaxing whirlpool tub draws you inside where a large walk-in closet and compartmental shower offer further benefits.

TO ORDER THIS PLAN CALL
1-800-947-7526

Nostalgia

Ackerly

❶ This charming design features lap siding and shutters to set off its All-American appeal.

❷ A large covered stoop opens to an informal floor plan with the kitchen located to the front.

❸ A snack bar serves the dinette, which could function both formally and informally.

❹ A media room – perfect for a family work area with home computer – could also become a dining room or hobby area.

❺ A cathedral ceiling centers on the fireplace in the dramatic family room.

❻ A nook in the master bedroom can be used as an entertainment center or bookshelf.

ALL PLANS COPYRIGHTED

For More Information on our Copyrights see page 154.

Nostalgia

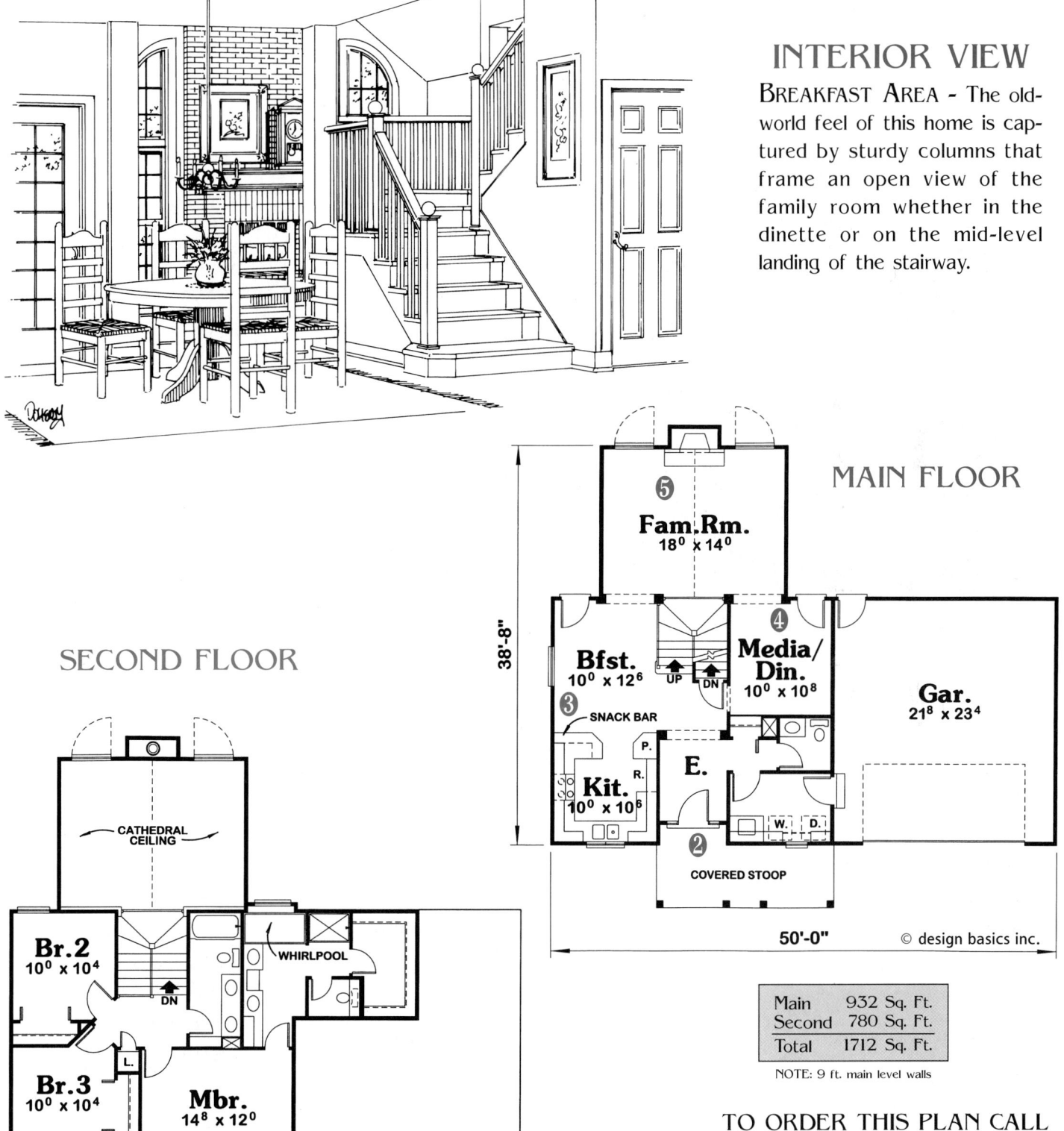

Rocklund

❶ Double doors seclude the parlor from the family room but also provide the possibility of expansion for larger groups.

❷ A built-in curio cabinet in the family room is a great place to decorate with books or family photos.

❸ A walk-in pantry offers storage to both the kitchen and breakfast area.

❹ Plenty of storage space in the garage is perfect for a work bench or lawn equipment.

❺ Expansion space above the garage provides the option to expand the master suite closet or create a storage area.

❻ Two linen closets provide extra storage on the second floor.

AVAILABLE FOR ALL PLANS

For More Information on Reverse Plans see page 158.

9K -4997 PRICE CODE **17**

SECOND FLOOR

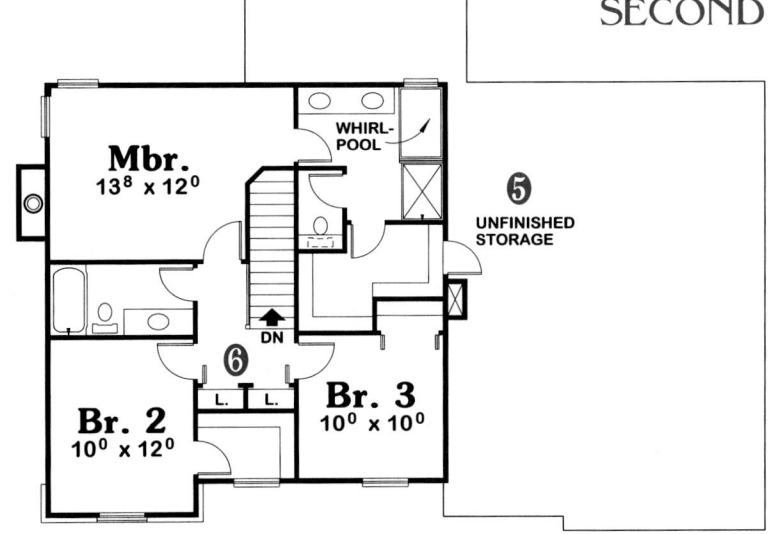

Main	1003 Sq. Ft.
Second	775 Sq. Ft.
Total	1778 Sq. Ft.

NOTE: 9 ft. main level walls

EXTERIOR HIGHLIGHT

Wide brick steps and pilasters help bring back the feel of homes from the Arts and Crafts era. An extension of this brick is carried on throughout the exterior of this facade.

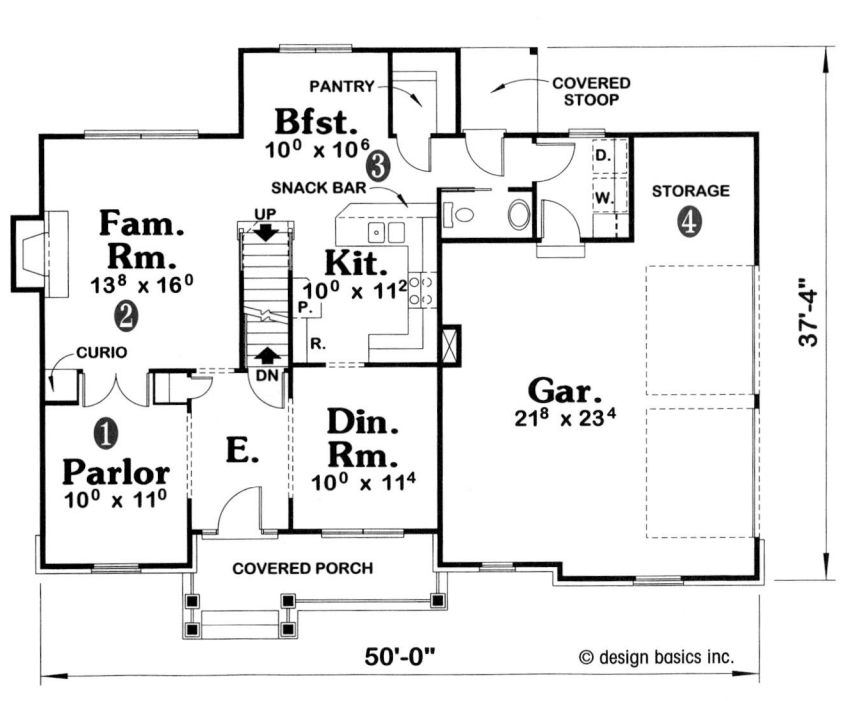

MAIN FLOOR

TO ORDER THIS PLAN CALL
1-800-947-7526

design basics inc.
HOME PLAN DESIGN SERVICE

Nostalgia
113

Cohasset

❶ This captivating design features beautiful windows set off with traditional, simplified trim.

❷ Upon walking in, the front room has a variety of options including a parlor or, with its close vicinity to the kitchen, a dining room.

❸ Bookshelves and a fireplace add a comfortable atmosphere to the family room.

❹ Extra storage space in the garage welcomes shelves or a work bench.

❺ Ample space is offered in the secondary bedrooms, both of which have a walk-in closet.

❻ Unfinished storage above the garage would make a great addition to the master suite's closet, especially for seasonal storage.

AVAILABLE FOR ALL PLANS

For More Information on our Roof Construction Package see page 158.

Nostalgia

9K-5084 PRICE CODE 18

SECOND FLOOR

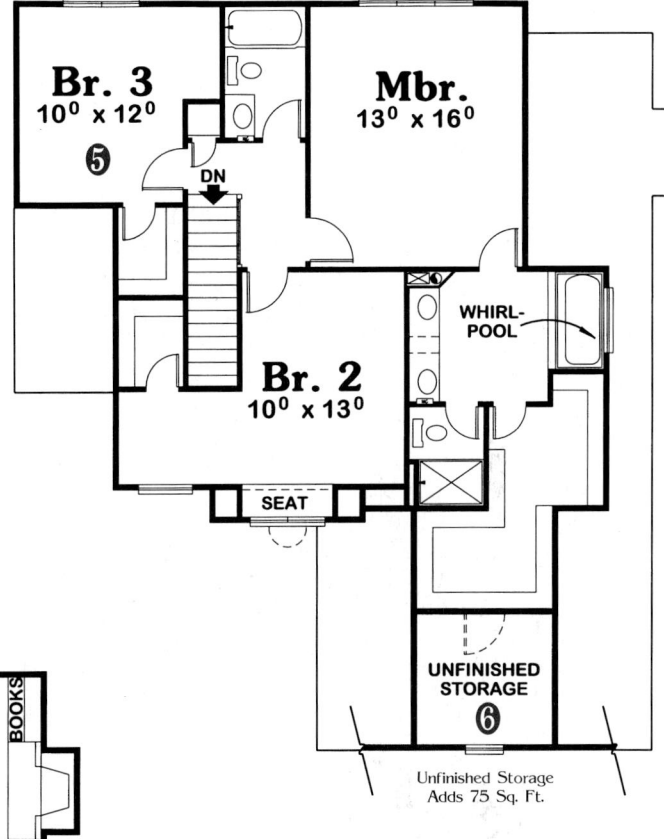

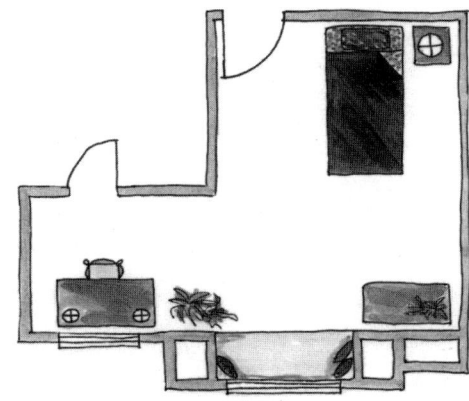

DECORATOR DESIGN TIPS

BEDROOM 2 – This bedroom has the perfect shape to arrange special areas. By tucking a desk in front of the window, a private study area is created. The window seat allows for a comfortable space to read in the sun.

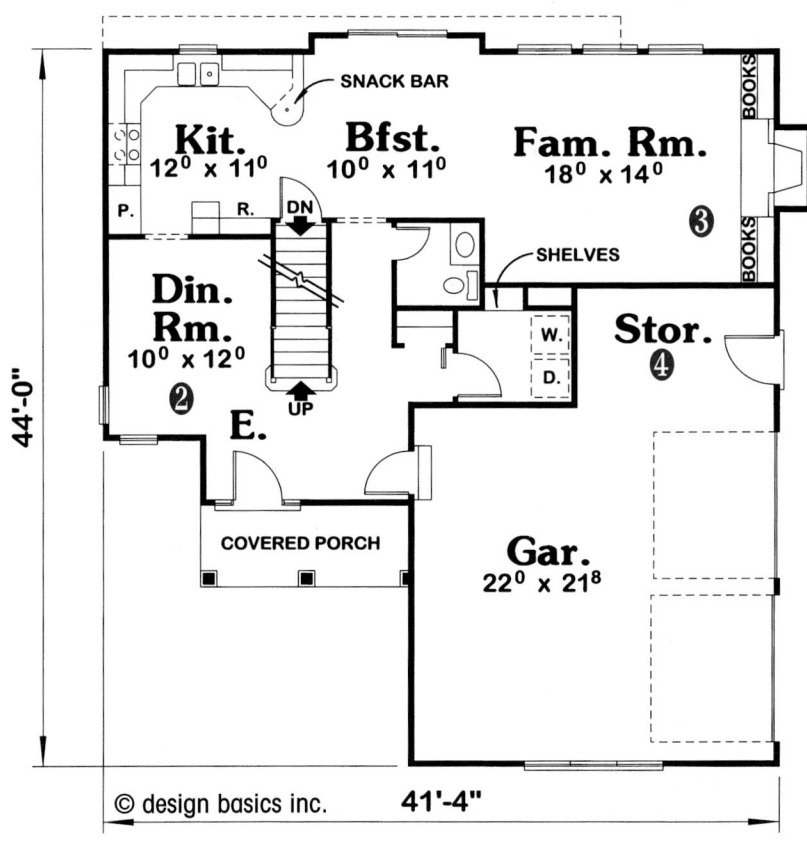

Main	920 Sq. Ft.
Second	973 Sq. Ft.
Total	1893 Sq. Ft.

NOTE: 9 ft. main level walls

MAIN FLOOR

TO ORDER THIS PLAN CALL
1-800-947-7526

design basics inc.
HOME PLAN DESIGN SERVICE

Branford

❶ Soldier coursing charms the windows of this home, which will make a good candidate for a narrower lot situation.

❷ In its traditional role, the living room in this home welcomes guests as they walk in the door.

❸ The hearth room offers a bookcase and shares a see-thru fireplace with the living room.

❹ A computer area at the top of the stairway is perfect for homework or finishing up office work.

❺ The unfinished bonus room on the second-floor, is a great place to expand into a studio.

❻ 9-foot main level walls bring a sense of spaciousness to all rooms on the first floor.

AVAILABLE FOR ALL PLANS

For More Information on Parade Home Packages see page 158.

Nostalgia
116

9K-5085 PRICE CODE 19

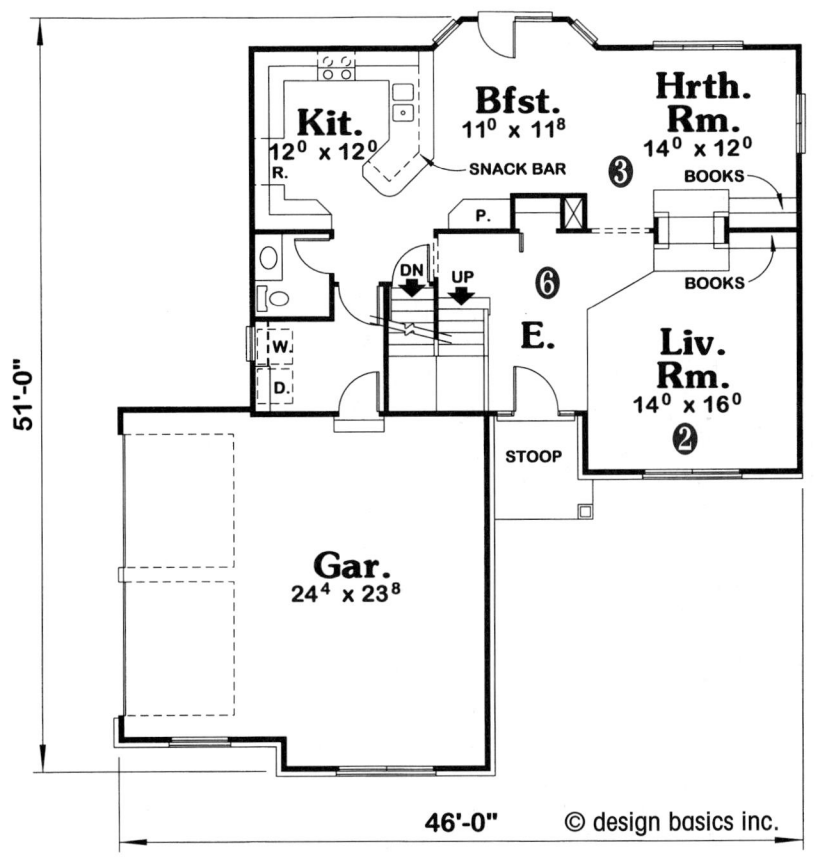

MAIN FLOOR

Main	1002 Sq. Ft.
Second	926 Sq. Ft.
Total	1928 Sq. Ft.

NOTE: 9 ft. main level walls

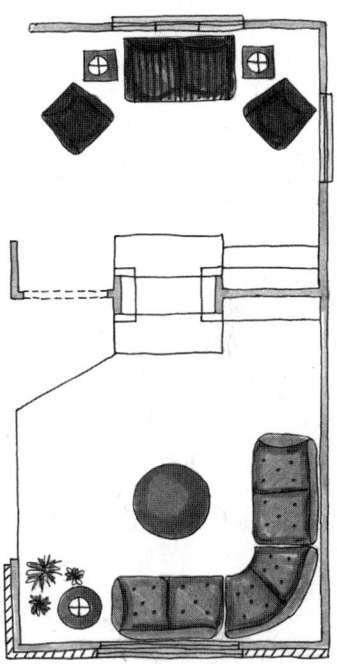

DECORATOR DESIGN TIPS

LIVING/HEARTH ROOM – These fairly open living spaces require an easy transition from one room to another. By using a large sectional piece in the living room, and smaller pieces in the hearth room, a nice composition of scale and shape is created. Too many pieces of the same size and proportion makes a space feel overdone and "busy."

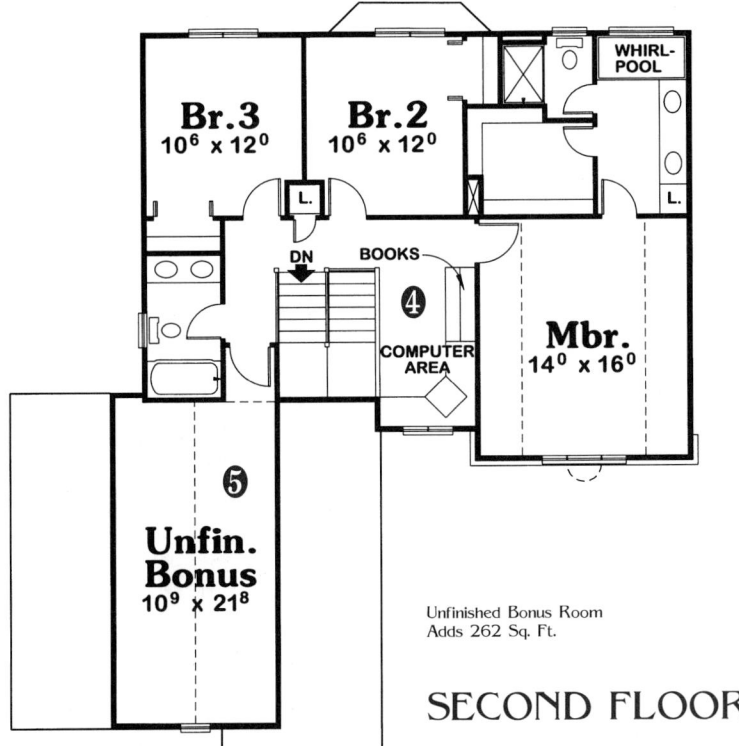

Unfinished Bonus Room Adds 262 Sq. Ft.

SECOND FLOOR

TO ORDER THIS PLAN CALL
1-800-947-7526

design basics inc.
HOME PLAN DESIGN SERVICE

Darius

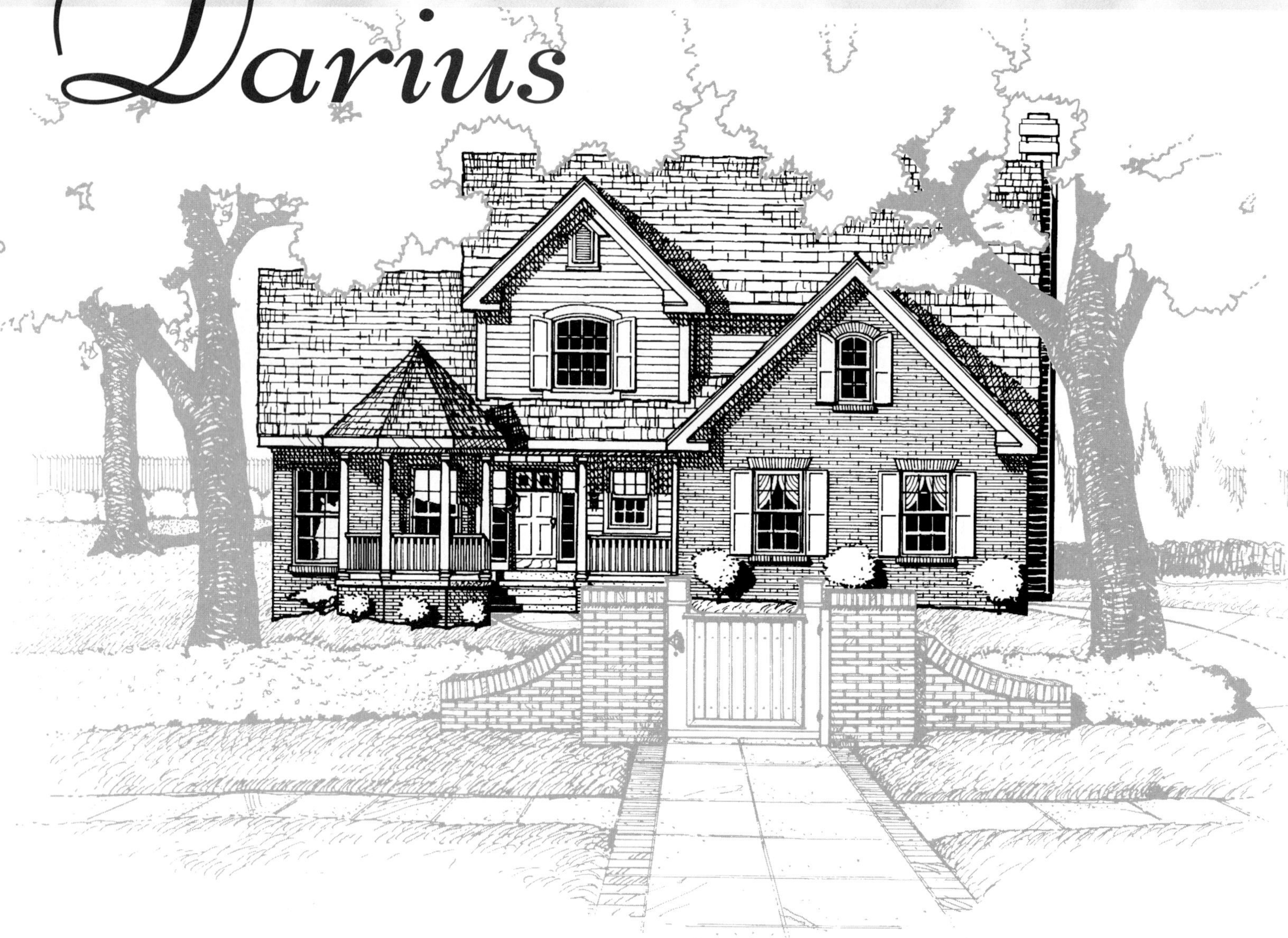

❶ With its wistful gazebo porch and subtle outside window details, viewing this home brings to life memories of homes of the past.

❷ A view of the living room, with elegant columns, sets the mood for the rest of the home.

❸ The dining room, when paired with the living room, shares space for formal occasions.

❹ The kitchen and breakfast area open spaciously to the family room, and are ideal for family celebrations.

❺ Upstairs, the master bedroom offers many options with its unfinished bonus space, great for storage or especially a private office.

❻ The master bath is lavish with its corner whirlpool tub and novel sloped ceiling.

AVAILABLE FOR ALL PLANS

For More Information on our Custom Changes see page 157.

9K-4949 PRICE CODE 19

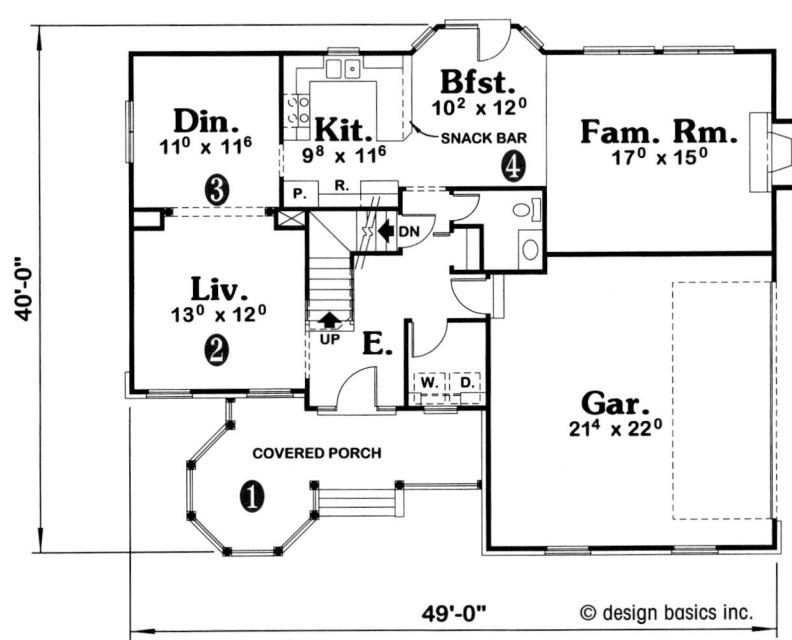

MAIN FLOOR

Main	1091 Sq. Ft.
Second	847 Sq. Ft.
Total	1938 Sq. Ft.

NOTE: 9 ft. main level walls

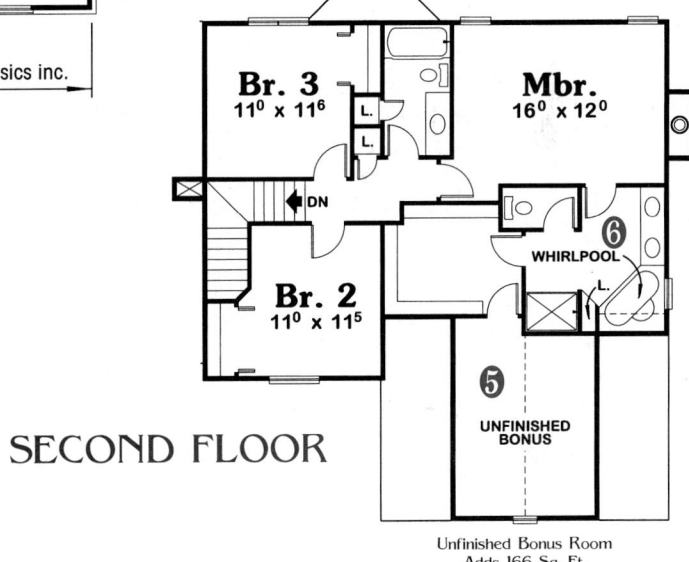

SECOND FLOOR

Unfinished Bonus Room Adds 166 Sq. Ft.

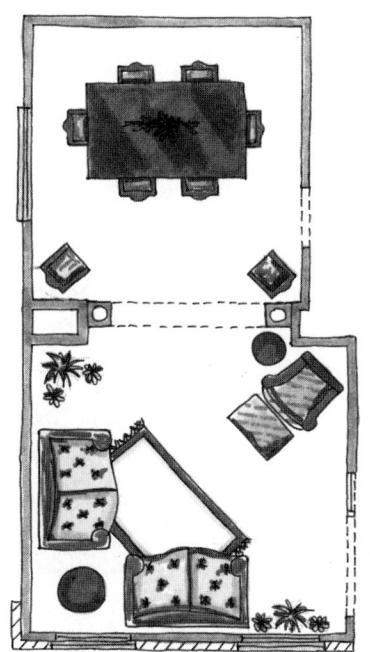

DECORATOR DESIGN TIPS

LIVING/DINING ROOM - The decorating choices in the living and dining rooms need to coincide since they are open to each other. In the living room, an angled rug ties two loveseats together to form a nice conversation area. Since this is a smaller room, loveseats work better together than larger furniture pieces. Also, choosing a more delicate style of furniture won't over-fill the space.

TO ORDER THIS PLAN CALL
1-800-947-7526

Nostalgia

Amesbury

❶ Upon walking in, a formal room easily adaptable as a dining room or living room is enhanced with a bayed window.

❷ Prominent columns and a ceiling sloped on two sides adds an airy comfort to the great room.

❸ A butcher's block, pantry and oven form an efficient working triangle in the kitchen.

❹ Storage space in the garage is a welcome amenity for a work bench or equipment storage.

❺ The second-floor corridor overlooks the entry and leads to two secondary bedrooms that share a full bath.

❻ The master bedroom is enhanced with a vaulted ceiling and shelves for displaying books.

ALL PLANS COPYRIGHTED

For More Information on our Copyrights see page 154.

Nostalgia

9K-4996 PRICE CODE 20

EXTERIOR HIGHLIGHT

To recess a porch such as this, on a home that already has a deep-set entry, could potentially "de-emphasize" the entry. The treatment works on this home because the Doric column detailing and the large sidelights and transom around the front door serve to capture attention.

SECOND FLOOR

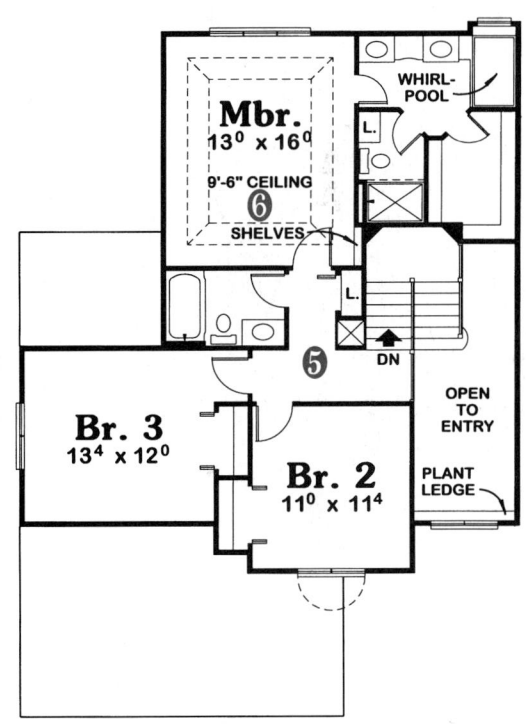

MAIN FLOOR

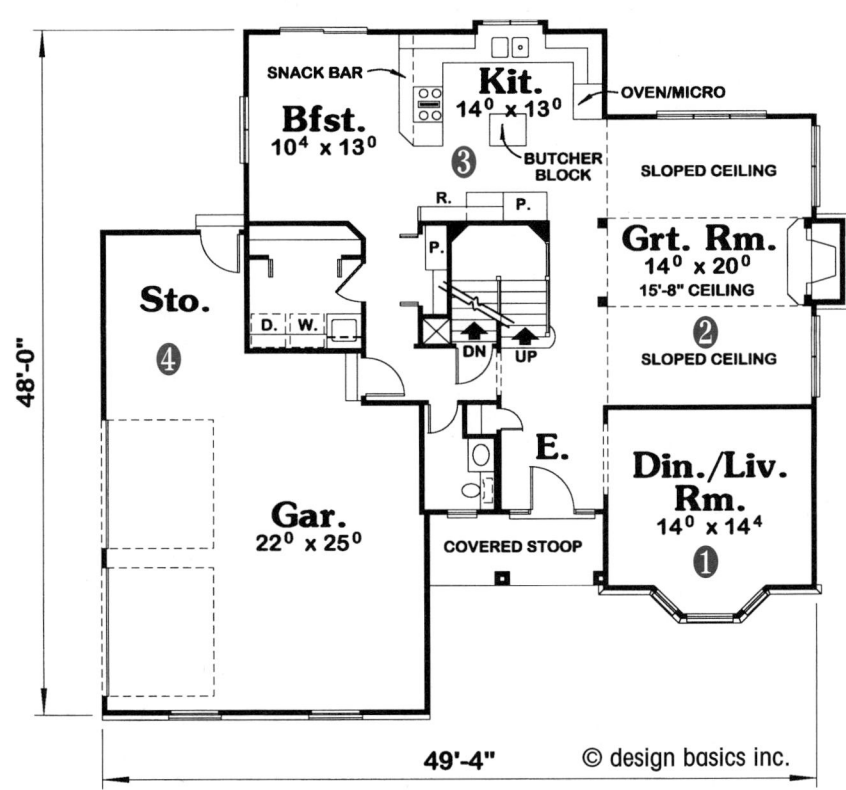

Main	1209 Sq. Ft.
Second	860 Sq. Ft.
Total	2069 Sq. Ft.

NOTE: 9 ft. main level walls

TO ORDER THIS PLAN CALL
1-800-947-7526

Nostalgia
121

Caldera

❶ Through the front covered porch is a lovely entry that views the staircase, and offers a large coat closet with old-fashioned double doors.

❷ The great room is warmed by a fireplace and opens to the dining room for ease when entertaining.

❸ The kitchen has ample counter space and a snack bar that serves the breakfast area.

❹ The master suite is spacious, with its giant walk-in closet that further opens to more storage space.

❺ Three secondary bedrooms, one with a handy built-in desk, share a full hall bath.

❻ A pocket door leads to the laundry room providing a soaking sink.

AVAILABLE FOR ALL PLANS

For More Information on Reverse Plans see page 158.

Nostalgia

9K-4952 PRICE CODE 21

EXTERIOR HIGHLIGHT

The recessed, arched entry on this home helps keep the frontage to a minimum. For that reason this home would work well on a narrower lot.

SECOND FLOOR

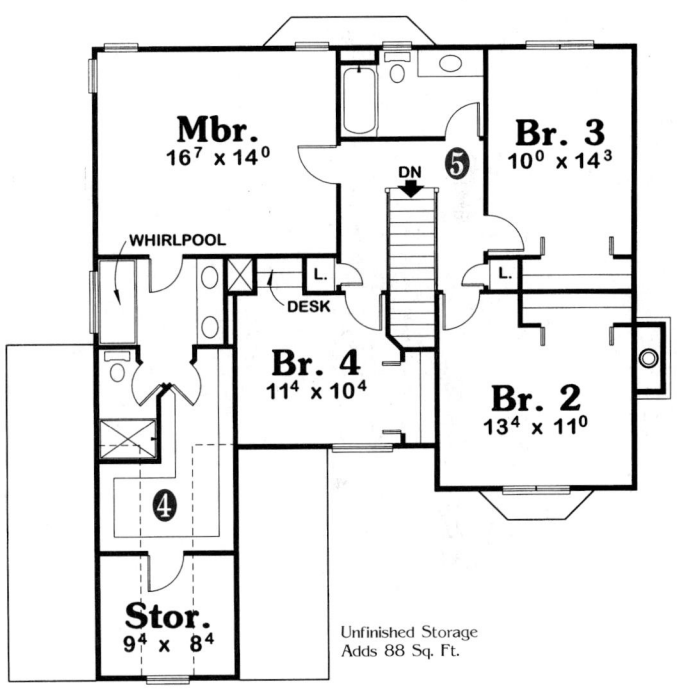

- Mbr. $16^7 \times 14^0$
- Br. 3 $10^0 \times 14^3$
- Br. 4 $11^4 \times 10^4$
- Br. 2 $13^4 \times 11^0$
- Stor. $9^4 \times 8^4$

Unfinished Storage Adds 88 Sq. Ft.

MAIN FLOOR

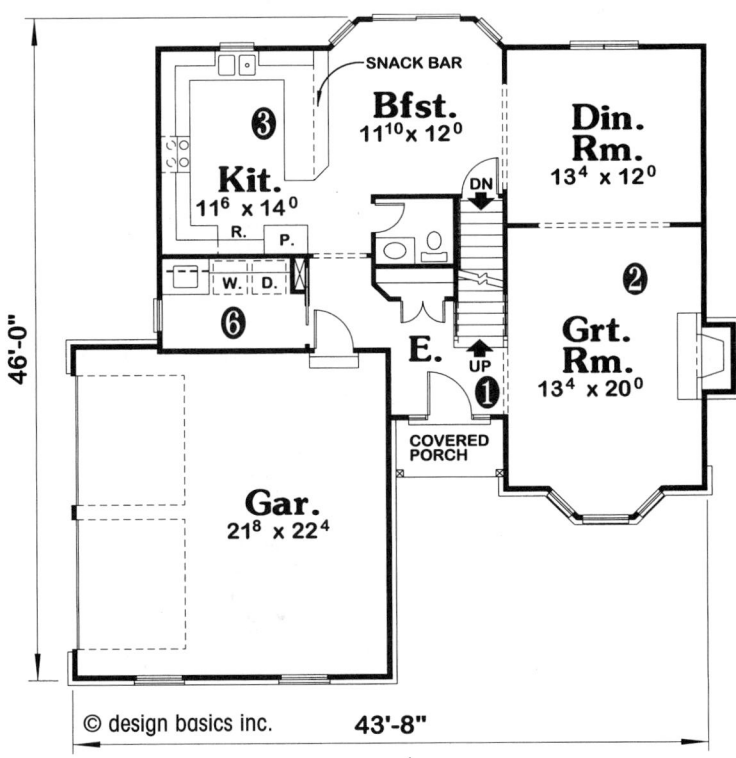

- Kit. $11^6 \times 14^0$
- Bfst. $11^{10} \times 12^0$
- Din. Rm. $13^4 \times 12^0$
- Grt. Rm. $13^4 \times 20^0$
- Gar. $21^8 \times 22^4$

46'-0" × 43'-8"

© design basics inc.

Main	1008 Sq. Ft.
Second	1136 Sq. Ft.
Total	2144 Sq. Ft.

NOTE: 9 ft. main level walls

TO ORDER THIS PLAN CALL
1-800-947-7526

design basics inc.
HOME PLAN DESIGN SERVICE

Nostalgia

Rochdale

❶ Whether used as a dining or living room, this lovely space will draw guests inside from the porch.

❷ The kitchen, dinette and family room function as a core at the rear of the home and comprise the main living areas.

❸ The master bedroom, located above the garage, offers a massive walk-in closet.

❹ With ample space to dress, the master bath features a dual-sink vanity and corner whirlpool tub.

❺ A sunlit walk-in closet in bedroom 3 provides room for storage.

❻ A large laundry room/mud room on the main floor includes a handy closet.

AVAILABLE FOR ALL PLANS

For More Information on our Roof Construction Package see page 158.

Nostalgia

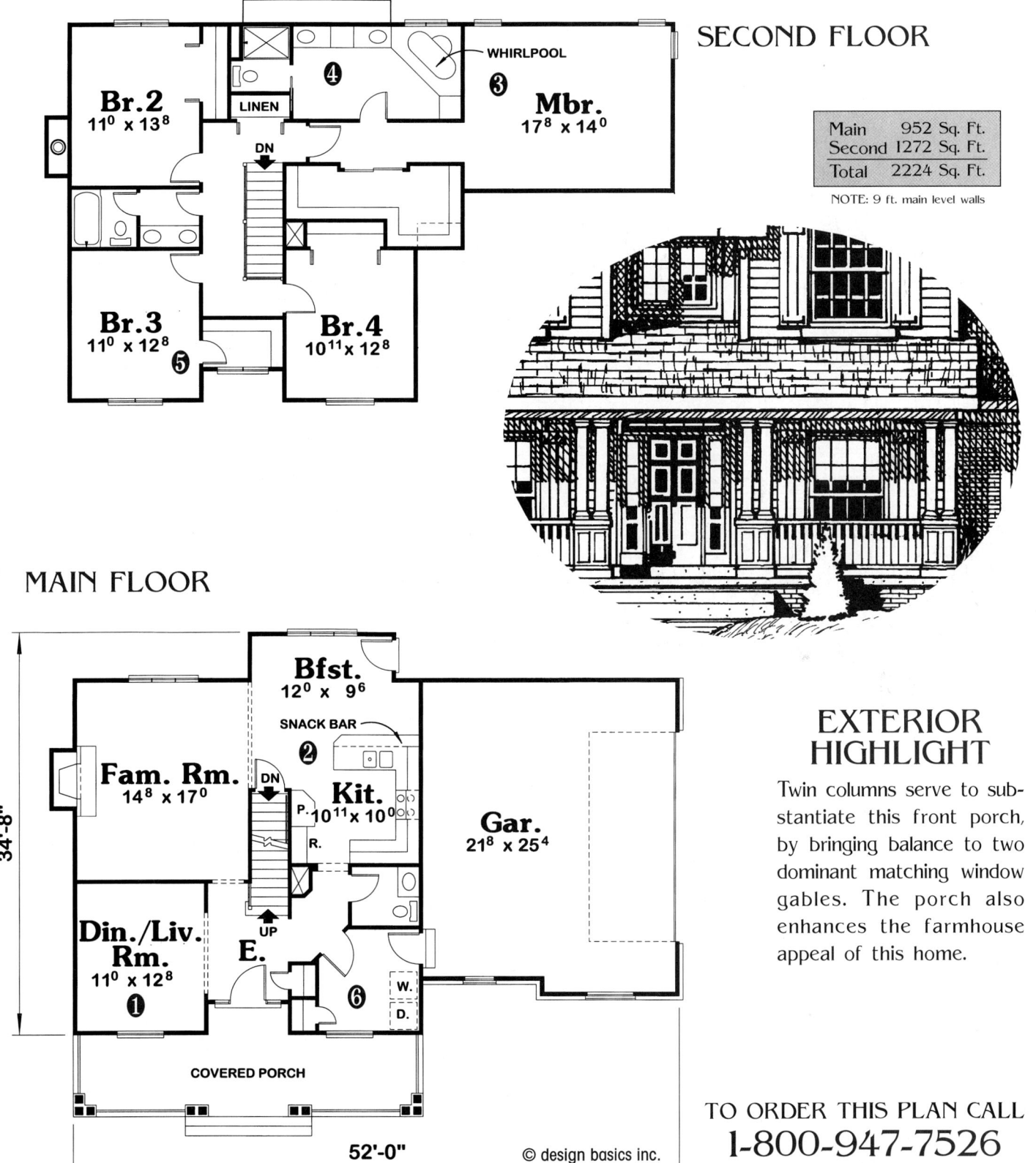

9K-5002 PRICE CODE 22

SECOND FLOOR

Main 952 Sq. Ft.
Second 1272 Sq. Ft.
Total 2224 Sq. Ft.

NOTE: 9 ft. main level walls

MAIN FLOOR

EXTERIOR HIGHLIGHT

Twin columns serve to substantiate this front porch, by bringing balance to two dominant matching window gables. The porch also enhances the farmhouse appeal of this home.

TO ORDER THIS PLAN CALL
1-800-947-7526

design basics inc
HOME PLAN DESIGN SERVICE

Nostalgia

Eldon

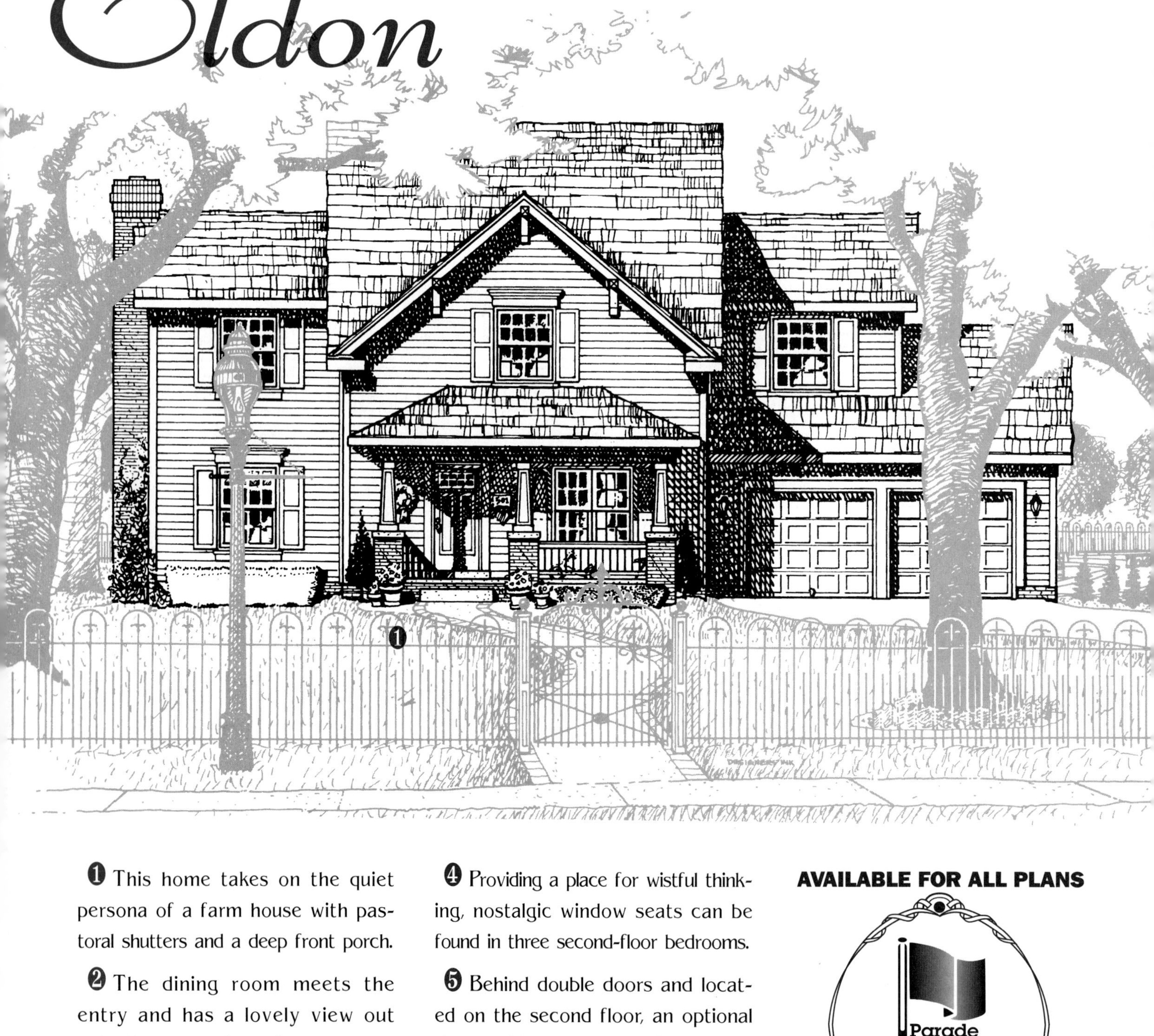

❶ This home takes on the quiet persona of a farm house with pastoral shutters and a deep front porch.

❷ The dining room meets the entry and has a lovely view out onto the covered porch.

❸ A fireplace warms the family room that has close ties to the kitchen and breakfast area.

❹ Providing a place for wistful thinking, nostalgic window seats can be found in three second-floor bedrooms.

❺ Behind double doors and located on the second floor, an optional den could become a quiet retreat for the whole family to enjoy.

❻ Stepping down into bedroom 3 provides the spaciousness of a nine-foot ceiling.

AVAILABLE FOR ALL PLANS

For More Information
on Parade Home Packages see page 158.

9K-4105 PRICE CODE 22

MAIN FLOOR

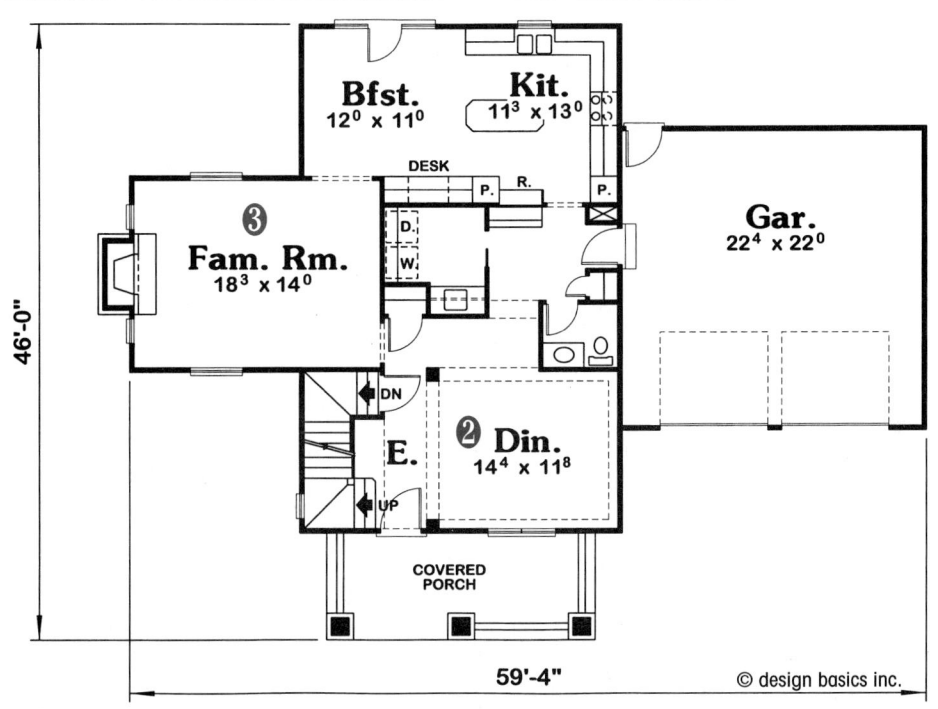

Main   1098 Sq. Ft.
Second 1184 Sq. Ft.
Total 2282 Sq. Ft.

NOTE: 9 ft. main level walls

INTERIOR VIEW

Dining Room - This spacious dining room offers plenty of room for large family gatherings. Whether decorated formally or informally, the open stairway will be a delightful view.

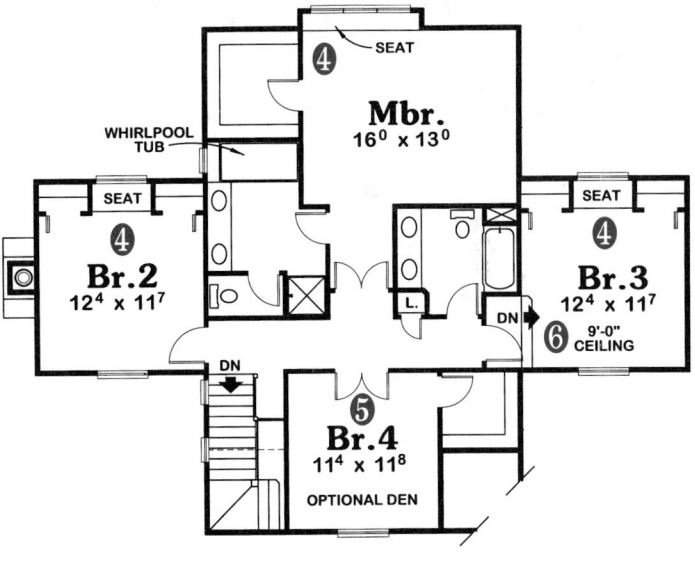

SECOND FLOOR

TO ORDER THIS PLAN CALL
1-800-947-7526

design basics inc.
HOME PLAN DESIGN SERVICE

Nostalgia

Ainsley

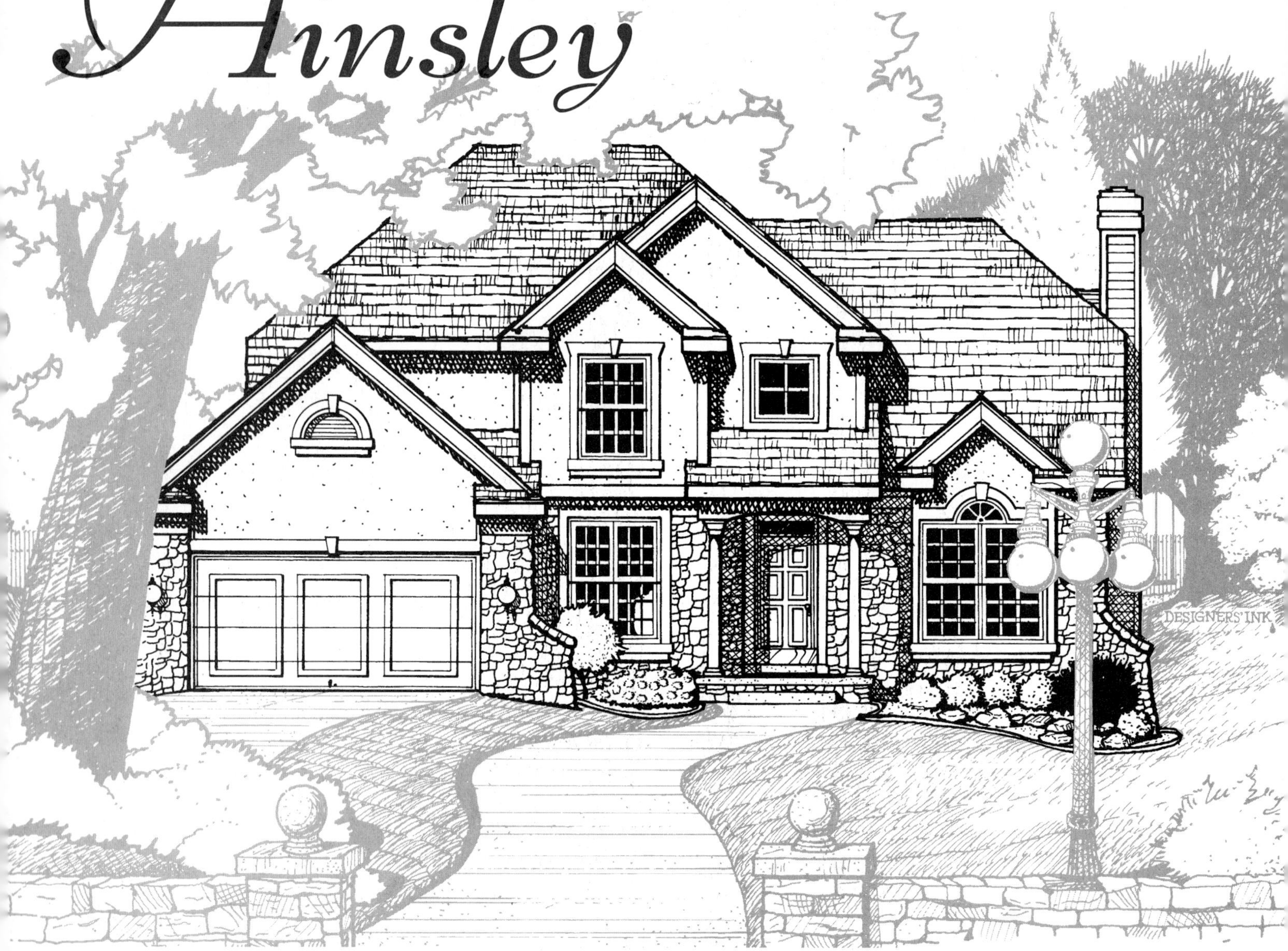

❶ Plant shelves and stylish arches add beauty to the entry.

❷ A spacious kitchen accommodates an island counter and large pantry, and is open to the bayed breakfast area and great room.

❸ The T-shaped stairway facilitates traffic to the second floor.

❹ A built-in dresser leaves room for more furniture in the master bedroom.

❺ Reminiscent of an antique buffet, yet modernized for convenience, a servery near the dining room cuts down on trips to the kitchen.

❻ The oversized laundry room has ample space to set up an ironing board.

AVAILABLE FOR ALL PLANS

For More Information on our Custom Changes see page 157.

9K-4145 PRICE CODE 23

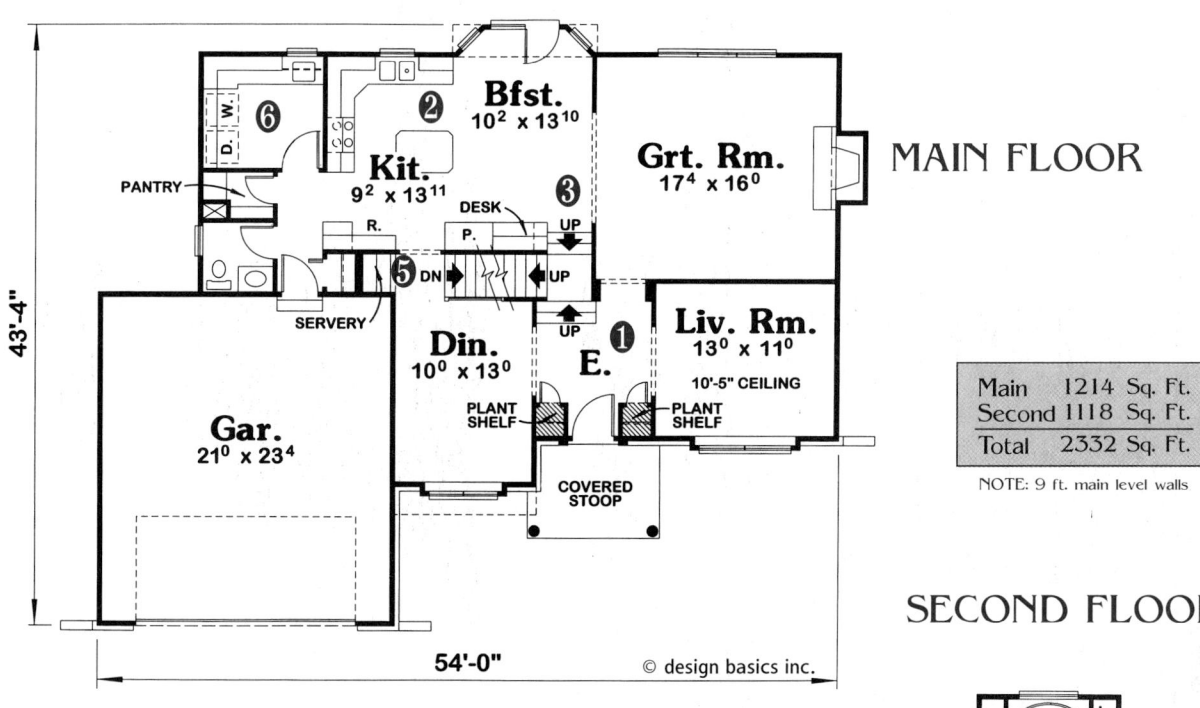

MAIN FLOOR

Main	1214 Sq. Ft.
Second	1118 Sq. Ft.
Total	2332 Sq. Ft.

NOTE: 9 ft. main level walls

SECOND FLOOR

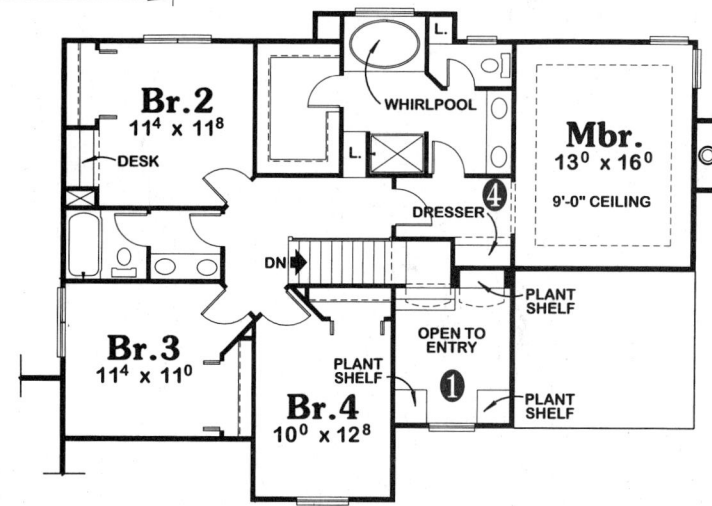

© design basics inc.

EXTERIOR HIGHLIGHT

The use of stone on this home, while adding an old world feel, does not take away from this home's entry. Designing a wider front stoop also calls attention to its welcome.

TO ORDER THIS PLAN CALL
1-800-947-7526

Nostalgia

Gerard

❶ The elevation's understated styling is enhanced by the use of a variety of timeless architectural elements, such as its double-hung windows and shutters.

❷ A wet bar in the family room is convenient when entertaining formally or informally.

❸ The living and dining rooms will comfortably entertain guests and make beautiful places to show off antiques.

❹ Bedroom 2 with its own private bath, makes the perfect guest bedroom or in-law suite.

❺ Unfinished storage offers the potential for expansion.

❻ At 50 feet in width, the Gerard helps solve a narrow lot situation.

ALL PLANS COPYRIGHTED

For More Information on our Copyrights see page 154.

9K -4135 PRICE CODE 23

MAIN FLOOR

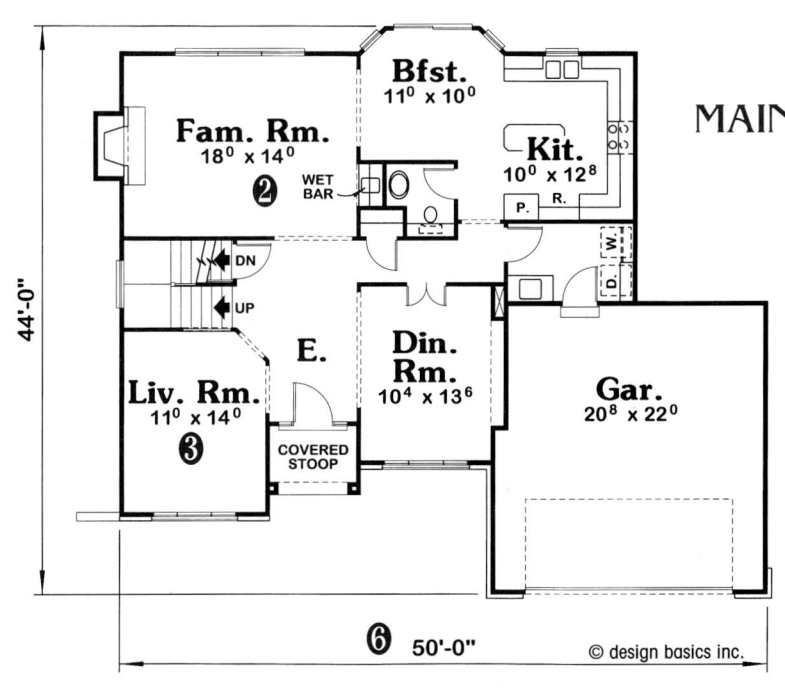

SECOND FLOOR

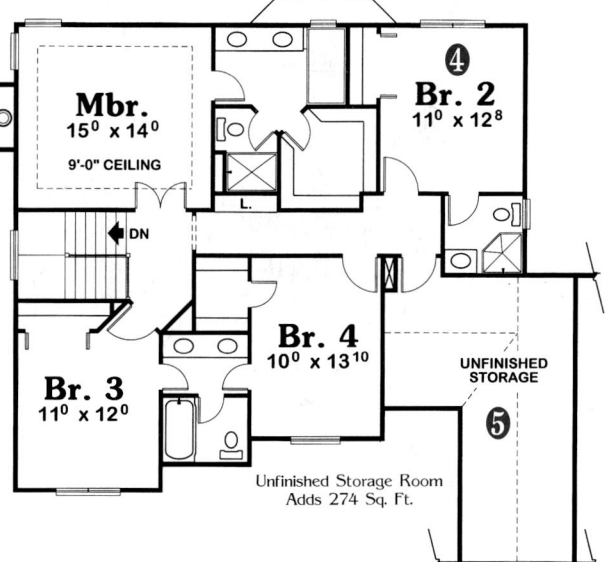

Unfinished Storage Room Adds 274 Sq. Ft.

Main 1199 Sq. Ft.
Second 1150 Sq. Ft.
Total 2349 Sq. Ft.

NOTE: 9 ft. main level walls

EXTERIOR HIGHLIGHT

Keystones showcased on decorative trim board and soldier coursing are repeated throughout the windows on this home. This detailing, mixed with a stucco and brick combination, makes a perfect design presentation.

TO ORDER THIS PLAN CALL
1-800-947-7526

design basics inc.
HOME PLAN DESIGN SERVICE

Nostalgia
131

Patagonia

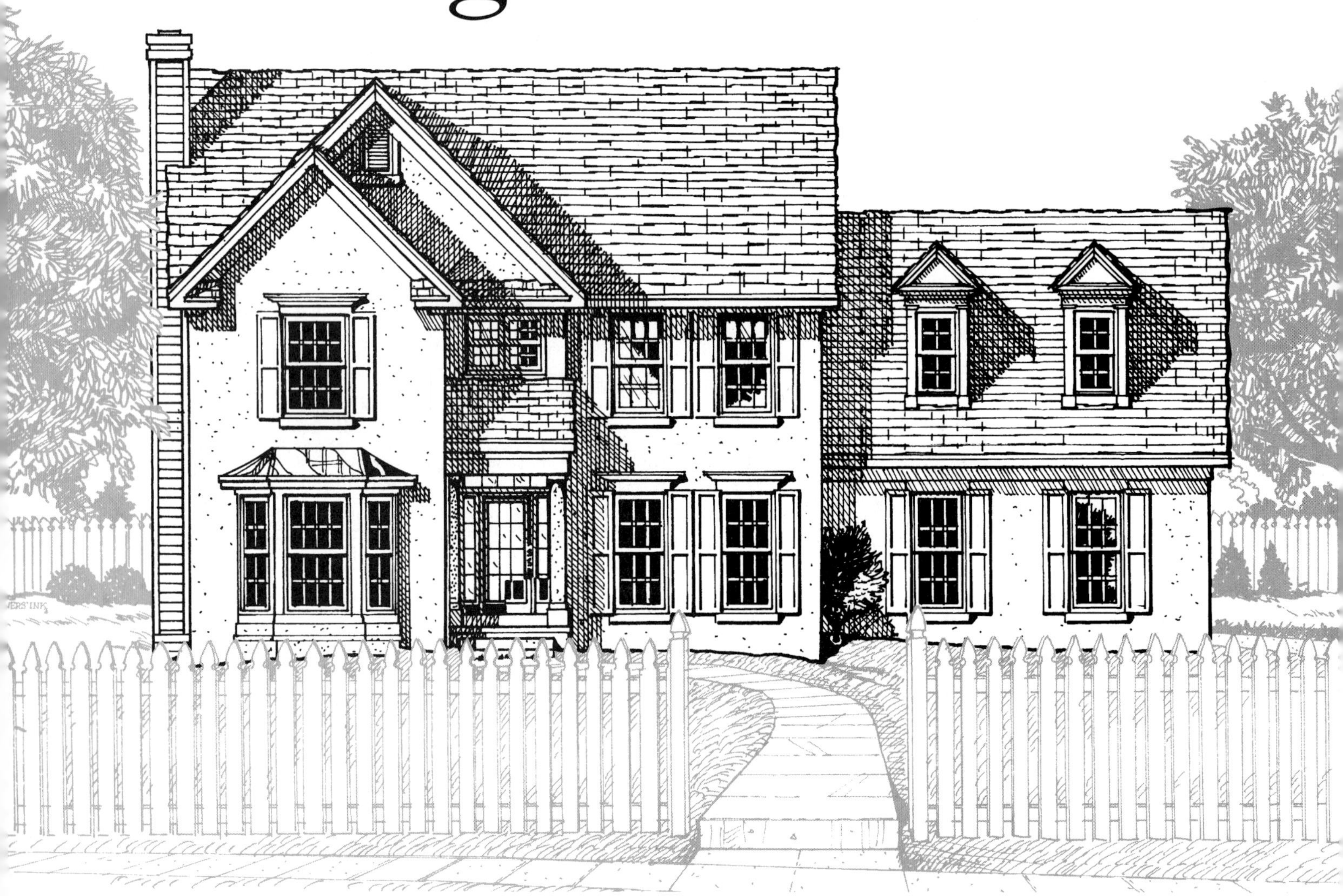

❶ French doors can be added to the bayed study to expand the family room.

❷ A built-in serving cabinet is strategically placed between the dining room and kitchen.

❸ A roll-a-way butcher block island is functional for the kitchen, but can easily be stored until needed.

❹ A rear covered porch is accessible from the breakfast area and is a great place to relax after a meal.

❺ The laundry room is conveniently located near the second-floor bedrooms.

❻ Unfinished storage above the garage is beneficial for keeping season items.

AVAILABLE FOR ALL PLANS

For More Information on Parade Home Packages see page 158.

9K-5086 PRICE CODE 24

SECOND FLOOR

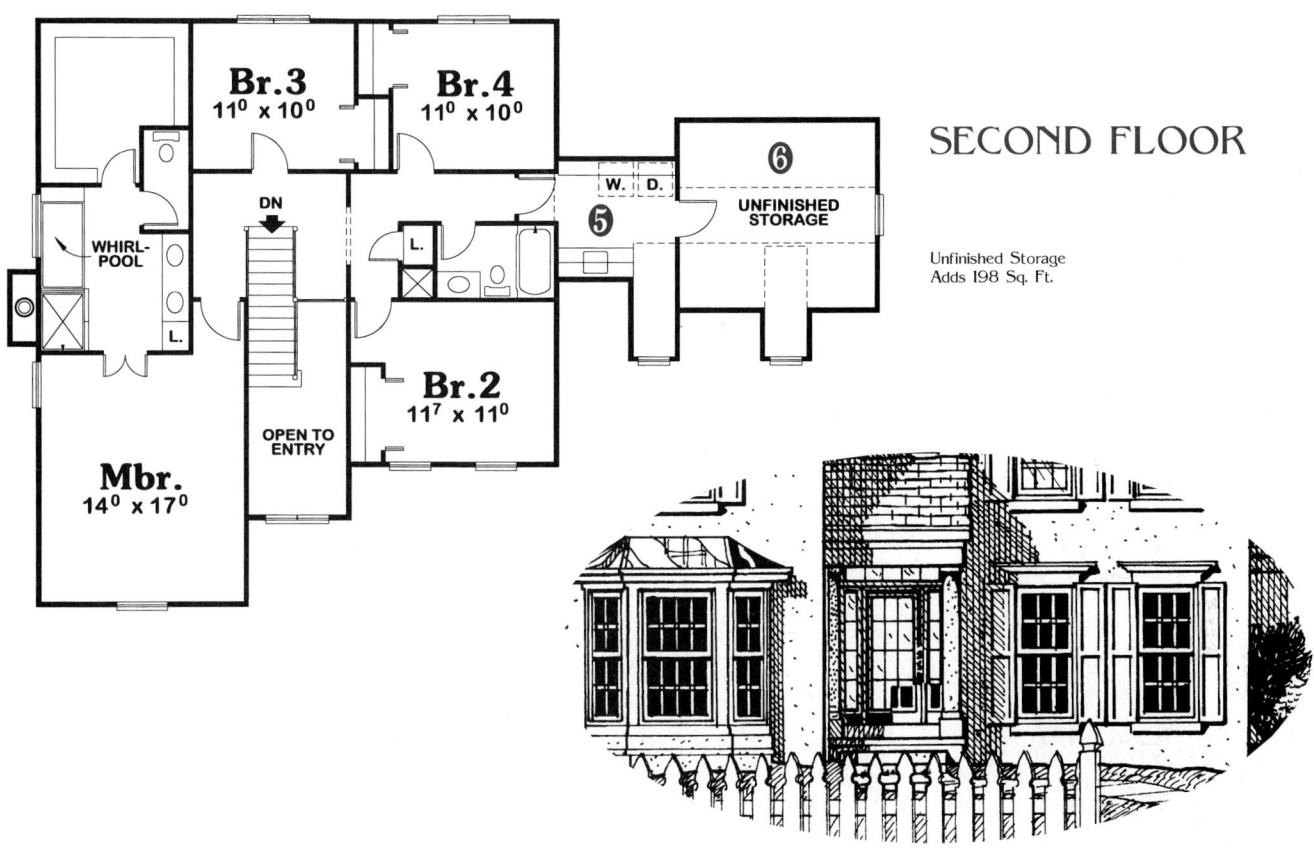

Unfinished Storage Adds 198 Sq. Ft.

MAIN FLOOR

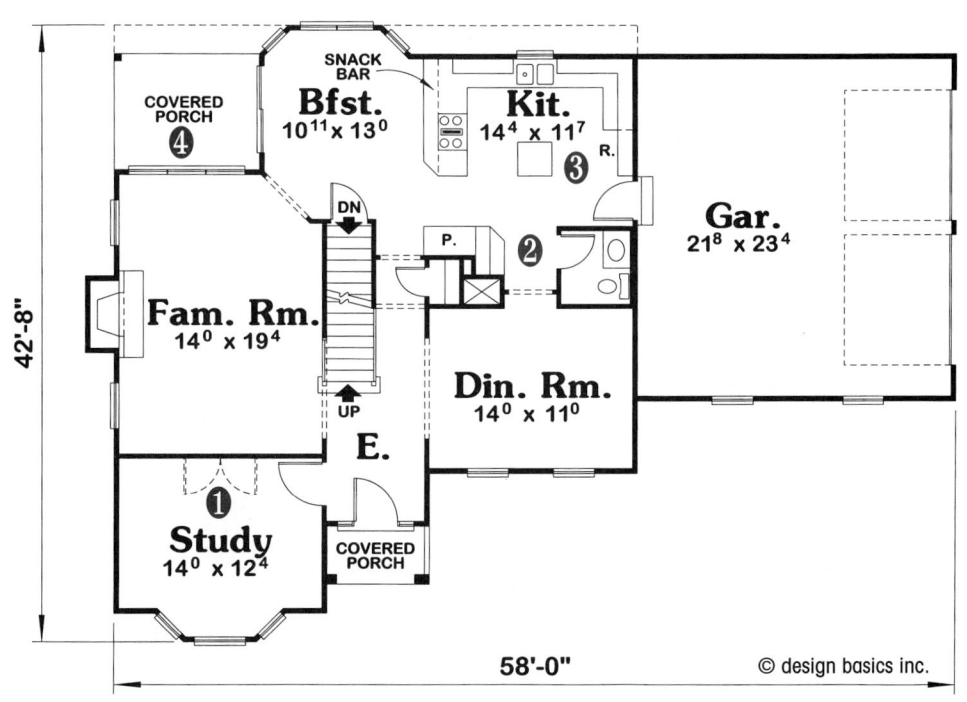

EXTERIOR HIGHLIGHT

Colonial pediments are nicely offset by the French influence of this design. A copper-clad eave over a bay window is one of the many charming focal points on this home's entry.

Main	1162	Sq. Ft.
Second	1255	Sq. Ft.
Total	2417	Sq. Ft.

NOTE: 9 ft. main level walls

TO ORDER THIS PLAN CALL
1-800-947-7526

Nostalgia

Norwood

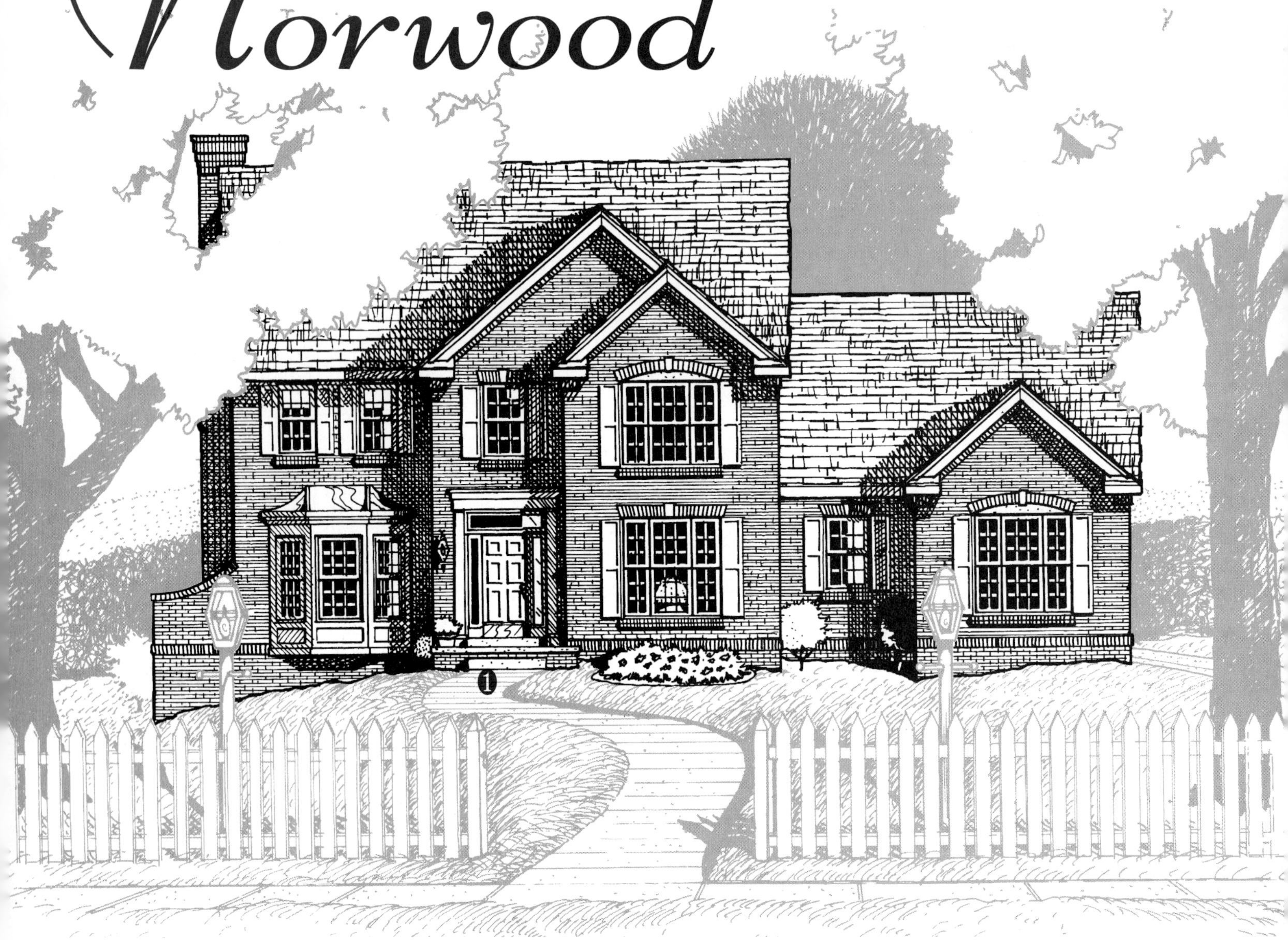

❶ A cantilevered bayed window, wing wall and all-brick facade bring to life the hospitality of this home.

❷ A butler's pantry adjoins the kitchen and dining room helping assist serving formal meals.

❸ The spacious laundry room doubles as a mud room with a coat closet and soaking sink.

❹ A second-floor cedar closet benefits storing clothing for the season.

❺ An accommodating master suite provides a built-in entertainment center along with a walk-in closet featuring his and her sections.

❻ Twin dormers add a view to the back in an exceptionally large bonus room.

AVAILABLE FOR ALL PLANS

For More Information on Reverse Plans see page 158.

9K-5049   PRICE CODE 24

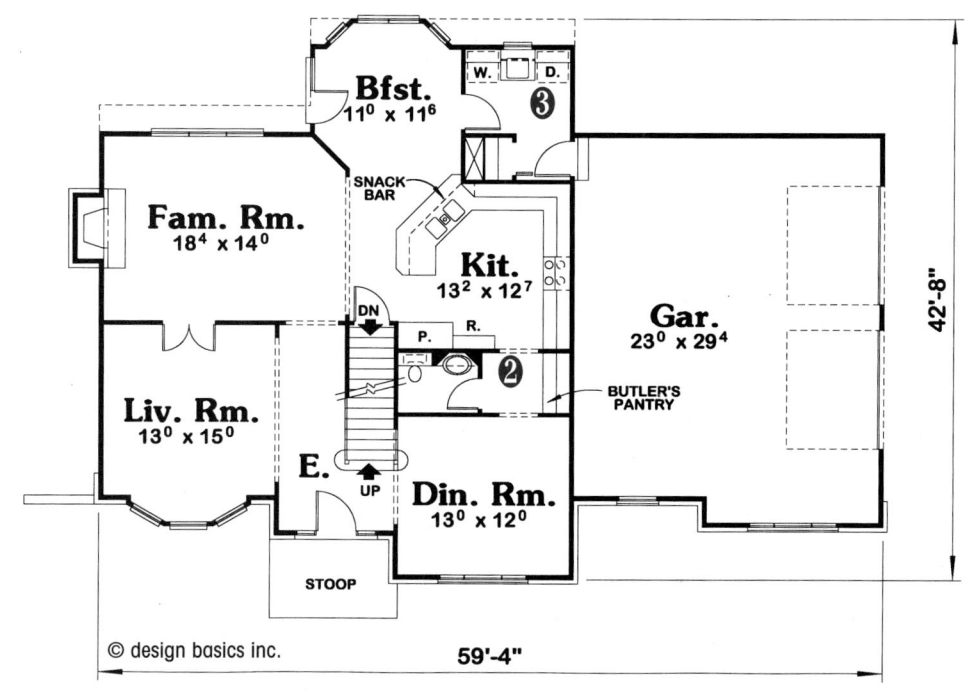

MAIN FLOOR

Main	1277 Sq. Ft.
Second	1198 Sq. Ft.
Total	2475 Sq. Ft.

NOTE: 9 ft. main level walls

DECORATOR DESIGN TIPS

MASTER BEDROOM - A built-in entertainment unit in the master suite calls for the bed to be placed for easy viewing. If there is room, including a piece of upholstry, such as a chair, is always a plus since it comes in handy for putting shoes on, etc. when getting ready.

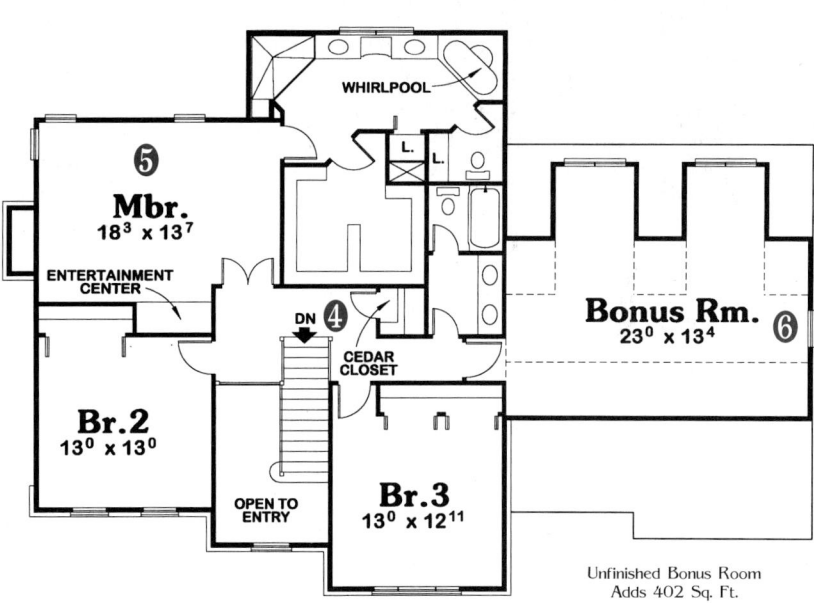

SECOND FLOOR

Unfinished Bonus Room Adds 402 Sq. Ft.

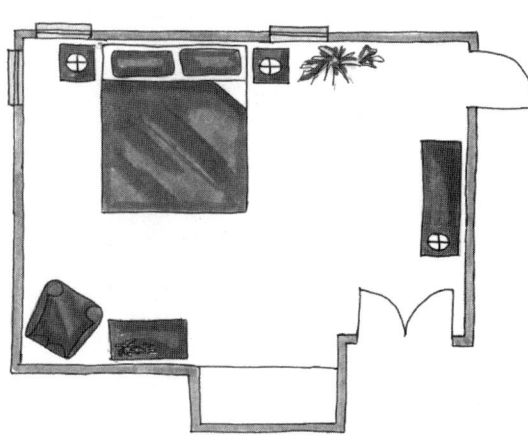

TO ORDER THIS PLAN CALL
1-800-947-7526

design basics inc.
HOME PLAN DESIGN SERVICE

Nostalgia
135

Castine

❶ Three narrow dormers solidify this home's romantic appeal.

❷ A set of French doors encloses the living room located just inside the entry.

❸ Offering a great place to kick back, the large family room features a volume ceiling.

❹ Twin closets frame a window seat in the den which also works as a bedroom with pocket-door access to the main bath.

❺ A walk-in pantry serves the kitchen and breakfast area.

❻ The spacious master bath has plenty of room to function as a dressing area and is well-lit by a dormer that could accommodate a dresser or towel rack.

AVAILABLE FOR ALL PLANS

For More Information on our Roof Construction Package see page 158.

9K -5132 PRICE CODE 25

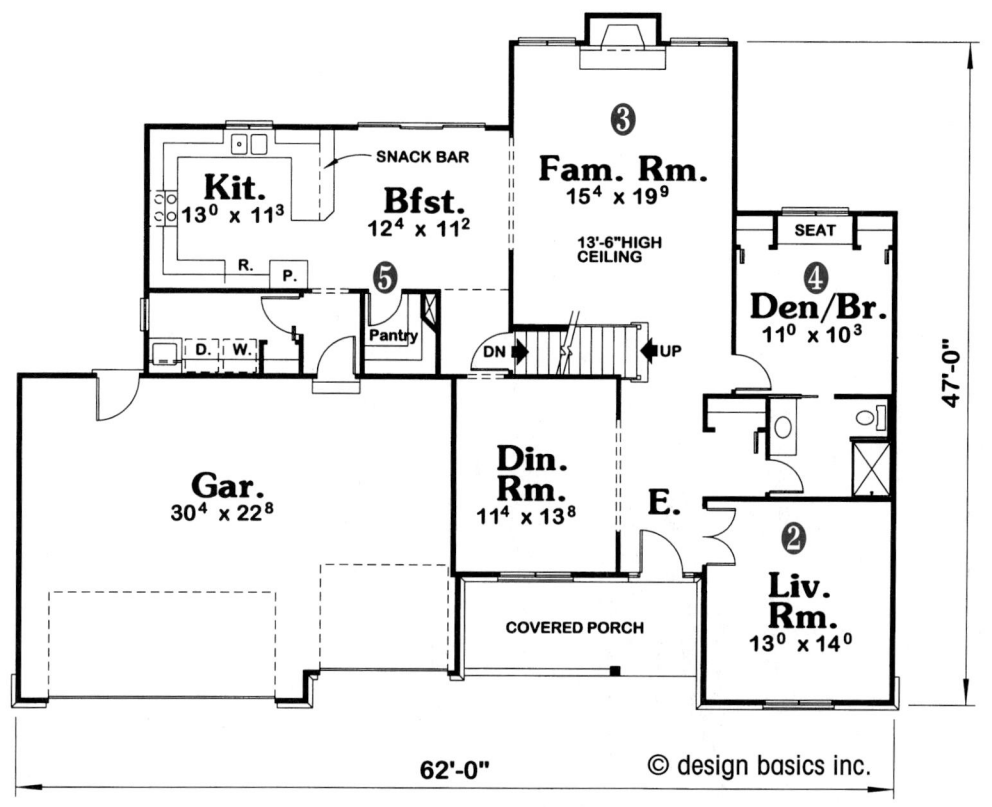

MAIN FLOOR

Main	1544 Sq. Ft.
Second	962 Sq. Ft.
Total	2506 Sq. Ft.

NOTE: 9 ft. main level walls

DECORATOR DESIGN TIPS

MASTER BEDROOM - This unique bedroom showcases two narrow dormers which provide exciting features to decorate. Plants logically complement one of the dormers. A small chair and reading lamp tucked in the other will provide a quiet place to sip a morning cup of coffee.

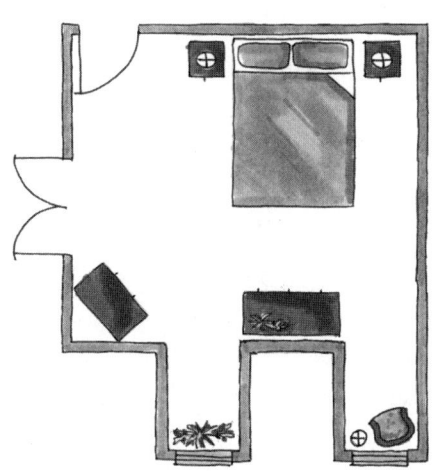

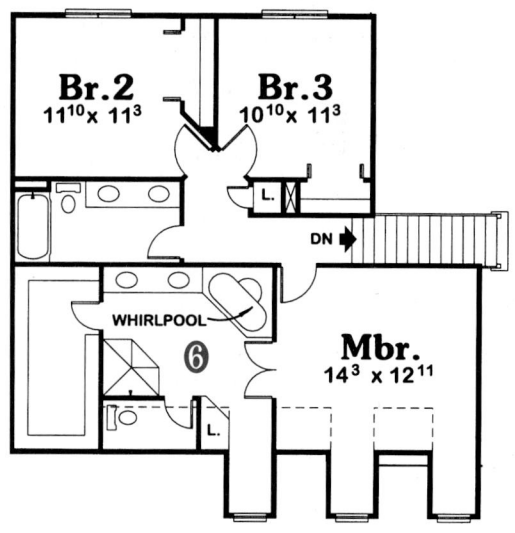

SECOND FLOOR

TO ORDER THIS PLAN CALL
1-800-947-7526

Nostalgia
137

Emery

❶ With shake siding and gingerbread details, this design has all the flair and ease of a modern Victorian home.

❷ An open parlor and bayed dining room have the ability to showcase the home's finest belongings.

❸ The secluded family room features a casual atmosphere with its fireplace and connection to the kitchen and breakfast area.

❹ A spacious study, open on the second floor, is ideal as the family office.

❺ A window seat, his and her vanities, an enormous walk-in closet and whirlpool imbue the master suite.

❻ The two secondary bedrooms share a full bath, with a compartmental vanity area.

AVAILABLE FOR ALL PLANS

Parade Home Package

For More Information on Parade Home Packages see page 158.

9K -4125 PRICE CODE 25

MAIN FLOOR

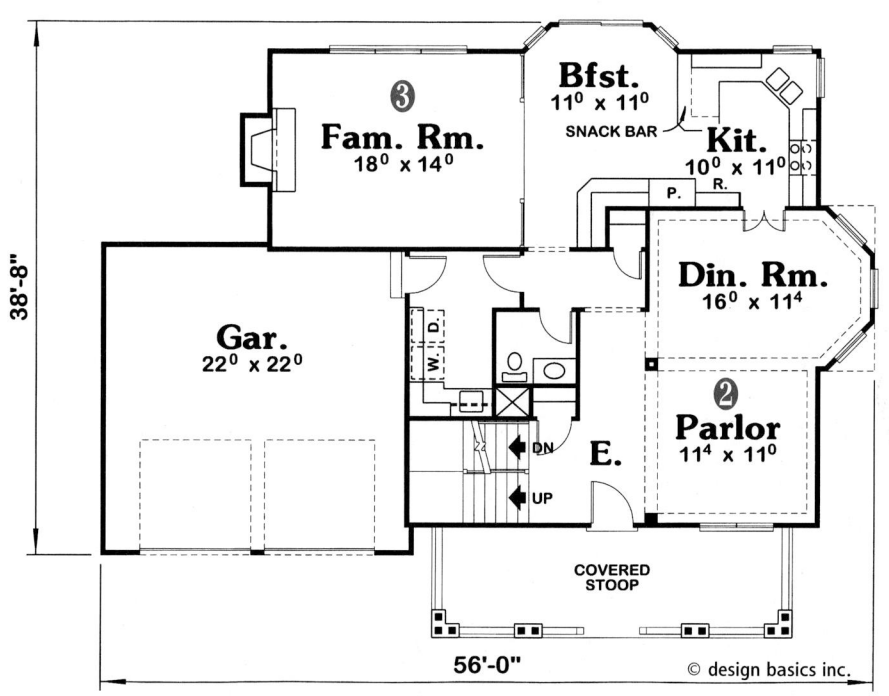

Main	1240 Sq. Ft.
Second	1283 Sq. Ft.
Total	2523 Sq. Ft.

NOTE: 9 ft. main level walls

DECORATOR DESIGN TIPS

STUDY - The study could easily become a favorite place in this house. A wall of bookcases fills one end of the room accompanied by two comfy chairs highlighted with reading lamps. A small table was included in this study, which could be used for studying, playing cards, etc. It is important not to overfill this space since it is located at the top of the staircase and will be a major traffic hub.

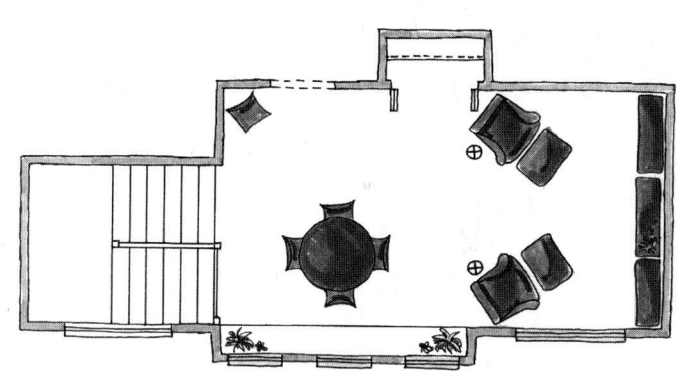

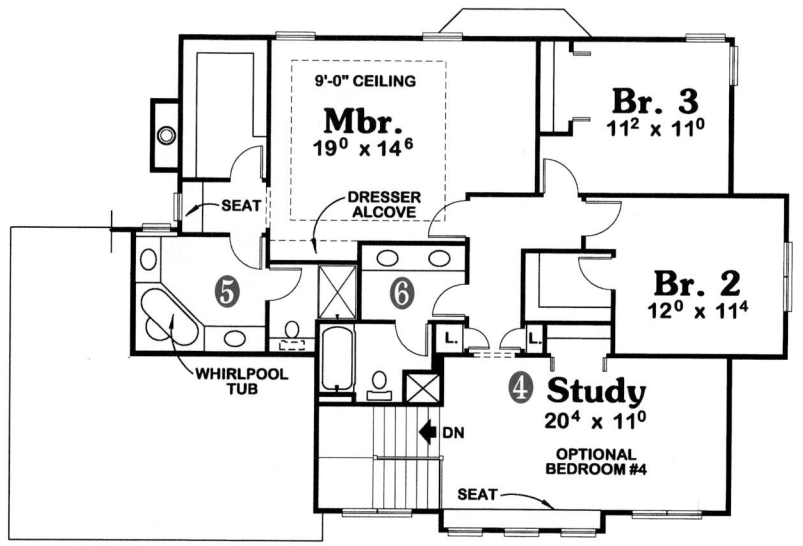

SECOND FLOOR

TO ORDER THIS PLAN CALL
1-800-947-7526

design basics inc
HOME PLAN DESIGN SERVICE

Nostalgia

Laveen

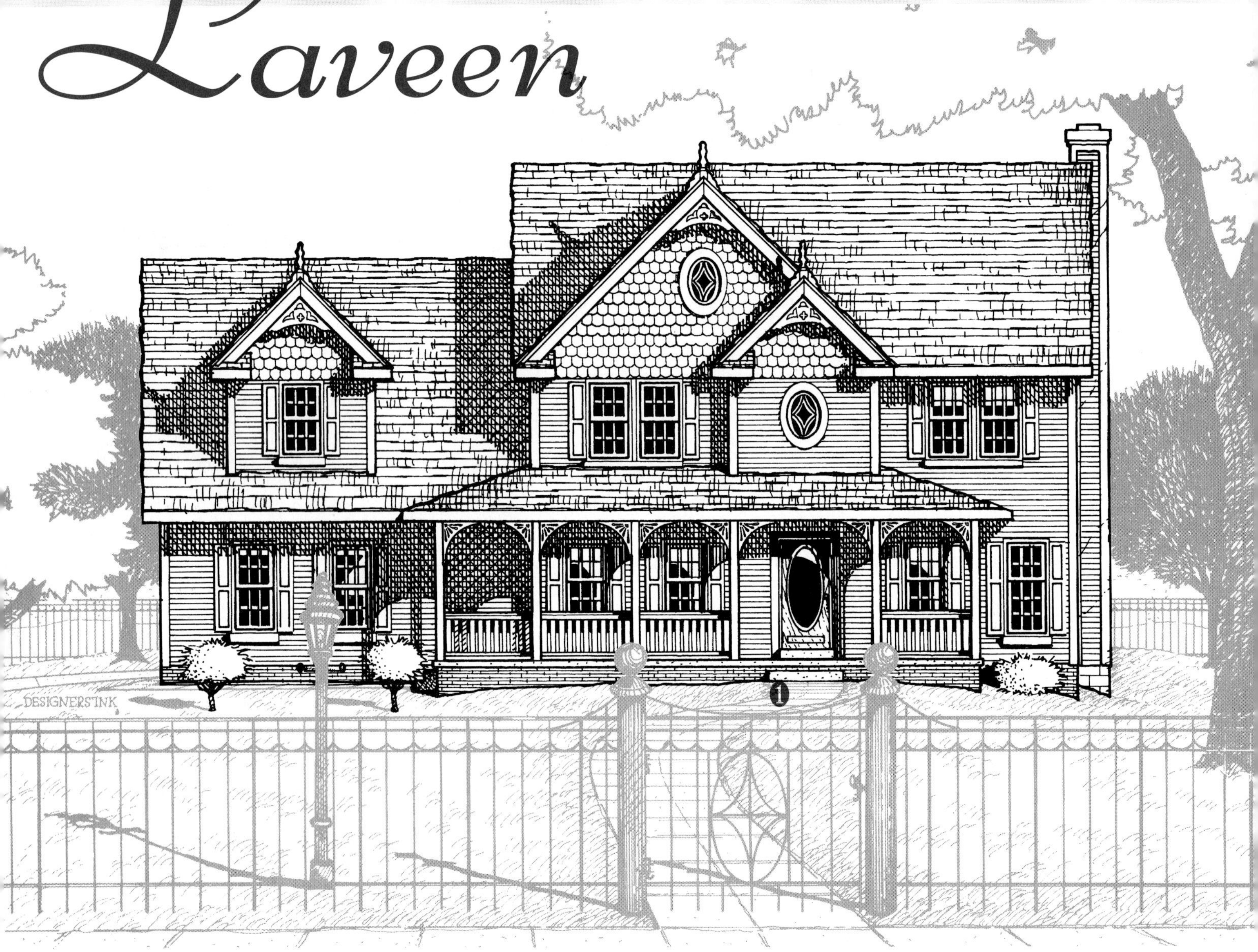

❶ This Victorian-inspired design is enhanced with finials and scalloped shingles.

❷ A deep alcove in the dining room will accommodate a cherished antique hutch.

❸ French doors enclose the living room or expand it into the family room.

❹ The island kitchen is accommodated with a large pantry and is brightened by the breakfast area.

❺ All second-floor bedrooms offer large walk-in closets.

❻ The second-floor corridor overlooks the two-story entry with a large plant shelf.

AVAILABLE FOR ALL PLANS

For More Information on our Custom Changes see page 157.

9K -5209 PRICE CODE 25

EXTERIOR HIGHLIGHT

Nothing reveals more about a Victorian home than its front porch. Spider web trim and an antique oval front door bring the early part of the 20th Century to life. Designed with farmhouse appeal, the wrapping front porch beckons a swing.

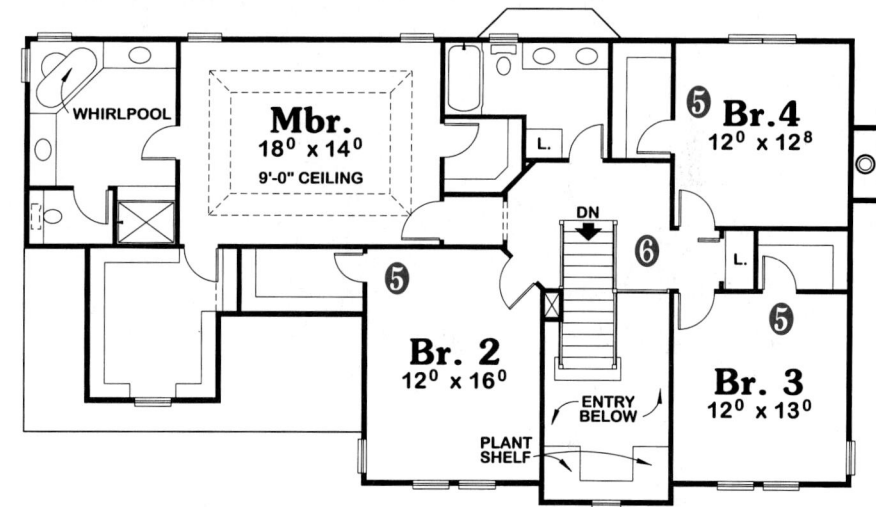

SECOND FLOOR

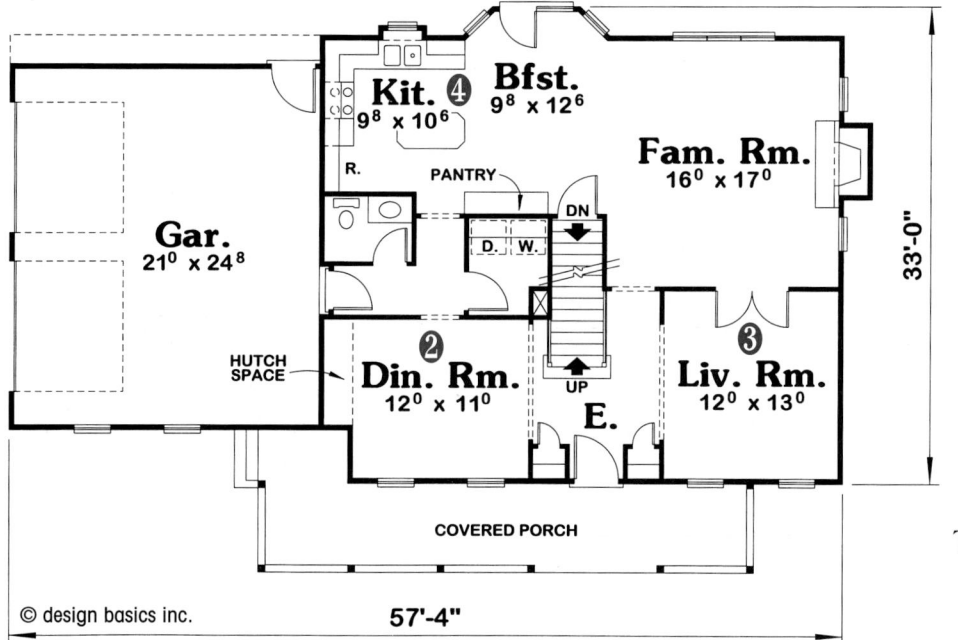

Main	1122 Sq. Ft.
Second	1409 Sq. Ft.
Total	2531 Sq. Ft.

NOTE: 9 ft. main level walls

MAIN FLOOR

TO ORDER THIS PLAN CALL
1-800-947-7526

design basics inc.
HOME PLAN DESIGN SERVICE

Nostalgia

Karlynda

❶ Designed to appeal to the country-at-heart, this home welcomes guests with its deep front porch and nostalgic shutters.

❷ A large area for a hutch in the dining room will accomodate an antique.

❸ The kitchen and breakfast area feature a walk-in pantry, island counter and bayed windows.

❹ A large plant shelf, corner whirlpool tub and large walk-in closet with iron-a-way comprise a luxurious master suite.

❺ A clothes chute is convenient to the secondary bedrooms within the main second-floor bath.

❻ Extra storage in the garage allows room for a work bench or sports equipment.

ALL PLANS COPYRIGHTED

For More Information on our Copyrights see page 154.

Nostalgia

9K -4156 PRICE CODE 25

MAIN FLOOR

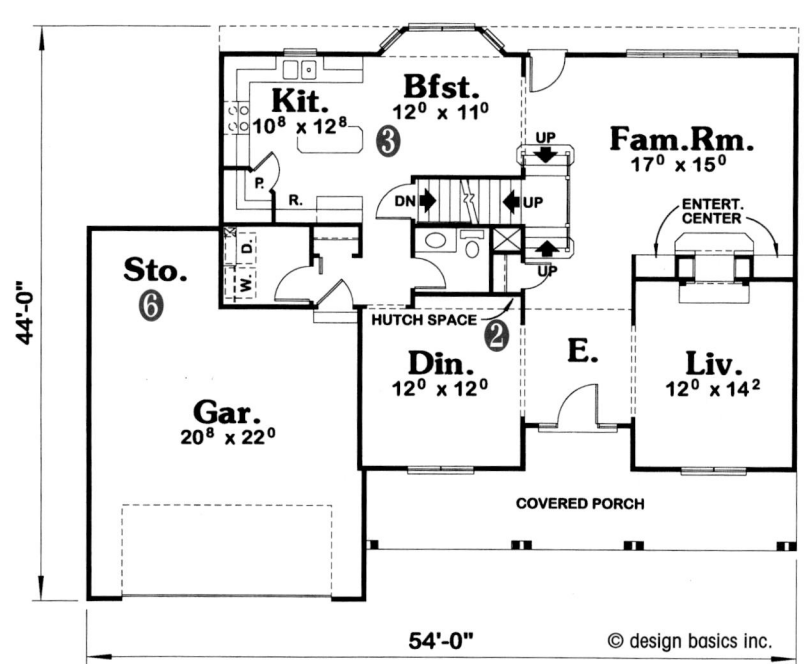

Main 1266 Sq. Ft.
Second 1292 Sq. Ft.
Total 2558 Sq. Ft.

NOTE: 8 ft. main level walls

SECOND FLOOR

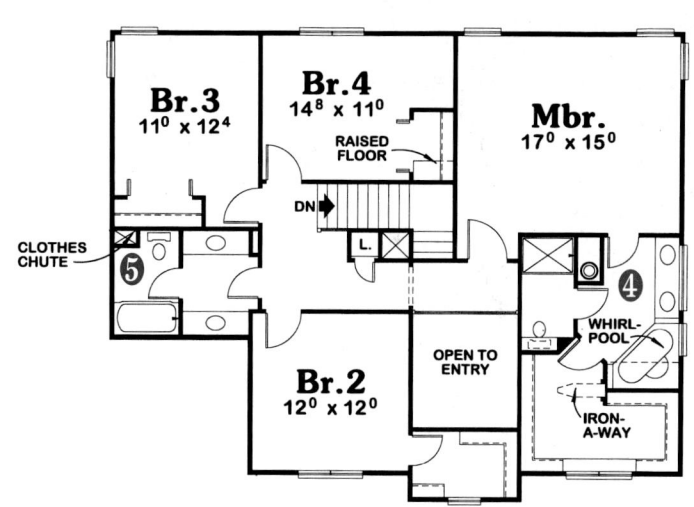

INTERIOR VIEW

FAMILY ROOM - An open T-shaped stairway creates a "cabin" feel in the family room, while leading traffic to the second-floor bedrooms. Built-in shelves and a see-through fireplace accentuate its lodge-like appeal.

TO ORDER THIS PLAN CALL
1-800-947-7526

Nostalgia

Suffolk

❶ Romantic quoins and subtle window detailing, will appeal to the most particular of buyers.

❷ Warming the great room is a raised-hearth fireplace and a wall of windows.

❸ The kitchen and bayed breakfast area are situated just off the great room allowing for casual entertaining.

❹ An ideal laundry facility is near the kitchen, with a soaking sink, hanging rod and folding counters.

❺ The master suite enjoys a vaulted ceiling and a luxurious bath complete with an elevated whirlpool tub, his and her vanity and spacious walk-in closet.

❻ A cedar closet offers a great place to store seasonal clothing.

AVAILABLE FOR ALL PLANS

For More Information on Reverse Plans see page 158.

Nostalgia

9K-5037 PRICE CODE 25

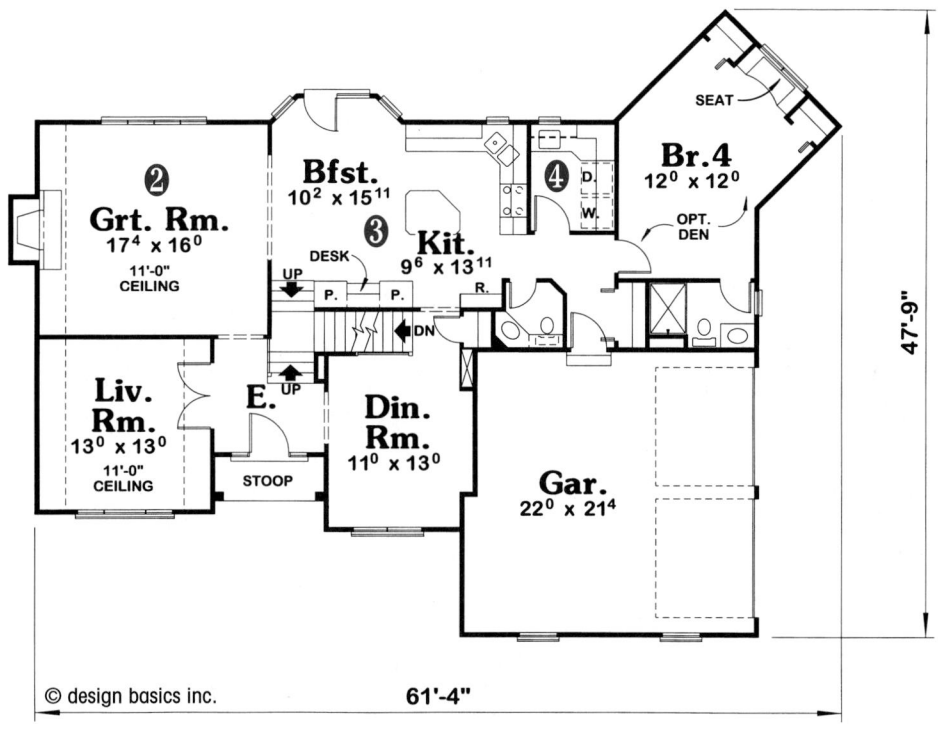

MAIN FLOOR

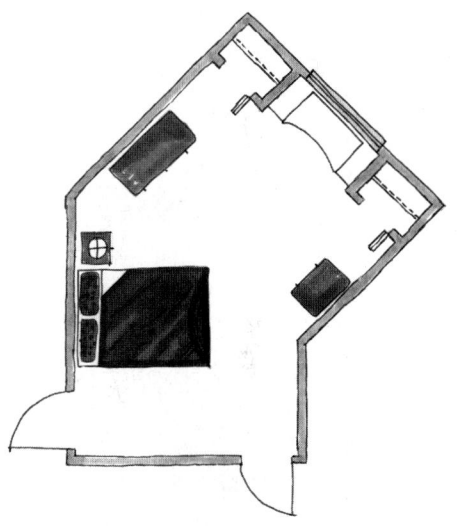

Main	1475 Sq. Ft.
Second	1085 Sq. Ft.
Total	2560 Sq. Ft.

NOTE: 9 ft. main level walls

DECORATOR DESIGN TIPS

BEDROOM 4 - An angled bedroom such as this requires special planning. The window wall consists of closets flanking a built-in seat which gives that end of the room a lot of visual weight. The bed, which also adds visual weight to the room, works best located away from the wall to create a pleasant balance.

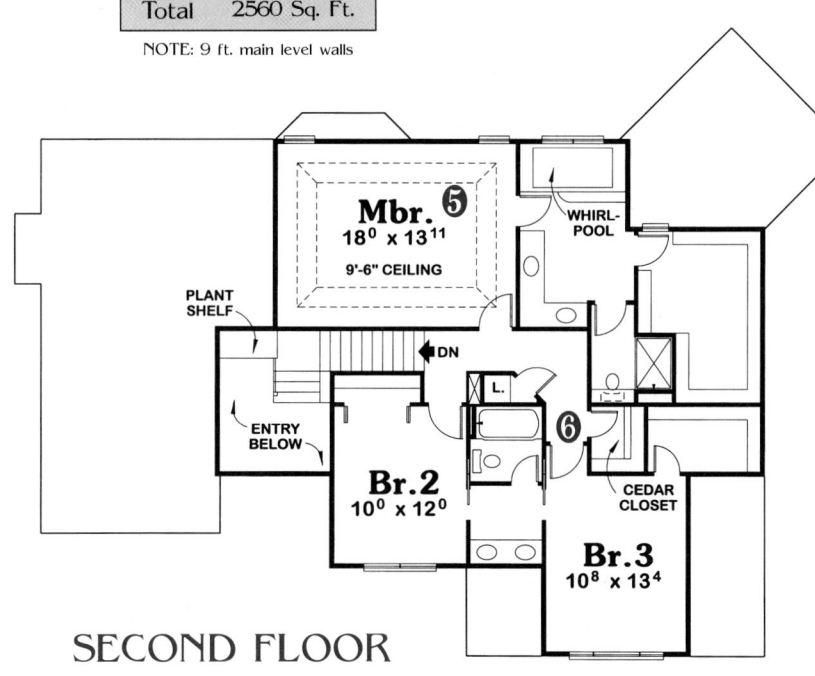

SECOND FLOOR

TO ORDER THIS PLAN CALL
1-800-947-7526

Calabretta

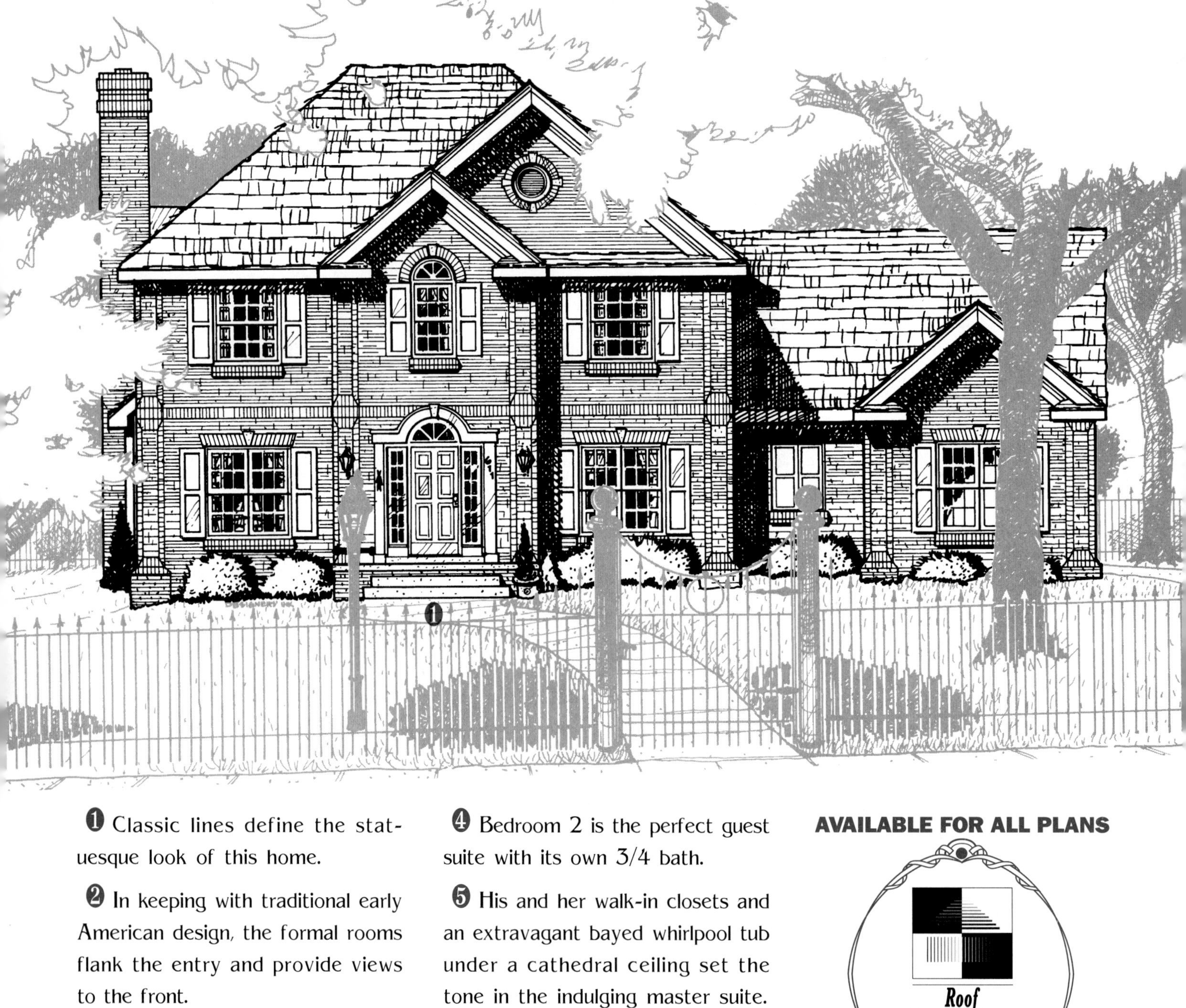

❶ Classic lines define the statuesque look of this home.

❷ In keeping with traditional early American design, the formal rooms flank the entry and provide views to the front.

❸ An angled snack bar in the kitchen serves the breakfast area that is bathed in natural light.

❹ Bedroom 2 is the perfect guest suite with its own 3/4 bath.

❺ His and her walk-in closets and an extravagant bayed whirlpool tub under a cathedral ceiling set the tone in the indulging master suite.

❻ A large bonus room has the potential to meet the preferences of many buyers.

AVAILABLE FOR ALL PLANS

For More Information on our Roof Construction Package see page 158.

9K-4106 PRICE CODE 26

INTERIOR VIEW

LIVING ROOM - The formal living room provides a view into an area showcasing a quaint window seat with optional wet bar. Whether solely entertaining in the living room or joined with the family room, this area offers perfect service to guests.

MAIN FLOOR

- Bfst. 11⁰ x 11⁰
- Fam. Rm. 18⁰ x 15⁰
- Kit. 11⁸ x 12⁰
- Gar. 21⁸ x 29⁴
- Liv. 14⁰ x 11⁰
- Din. 14⁰ x 11⁰
- 44'-4"
- 58'-0"

© design basics inc.

Main	1333 Sq. Ft.
Second	1280 Sq. Ft.
Total	2613 Sq. Ft.

NOTE: 9 ft. main level walls

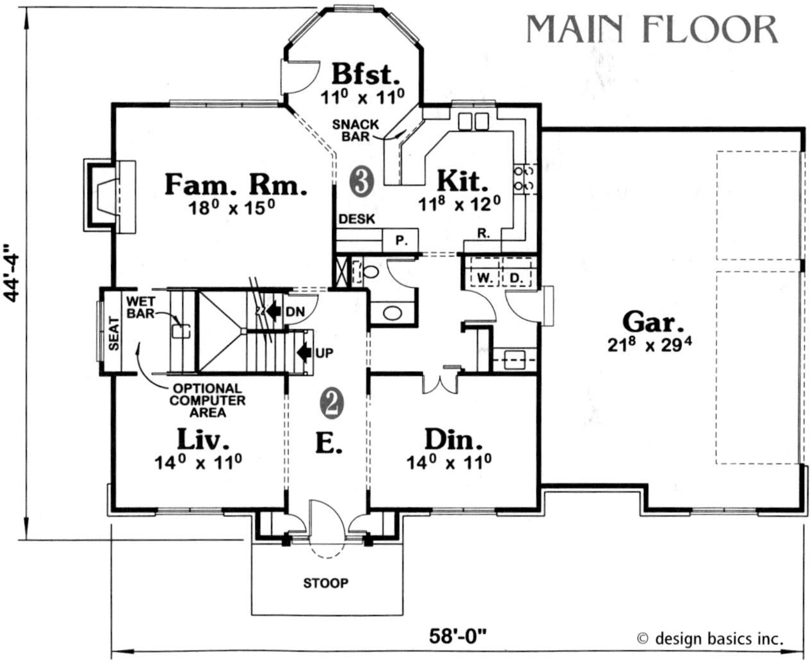

SECOND FLOOR

- Mbr. 15⁰ x 15⁰ (9'-0" CEILING)
- Br.2 12⁰ x 12⁰
- Br.3 13⁰ x 11⁰
- Br.4 13⁰ x 11⁰
- Unfinished Bonus 21⁸ x 14⁰
- WHIRLPOOL TUB / CATHEDRAL CEILING

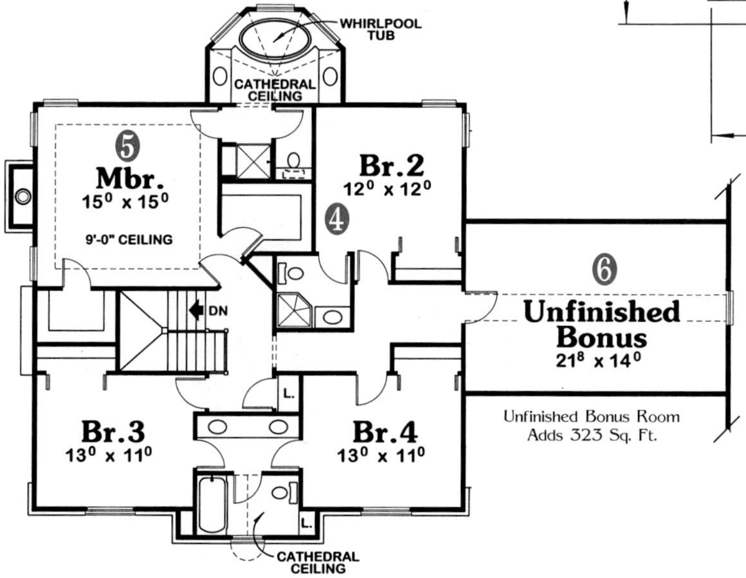

Unfinished Bonus Room Adds 323 Sq. Ft.

TO ORDER THIS PLAN CALL
1-800-947-7526

design basics inc.
HOME PLAN DESIGN SERVICE

Nostalgia
147

Sutter

❶ A subdued exterior hints at this home's colonial roots.

❷ The two-story entry is enhanced with an open, second-floor balcony.

❸ A barrel-vault ceiling leads to the great room which offers a comforting see-through fireplace.

❹ The kitchen, with an island counter and double oven, is conveniently near the dining room and bayed breakfast area.

❺ Pampering the master suite is a boxed ceiling, oval whirlpool tub and French doors.

❻ Bedroom 4 can be an optional sitting room with access from the master suite.

AVAILABLE FOR ALL PLANS

For More Information on our Custom Changes see page 157.

Nostalgia
148

9K -4147 PRICE CODE 26

INTERIOR VIEW

LIBRARY - A spider-beamed ceiling and bright windows characterize this library. Built-in bookshelves provide a wonderful place for favorite novels, reference books and family encyclopedias.

SECOND FLOOR

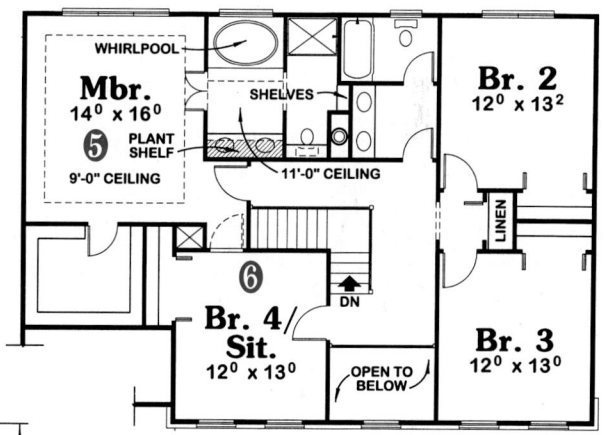

MAIN FLOOR

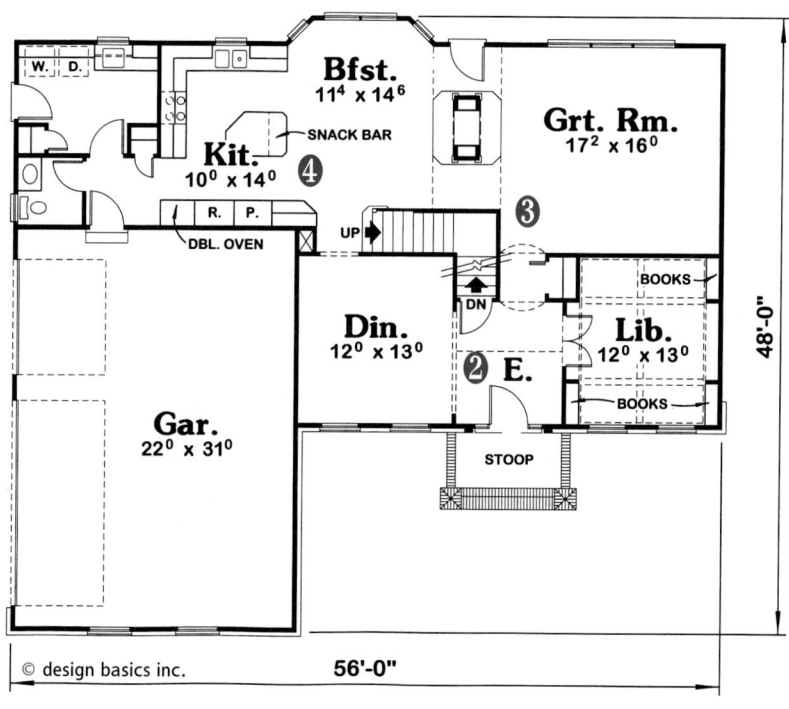

Main	1357 Sq. Ft.
Second	1285 Sq. Ft.
Total	2642 Sq. Ft.

NOTE: 9 ft. main level walls

TO ORDER THIS PLAN CALL
1-800-947-7526

Attleboro

❶ This home, while making a smart impression from the street, features a roofline that can easily be trussed.

❷ An optional guest bedroom on the main floor offers flexibility as family needs change.

❸ A walk-in pantry in the island kitchen accommodates the needs of the whole family.

❹ 9-foot main level walls gives a sense of spaciousness to main level rooms.

❺ Sturdy columns frame the dining room, sure to make it memorable on special occasions.

❻ The whole family will be accommodated with three bedrooms and a master suite on the second level.

ALL PLANS COPYRIGHTED

For More Information on our Copyrights see page 154.

9K-5083 PRICE CODE 27

MAIN FLOOR

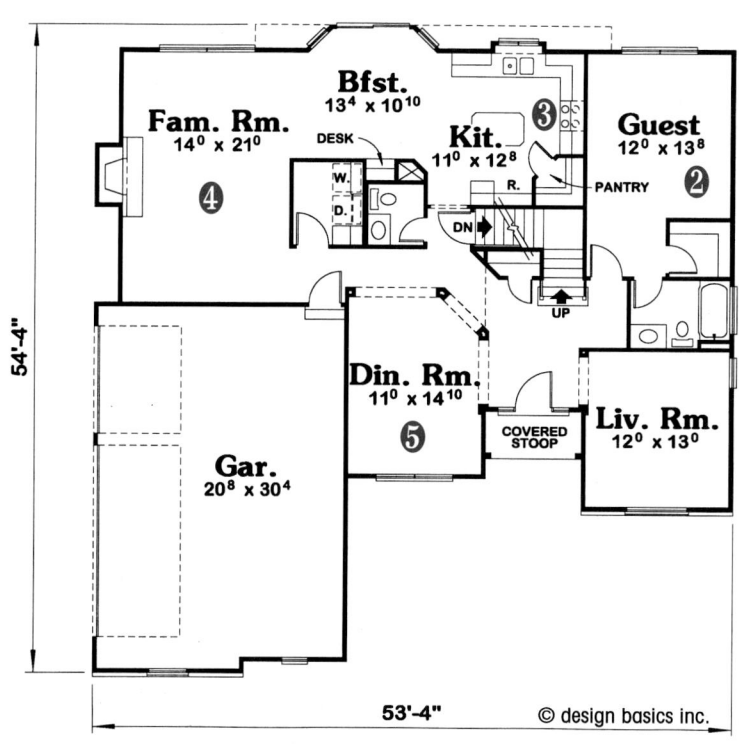

Main	1582 Sq. Ft.
Second	1170 Sq. Ft.
Total	2752 Sq. Ft.

NOTE: 9 ft. main level walls

SECOND FLOOR

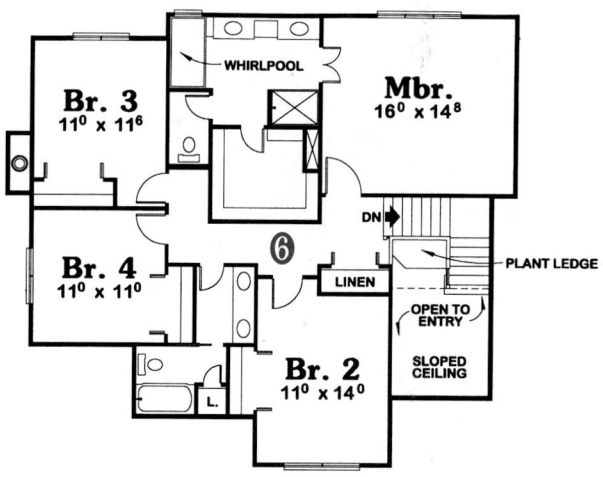

EXTERIOR HIGHLIGHT

Brick and stucco are effortlessy blended together on this veneer. Helping to make it all come together are repeating design themes such as the arches showcased on the covered stoop and windows.

TO ORDER THIS PLAN CALL
1-800-947-7526

design basics inc.
HOME PLAN DESIGN SERVICE

Nostalgia

Neville

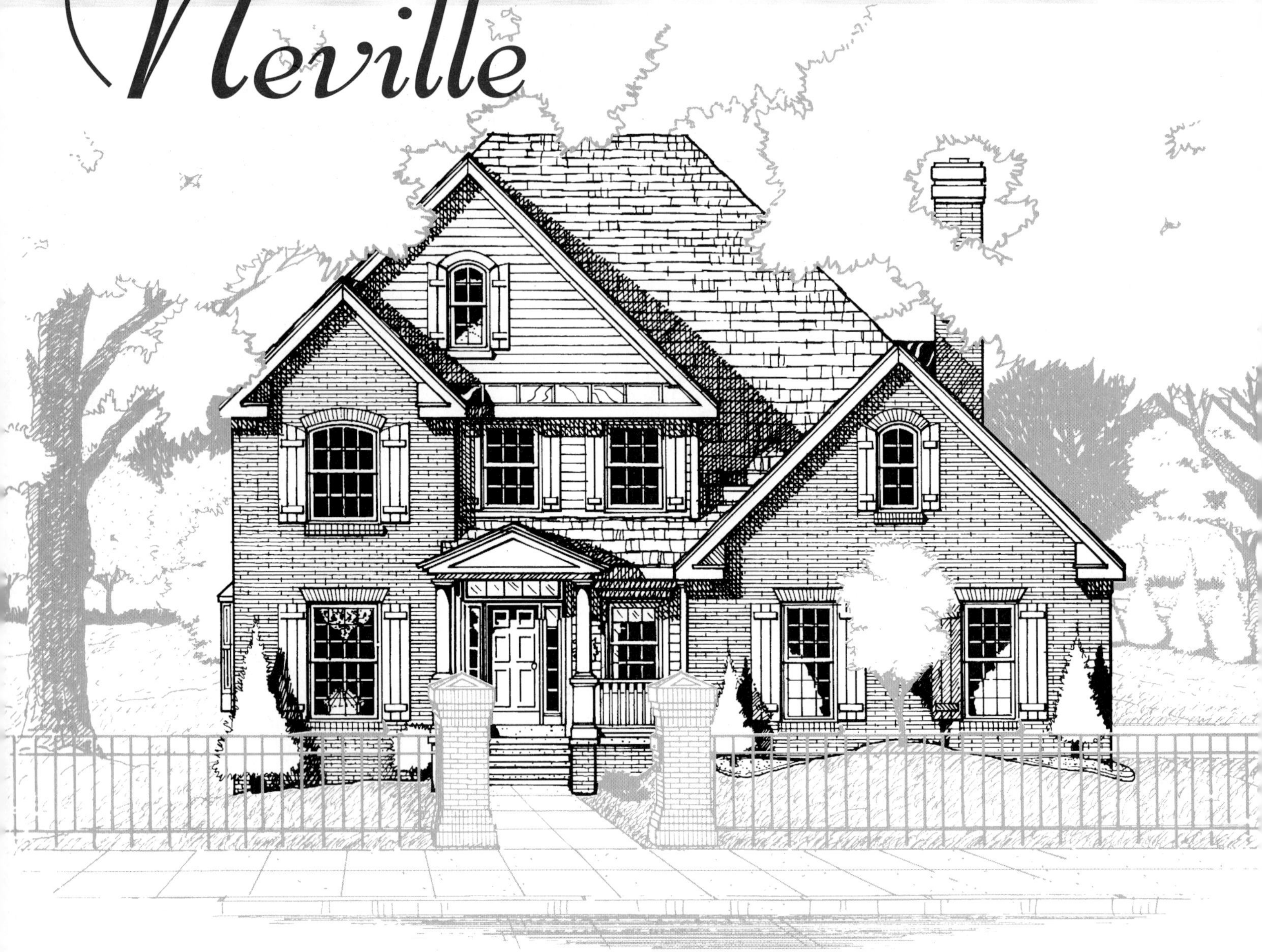

❶ A covered porch with columns is an inviting way to lure guests inside this home, while remaining a perfect place to observe the neighborhood from a porch swing.

❷ The double doors that open to the dining room allow for quiet dining and are a signature trait of this home.

❸ The master suite offers a walk-in closet with his-and-her aisles.

❹ Window benches in the upstairs landing and bedroom 4 add to the home's subtle charm.

❺ Optional storage space off of bedroom 4 allows for expansion of its walk-in closet.

❻ An unfinished attic offers abundant yet careful storage of a family's memories.

AVAILABLE FOR ALL PLANS

For More Information on Reverse Plans see page 158.

9K-4950 PRICE CODE 28

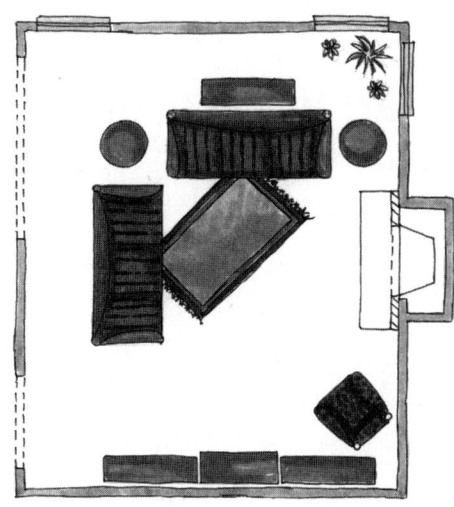

DECORATOR DESIGN TIPS

FAMILY ROOM - This room is large enough for two sofas. By placing them in an "L" shape, an intimate, cozy area is created by the fireplace. Traffic is kept behind the conversation area. The only wall without an opening or window works well to place an entertainment unit surrounded by bookcases. Tucking a chair by the fireplace makes a great place to read.

MAIN FLOOR

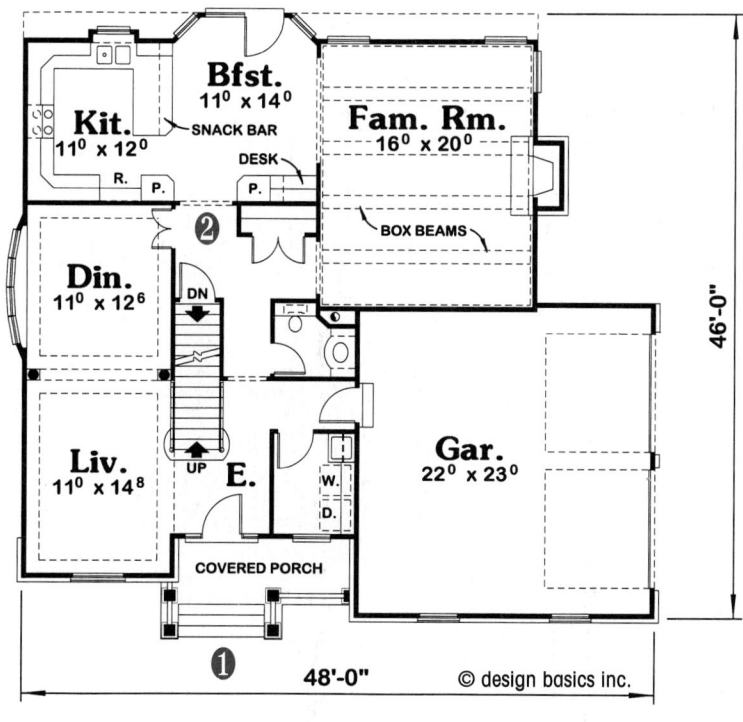

SECOND FLOOR

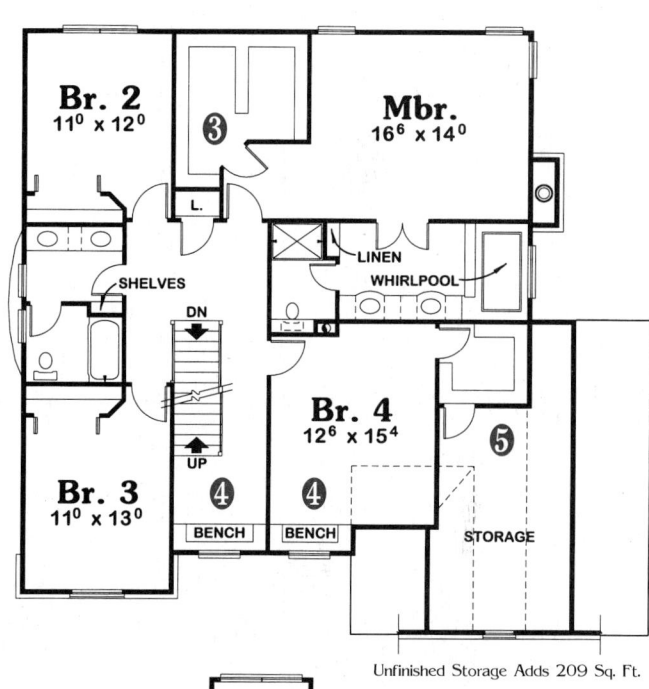

Unfinished Storage Adds 209 Sq. Ft.

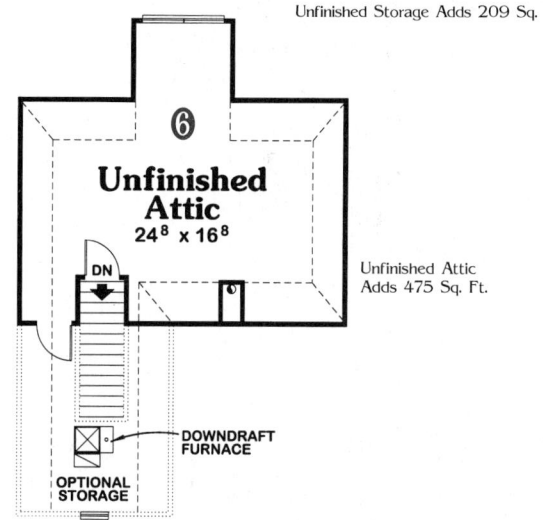

Unfinished Attic Adds 475 Sq. Ft.

Main	1304 Sq. Ft.
Second	1504 Sq. Ft.
Total	2808 Sq. Ft.

NOTE: 9 ft. main level walls

TO ORDER THIS PLAN CALL
1-800-947-7526

Nostalgia
153

What Are You REALLY Buying When You Order A Design Basics Home Plan?

You get more than just a set of construction drawings...

You receive a construction license that grants you, the purchaser, the right to build the home as many times as you wish, with no re-use fee. You also receive the right to make modifications to vellum copies of the original design and the right to make blueprints from vellum copies for construction purposes only. For more details see the example construction license at left.

More Importantly...

When you purchase one of our home plans, you tap into the design expertise that has made Design Basics the largest home plan design firm in the nation.

If you've ever paid to have a home plan designed from scratch, you know it's expensive – and time consuming. We invest thousands of dollars and a vast amount of time to painstakingly develop each one of our home plans. But because of our plan service approach, we can offer our award-winning designs for only a fraction of the cost. Plus, you'll have them within two business days.

For Your Protection

To discourage illegal usage of our home plans, and to help protect your rights as the legal holder of a Design Basics construction license, the symbol shown below now appears on all of our construction drawings. It is a reminder to all, that as the purchaser of a Design Basics home plan, you have specific legal rights that need to be protected.

Design Basics Copyright facts to remember.

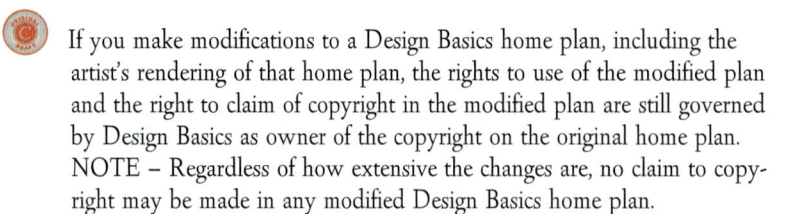

- Every home plan (as well as the artists' renderings of every home plan) featured in this publication has been registered with the U.S. Copyright Office by Design Basics Inc.

- When you purchase a Design Basics home plan, you receive a validated construction license. The construction license gives the purchaser legal rights, including the right to build the plan as many times as desired and to modify the construction drawings in connection with that construction.

- If you make modifications to a Design Basics home plan, including the artist's rendering of that home plan, the rights to use of the modified plan and the right to claim of copyright in the modified plan are still governed by Design Basics as owner of the copyright on the original home plan. NOTE – Regardless of how extensive the changes are, no claim to copyright may be made in any modified Design Basics home plan.

- Redrawing and/or constructing a home that utilizes design elements, either in whole or in part, based on a copyrighted Design Basics home plan, without first obtaining a valid Design Basics construction license constitutes infringement of U.S. copyright law and can carry penalties of up to $100,000 per violation.

- With your purchase of a Design Basics plan, you also receive a copyright release for our artwork. This gives you our permission to use our rendered elevation and floor plan(s) of the design in your promotional materials. However, Design Basics' name and copyright must appear along with the rendered artwork.

THE ABOVE POINTS ARE PROVIDED AS GENERAL GUIDELINES ONLY.

I LOVE this floor plan but...

I WANT TO SEE THE HOME IN MORE DETAIL, BEFORE I BUY THE PLANS.

HOW DOES IT LOOK FROM ALL SIDES?
WILL MY GRANDMA'S HUTCH FIT?
WILL I NEED TO ALTER THE ROOM SIZES?

We understand that comprehending the finished home from a set of floor plans is a challenge. Our Study Print & Furniture Layout Guide was designed to help you better understand how your Design Basics' home will "live." This helpful home planning tool comes with a Study Print showing views of all exterior elevations and aerial views of the roof. It also includes the Furniture Layout Guide, made up of a 1/4" scale floor plan and over 100 reusable furniture pieces allowing you to plan furniture placement and determine adequate room sizes. The Study Print & Furniture Layout Guide™ is available for any Design Basics' home plan. Order today by calling (800) 947-7526.

The Study Print & Furniture Layout Guide™
Only $29.95

Quality Plans ~ Dependable Designs

Design Basics home plans come to you on high-quality, erasable, reproducible vellums and include the following:

1. **COVER PAGE.** Each Design Basics home plan features the rendered elevation and informative reference sections including: general notes and design criteria*; abbreviations; and symbols for your Design Basics plan. 2. **ELEVATIONS.** Fully detailed showing materials used, and drafted at 1/4" scale for the front and 1/8" scale for the rear and sides. An aerial view of the roof is provided showing all hips, valleys and ridges. For a more thorough understanding, a Roof Construction Package (see pg. 158) is available showing roof framing and dimensional layouts. Additionally, fascia and railing sections are provided when necessary. 3. **FOUNDATIONS.** Drafted at 1/4" scale. Block foundations and basements are standard. We also show the suggested HVAC layout, structural information*, steel beam and pole locations and the direction and spacing of the floor system above. 4. **MAIN LEVEL FLOOR PLAN.** 1/4" scale. Fully dimensioned from stud to stud for ease of framing. 2"x4" walls are standard. The detailed drawings include such things as ceiling treatments, structural header locations*, flooring materials, framing layout, supply air locations and kitchen layout.

5. **SECOND LEVEL FLOOR PLAN.** 1/4" scale. Dimensioned from stud to stud and drafted to the same degree of detail as the main level floor plan*. 6. **ATTIC SPACE.** (Included when applicable.) 1/4" scale. Dimensioned from stud to stud and drafted to the same degree of detail as the main and second level floor plans*.
7. **INTERIOR ELEVATIONS.** Useful for the cabinet and bidding process, this page shows all kitchen and bathroom cabinets as well as any other cabinet elevations. Also shown is the elevation of the fireplace face, designed to complement the overall theme of the house.
8. **OVERALL CROSS SECTION.** General section view of the whole house. Includes overall structural detail. 9. **ELECTRICAL AND SECTIONS.** Illustrated on a separate page for clarity, the electrical plan shows suggested electrical layout for the foundation, main and second-level floor plans. Typical wall, cantilever, stair, brick and fireplace sections are provided to further explain construction of these areas.

CODES AND CONDITIONS
*Our plans are drafted to meet average codes and conditions in the state of Nebraska, at the time they are designed. Because codes and requirements can change and may vary from jurisdiction to jurisdiction, Design Basics Inc. cannot warrant compliance with any specific code or regulation. All Design Basics plans can be adapted to your local building codes and requirements. It is the responsibility of the purchaser and/or builder of each plan to see that the structure is built in strict compliance with all governing municipal codes (city, county, state and federal).

ERASABLE VELLUMS. Before making changes to your plan, PLEASE NOTE the following: ➤ To erase, you must use an electric eraser with a white #73 refill (we recommend a Eberhard Faber refill #75214.) ➤ Use a 2H graphite lead to re-draft. If you have any further questions, contact our Customer Support Specialists at (800) 947-7526.

CUSTOMIZED PLAN CHANGES

PRICE SCHEDULE

2 X 6 EXTERIOR WALLS $150
FROM STANDARD 2 X 4 TO 2 X 6 EXTERIOR WALLS

EACH GARAGE ALTERATION $275
- FRONT-ENTRY TO SIDE LOAD (OR VICE VERSA)
- 2-CAR TO 3-CAR (OR VICE VERSA)
- 2-CAR FRONT-ENTRY TO 3-CAR SIDE-LOAD (OR VICE VERSA)
- 3-CAR FRONT-ENTRY TO 2-CAR SIDE-LOAD (OR VICE VERSA)

WALK-OUT BASEMENT $175

CRAWL SPACE FOUNDATION $225

SLAB FOUNDATION $225

STRETCH CHANGES .... $5 per lineal foot of cut

ADDITIONAL BRICK TO SIDES & REAR $325

ADDITIONAL BRICK TO FRONT,
    SIDES AND REAR $425

ALTERNATE PRELIMINARY ELEVATION $150

9-FOOT MAIN LEVEL WALLS .... starting at $150

SPECIFY WINDOW BRAND $95

POURED CONCRETE FOUNDATION $25
ONLY WITH OTHER CHANGES

ADDING ONE COURSE (8") TO THE FOUNDATION HEIGHT ... $25
ONLY WITH OTHER CHANGES

NOTE
- All plan changes come to you on erasable, reproducible vellums.
- An unchanged set of original vellums is available for only $50 along with your plan changes.
- Design Basics changes are not made to the artist's renderings, electrical, sections or cabinets.
- Prices are subject to change.

As a part of our commitment to help you achieve the "perfect" home, we offer an extensive variety of plan changes for any Design Basics plan. For those whose decision to purchase a home plan is contingent upon the feasibility of a plan change, our Customer Support Specialists will, in most cases, be able to provide a FREE price quote for the changes.

call us toll-free at

(800) 947-7526

to order plan changes listed here, or if you have questions regarding plan changes not listed.

MORE ABOUT DESIGN BASICS ON THE
WORLD WIDE WEB
www.designbasics.com

▸▸ More Photographed Home Plan Designs ▸▸ Useful information about our Products and Services
▸▸ Commonly Asked Questions about Building a New Home ▸▸ Details about Design Basics Construction Prints
▸▸ Custom Change Information ▸▸ What's New from Design Basics ▸▸ All About Design Basics

E-MAIL info@designbasics.com

Don't Underestimate our Roofs!

Roof Construction Package
F O R • A L L • P L A N S

- Prepare accurate bids.
- Eliminate costly mistakes and waste.
- Save time and money during construction.

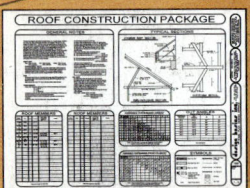 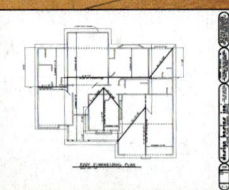 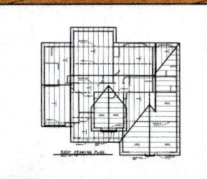

Available for each Design Basics plan, our Roof Construction Package is a complete roof framing and dimensional layout, including:

1) Aerial views of the roof showing hips, valleys, ridges, rafters and roof supports.
2) A dimensional plan showing lengths, runs, ridge heights and wall plate heights.

$100 at time of plan purchase. *$150 after plan purchase.
*Please have Construction License Number Available

Right-Reading Reverse Plans

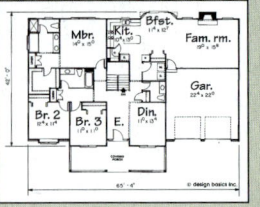
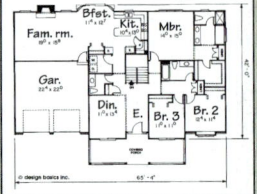

Get the convenience and flexibility of **Right-Reading Reverse Plans** on any Nostalgia home design. Our CAD-generated reverse versions are available at the same price as originally drafted plans.

Order both the original design and its reverse version at the same time for just an additional $100. Or order the reverse after plan purchase for $150.

Triple Your Sales Efforts!

Get all three products for only $149

available for all plans

ESTIMATOR'S MATERIAL LIST

Nostalgia Home Plans Estimator's Material List can help ensure accurate bids through detailed quantity take-offs for each Nostalgia home plan. An IBM-formatted disk version is available to save time in ensuring updated, accurate bids and eliminating cost overruns.

Disk and hard copy set, $50
Hard copy only, $35

PROMOTIONAL ARTWORK

Customize your Nostalgia Home Plans **Promotional Handout Artwork** with your name, address, phone number and company logo. The 8 1/2" x 11" reproducible master copy features a black and white rendered elevation and floor plan of your choice.

Available for $69

NOSTALGIA COLOR RENDERINGS

Spruce up your sales office or model home with a Nostalgia Home Plans **Color Rendering**. An artist's original, hand-colored portrayal of the front elevation and floor plan is available for the home of your choice.

Mounted in a 13" x 16" black metal frame, with a choice of grey marble or black matte.

Framed $99 – Unframed $79

FROM BUDGET-CONSCIOUS TO LUXURY...
DESIGN BASICS HAS THE PERFECT PLANS FOR YOUR MARKET NICHE.

1. Nostalgia Home Plans Collection™ – A New Approach to Time-Honored Design. 70 designs showcasing enchanting details and unique "special places." From 1339' to 3480'. Just $9.95

2. Gold Seal™ Home Plan Book Set. 442 of today's most sought-after one-story, 1½ and 2-story home plan ideas. $19.95 each

SPECIAL OFFER – all 5 for $84.95 Homes of Distinction – 86 plans under 1800' • Homes of Sophistication – 106 plans, 1800' - 2199' • Homes of Elegance – 107 plans, 2200' - 2599' • Homes of Prominence – 75 plans, 2600' - 2999' • Homes of Grandeur – 68 plans, 3000' - 4000'

3. Timeless Legacy™, A Collection of Fine Home Designs by Carmichael & Dame. 52 breathtaking luxury home designs from 3300' to 4500'. Includes artful rear views of each home. Available for $25

4. Heartland Home Plans™. 120 plan ideas designed for every-day practicality. Warm, unpretentious elevations easily adapt to individual life-styles. From 1212' to 2631'. Just $8.95

Call for package pricing 1-800-947-7526.

5. Seasons of Life™ – Designs for Reaping the Rewards of Autumn. 100 home plans specially tailored to today's empty-nester. From 1212' to 3904'. Just $4.95

6. The Narrow Book™. 217 one-story, 1½ story and 2-story home plans that are from 26 to 50 feet wide. Many can be joined together to create customized duplex plans. Just $14.95

7. Photographed Portraits of an American Home™. 100 of our finest designs, beautifully photographed and tastefully presented among charming photo album memories of "home". A must for any sales center's coffee table. Only $14.95

8. Easy Living One-Story Designs™. 155 one-story home designs from the Gold Seal™, Heartland Home Plans™ and Timeless Legacy™ collections, together in one plan book. Just $7.95

9. On the Porch™ – A Designer's Journal of Notes and Sketches. 64 designs from Gold Seal™, Heartland Home Plans™ and Timeless Legacy™ – each one with a porch. Includes essays on the porch and its role in traditional design. Only $2.95 (Subject to availability)

Please include $2.95 Shipping & Handling when ordering one plan book, or $4.95 when ordering 2 or more plan books.

ORDERING INFORMATION – ATTENTION DEPT. 9K

Name _____ Company _____
Address _____ Title _____
(For UPS Delivery – Packages cannot be shipped to a P.O. Box.)
Above Address ☐ business address ☐ residence address
City _____ State _____ Zip _____
Phone (___) _____ FAX (___) _____

☐ Visa VISA ☐ AMEX
☐ MasterCard ☐ Discover
☐ Check enclosed

Credit Card: ☐☐☐☐☐☐☐☐☐☐☐☐☐☐☐☐   ☐☐ / ☐☐ Expiration Date

All COD's must be paid by Certified Check, Cashier's Check or Money Order.
(Additional $5.00 charge on COD orders)

Signature _____

Follow this example for ordering PLANS:

PLAN NUMBER	PLAN NAME	AMOUNT
9K - 4133	Marcell	$505
Additional set of prints w/plan purchase	ea. $10.00	
	SUBTOTAL	

Follow this example for ordering PRODUCTS and BOOKS:

PLAN NUMBER	DESCRIPTION	QTY.	AMOUNT
9K - 4133	Estimator's Material List	1	$50

BOOK NUMBER	BOOK NAME	QTY.	AMOUNT

SHIPPING & HANDLING (CONTINENTAL US)

Home plans
- 2nd Business Day .... N/C
- Next Business Day $15.00

Books & Products
- UPS Ground (4-5 business days) .... $ 4.95
- 2nd Business Day $10.00
- Next Business Day $20.00
- Any Single Plan Books .... $ 2.95
- Any Combination of Plan Books .... $ 4.95

SAME DAY SHIPPING IF ORDERED BY 2:00 P.M. CT.

SUBTOTAL OF PLANS, PRODUCTS AND BOOKS _____
NE Res. Add 6.5% Sales Tax _____
Shipping & Handling (see chart at left) _____

No refunds or exchanges, please.
All orders payable in U.S. funds only.   **TOTAL** _____

All Design Basics home plans come with a basement foundation. Alternate foundations available for additional charges. Home plans do not carry an architect's/engineer's stamp. You may need to obtain an architect's/engineer's stamp to comply with your local building codes.

Nostalgia HOME PLANS COLLECTION™

PLAN PRICE SCHEDULE

Plan Price Code	Total Square Feet	1 Set Master Vellums
13	1300' - 1399'	$465
14	1400' - 1499'	$475
15	1500' - 1599'	$485
16	1600' - 1699'	$495
17	1700' - 1799'	$505
18	1800' - 1899'	$515
19	1900' - 1999'	$525
20	2000' - 2099'	$535
21	2100' - 2199'	$545
22	2200' - 2299'	$555
23	2300' - 2399'	$565
24	2400' - 2499'	$575
25	2500' - 2599'	$585
26	2600' - 2699'	$595
27	2700' - 2799'	$605
28	2800' - 2899'	$615
29	2900' - 2999'	$625
30	3000' - 3099'	$635
31	3100' - 3199'	$645
34	3400' - 3499'	$675

Prices subject to change.

Free 2ND BUSINESS DAY DELIVERY

All plan orders received prior to 2:00 p.m. CT will be processed, inspected and shipped out the same afternoon via 2nd business day delivery within the continental U.S. All other product orders will be sent via UPS ground service or US Postal Service.

FOR FASTEST SERVICE CALL (800) 947-7526 OR FAX (402) 331-5507
Monday - Friday, 7:00 a.m. to 6:00 p.m. C.T.

Design Basics Inc. • 11112 John Galt Boulevard • Omaha, Nebraska 68137-2384

design basics inc. HOME PLAN DESIGN SERVICE

STANDARDS OF EXCELLENCE – *Each complete Nostalgia Home Plan design comes to you on high quality, erasable, reproducible vellum.*